Pelican Books
Pelican Geography and Environmental Studies
Editor: Peter Hall

Oil and World Power: Background to the Oil Crisis

Peter R. Odell was born in 1930 in Coalville in the centre
of the small Leicestershire coalfield, giving him an early
interest in energy problems. He graduated with first class
honours in geography from Birmingham University, where
he also received his Ph.D. After military service with the
R.A.F. and a year studying at an institution for training
'budding' diplomats – the Fletcher School of Law and
Diplomacy in Boston, U.S.A. – he took up a post in the
Economics Division of the Shell International Petroleum
Company in London. After several somewhat frustrating
years with Shell, overstaffed at that time in common with
other international oil companies as a result of an easy-profits
situation throughout most of the 1950s, he left in 1961 and
was appointed lecturer in the Department of Geography
at the London School of Economics. Seven years later, in
September 1968, he was appointed to the Chair of Economic
Geography at the Netherlands School of Economics,
Erasmus University in Rotterdam where he now lives with
his wife and four children. He is the author of *An Economic
Geography of Oil* (1963), *Oil: the New Commanding
Height* (1966), *Natural Gas in Western Europe: A Case Study
in the Economic Geography of Energy Resources* (1969),
Energy Needs and Resources (1974), and of many papers
and articles on his special interests.

Oil and World Power: Background to the Oil Crisis

Third edition

Peter R. Odell

Penguin Books

Penguin Books Ltd, Harmondsworth,
Middlesex, England
Penguin Books Inc., 7110 Ambassador Road,
Baltimore, Maryland 21207, U.S.A.
Penguin Books Australia Ltd, Ringwood,
Victoria, Australia
Penguin Books Canada Ltd, 41 Steelcase Road West,
Markham, Ontario, Canada
Penguin Books (N.Z.) Ltd, 182–190 Wairau Road,
Auckland 10, New Zealand

First published 1970
Second edition 1972
Third edition 1974
Copyright © Peter R. Odell, 1970, 1972, 1974

Made and printed in Great Britain by
Hazell Watson & Viney Ltd,
Aylesbury, Bucks
Set in Monotype Times

Contents

List of Maps and Figures

6

Acknowledgements

This book has emerged from some thirteen years of an increasing familiarization with the oil industry, first as an employee of Shell, the world's second largest and the most international of oil companies, and then as a student and observer of its continued growth both in size and complexity. During this time I have benefited from innumerable opportunities to learn through debate, discussion and argument something of the industry's problems and I would wish to acknowledge my debt in this respect to many people in the industry, in consultancies concerned with oil, in governments and in academic circles not only in London, where most of this book was written, but also in other parts of Europe, the United States and many countries of Latin America. Whilst I have not had opportunities to see the oil industry in action in the rest of the world, there are few countries with important oil interests whose problems I have not been better able to understand as a result of listening to their representatives talking about them on their visits to London and to conferences elsewhere. In a more strict academic context my greatest debt of gratitude lies with all who participated in the series of seminars on the economics and politics of the international oil industry that Professor E. Penrose and I jointly ran at the London School of Economics and the School of Oriental and African Studies from 1963 to 1967. The broad general idea for this book, as well as many specific ideas in it, emerged from sessions of that very successful seminar at which representatives of governments and companies gave willingly of their time.

Finally, I would like to thank: first, two secretaries who coped with the production of the manuscript – Miss Diane Dubury in London and Mrs. J.v.d. Heiden-Jenkins in Rotterdam. Their interest in the book exceeded the call of duty and I hope they will approve of the

Acknowledgements

final version. Secondly, my wife and children, who have accepted many hours of my preoccupation with the affairs of oil rather than with those of the family. I hope the final result will convince my wife and those of my children that are able to read that this was in a good cause. For the younger children, however, the only result will be a somewhat higher-than-normal interest on their part in the visual manifestations of the petroleum industry. In this respect though, I am still sure that the 'Shell-Spel', the 'Chevron-Colours' and the 'Esso Moon Race' competitions at their respective service stations have been even more effective, and would have been more so had their father been competent enough to secure one of the all-elusive tokens that would have won them a prize. Such is the fascination of oil.

Peter R. Odell, Rotterdam,
January 1970

Note on the Third Edition

The original version of this book was completed in January 1970. Since then there have not only been the quite normal run of events in the world of oil in terms of new discoveries, increasing production and changes in demand etc., but also a set of abnormal and quite traumatic developments which have completely undermined the traditional pattern of organization of the industry. Thus, the text for this third edition has been much changed from the original in order to include not only more recent facts and statistics on oil industry developments, but also comments on and explanations of the more fundamental changes in oil in the last three years. In addition there is an entirely new chapter, 'The World of Oil Power in 1974', which attempts to put these changes in perspective and to show how they open up many new options for the future of the industry.

P.R.O., Rotterdam,
February 1974

1 : Introduction:
The World's Oil Industry

A description of the world's oil industry demands the use of many superlatives. By any standards it is the world's leading industry in size; it is probably the only international industry that concerns every country in the world; and, as a result of the geographical separation of regions of major production and regions of high consumption, it is first in importance in its contribution to the world's tonnage of international trade and shipping. Because of these and other attributes, such as its involvement in both national and international affairs, a day rarely passes without oil being in the news. Often the significance of such news items is not apparent in isolation or without some background knowledge of the way in which the industry has been and is organized internationally and of its impact upon individual countries and groups of countries in which its operations and interests lie. This book aims at providing such a background by describing and analysing the oil industry's affairs and relationships around the world.

We shall be concerned almost exclusively with the period of about thirty years since the end of the Second World War, when growth in oil has exceeded growth in all other large-scale economic activities. Already by 1950 twice as much crude oil was produced as had been produced in 1945. Ten years later, in 1960, production had doubled again to 1,000 million tons. The rate of expansion continued, and it took only five years more for the next additional 500 million tons annual output to be achieved. In 1968, only three years later, another leap of 500 million tons in annual output to a total of 2,000 million tons was achieved and by now the prospect of an annual output of almost 3,000 million tons by 1975, and of 4,000 million tons by the early 1980s, is considered to be as near certain as any forecast can be. Thus, in spite of the massive developments to date the greatest possibilities for growth still lie ahead. In the light of this, more oil tankers on the roads and railways, new pipelines to major consuming centres, additional refineries on major estuaries and elsewhere, more and even larger tankers for moving oil around the world, and continued news items about oil exploration and development efforts in hitherto unexpected places such as the North Sea and off-shore China can be expected for as far ahead as we can see.

But generalizations about the world oil industry are somewhat misleading, particularly as it has never been a fully interlocking system and now seems likely, in view of recent events, to split up even more. There is, to start with, and as one would expect from the division between the communist group of countries and what the Americans call the 'free world' (a description often used in oil-company literature), a clear break between the industry of the communist nations and that of the rest of the world – though, as we shall see later, there are certain interrelationships which appear to be of increasing significance. On the other hand, within the communist world the increasingly deep cleavage between the Soviet Union and its European allies on one side and China and some of its friendly neighbours on the other is also reflected in a decreasing degree of contact between the oil industries of these countries. A few years ago, increases in Soviet oil output were planned on the assumption of an increasing import requirement by China. Today oil trade between the Soviet Union and China has been eliminated and China's efforts in securing a rapid expansion of its own oil industry have already made it self-sufficient and could soon make it an important exporter to other parts of the world.

In the rest of the world, in the post-war period, a split emerged between the oil industry of North America (mainly the U.S.A., but also including Canada and, to a lesser degree, Mexico) and that of the remaining non-communist world. Before the war, and up to 1945, in as far as wartime supply routes made this possible, the U.S.A. was the leading exporter of petroleum products to Europe and to other parts of the world, but it soon lost that position as its relatively slowly growing oil production was required at home to sustain the country's rapid economic development. Thus, its oil industry became a separate entity, with such differences in price levels and in organization from the rest of the world as to necessitate an increasingly autarkic policy on the part of the U.S.A., whose oil industry would have greatly diminished in size if it had been subjected to competition from outside in the 1950s and the 1960s. (This was no longer true by 1973 because of major increases in the price of international oil. See pages 36–7 for a reappraisal of the U.S. situation in the light of the changed world oil supply and price situation.) In this respect at least, the U.S.A. and the U.S.S.R. have had something in common, for the latter has also protected its domestic industry through the exclusion of imports.

Outside North America and the communist world we have the territory of the so-called 'international oil industry'; but 'international' used in this context does not imply an industry owned and/ or controlled by the world's many nations. Instead it refers simply to the fact that this is an industry which operates internationally, with a complex network of relationships connecting most countries of the world. Its ownership and direction still lie mainly in the hands of a very small group of companies known, in oil-industry terminology, as the 'international majors'. These companies are responsible for something like 80 per cent of all oil production in the world outside the communist countries and North America. In the same areas they own or control over 70 per cent of the total refining capacity and they operate either directly or indirectly, through long-term charter, well over 50 per cent of the tonnage of internationally operating tankers. Just a few years ago these percentage figures were even higher.

The companies concerned are international only in the sense that their operations are world-wide, in their employment of nationals of many countries, and in their having locally (that is nationally) registered subsidiaries in many countries of the world. But their ownership and ways and methods of working are limited to those of just three countries, with the U.S.A. as the dominant element. Thus of the seven 'international majors' no fewer than five have their headquarters and the overwhelming majority of their shareholders in the U.S.A., which also provides all the top management and a high proportion of the lower echelons as well. The largest is Standard Oil of New Jersey, which through most of the world trades under the Esso ('tiger in your tank') sign – except, ironically, in the U.S.A., where the nationally trading subsidiary was, until recently, rather amusingly in the light of the group's strength and size, known as Humble Oil! In

1972, however, there was a corporate decision, taken after considering many alternatives and after much debate by top management, to establish a new world-wide name for the company – the Exxon Corporation. This has already been generally adopted in the United States and is gradually spreading to other parts of the world. Another Standard company, Standard Oil of New York (almost every state in the U.S.A. secured a 'Standard' company when the coast-to-coast 'empire' of Rockefeller's Standard Oil was broken up by anti-monopoly legislation earlier in the century), is the parent company of many subsidiaries around the world trading as Mobiloil, while the other Standard Company which has achieved a place amongst the 'majors' is Standard Oil of California, which after many years of operating abroad jointly with one or other of the other majors, is now 'going it alone' under the Chevron sign. Gulf Oil, with headquarters in Pittsburg, has for long been a major producer of crude oil in the Middle East, having secured a 50 per cent interest in the extremely prolific Kuwait oilfields in the late 1930s, and through the 1950s and the 1960s increasingly diversified into refining and marketing operations throughout Europe and in parts of the Far East and South East Asia. Finally Texaco, which, as its name suggests, operates out of Texas, is an aggressive company with major overseas interests in the Caribbean and South America and with important shares in joint producing companies in the Middle East. It is also involved through a wide range of subsidiaries in refining and/or marketing oil products in some forty countries.

Though these companies have – and even deliberately foster – different corporate images they do have one overriding attribute in common: their Americanism. Although many of their subsidiaries have a management consisting mainly of nationals of the country concerned, it is seldom necessary to dig very deeply to find the key U.S. personnel whose job it is to ensure that American professionalism and expertise in oil reaches into the furthest parts of the company's empire and who at the same time will be responsible for ensuring that the policy of the subsidiary is in line with the authorized interpretation of centrally taken decisions. The communications infrastructure of these U.S.A.-centred 'international' firms certainly rivals that of the foreign services of the majority of the world's nations.

This is also true of the two remaining 'international majors' – the Royal Dutch/Shell group and British Petroleum. The former is an Anglo-Dutch enterprise with the shareholding interest of the Dutch parent making the Dutch element the more important in the ratio of 60:40 (reflected also in a 4:3 split of Managing Directorship in favour of the Dutch side) – but with operational and commercial head-quarters in London. It is second only to Standard Oil of New Jersey in the size and complexity of its operations, and there are only a hand-ful of countries in the world in which there is no local Shell Company. The latter, B.P., is a wholly British-owned enterprise (except for a little foreign ownership of its shares) in which, incidentally, the state had a more than 50 per cent holding from 1913 until it was reduced to 'only' 49 per cent in the early 1960s. However, this dominant state holding, much to the disbelief of foreigners, has not resulted in the British government as such exercising a dominant role in the company. In fact, successive governments have elected to exercise no role at all beyond that of nominating two directors to the seven-man board. These directors then remain quite free apparently to act as they them-selves think best, without even a formal obligation to report back to the government or to seek its advice when participating in company policy making. In other words the state is a sleeping partner and is content to let B.P. operate just as the other six private-enterprise international oil companies do, though this will be changed with the next Labour government in the U.K. when B.P. may be converted into a state oil company. Meanwhile, the state's interest lies only in drawing its not inconsiderable dividends from the company, which, like Gulf Oil, has had the advantage of access to massive supplies of crude oil in the Middle East in the post-war period and thus had the incentive to diversify into refining and marketing operations in an increasing number of countries. These include the U.S.A., where, after a series of small incursions to test the market, B.P. made up its mind in 1968 to go into refining and marketing in a very big way with take-over bids for a number of medium-sized oil companies. Favour-able decisions by the U.S. Department of Justice (which is responsible for investigating take-over bids in the light of the country's anti-trust legislation) gave the green light for the implementation of this major policy development, which will ultimately have the effect of

13

making B.P. about the ninth or tenth largest oil company in the United States and one of the very biggest producers as a result of its oil discoveries in Alaska.

These then are the seven 'majors', and, as the figures given earlier indicate, they made up the dominant element in the international oil industry until 1973. Before the Second World War they collectively constituted a near-cartel – having agreed on market shares. Effects of the war and U.S. anti-trust legislation eliminated formal agreements between them, but until recently – because of their organization and their continued control over supplies – they were able to have the industry work the way they wanted it, with mutual understanding over pricing policies ensuring high profits for them.

It should be noted, however, that their ability to dominate the industry has fallen away in recent years. This change is a result of the growth of new elements in the oil business. One is the rapid growth of important European enterprises such as Compagnie Française des Pétroles (C.F.P.) of France and Ente Nazionale Idrocarburi (E.N.I.), the Italian state company. Their interests, moreover, have not remained confined to Europe – though this is where they remain at their strongest – but have spread to many other parts of the world, where they are participating not only in production ventures but also in refining and marketing.

Even more important were the activities of U.S. oil companies which used to have interests only within the U.S.A. but which, since the early 1950s, sought both oil and markets abroad. They did this at first to obtain lower-cost crude-oil supplies than they had available from their fields in the U.S.A. with a view to shipping them back home and so increasing the profitability of their domestic refining and marketing operations. But when the U.S. government imposed oil import quotas in 1959, so limiting the amounts of oil they could send from overseas to the U.S.A., they had to diversify into refining and selling oil in other parts of the world – notably Western Europe – in order to obtain revenues from the crude-oil supplies that they have discovered and developed, often at a high capital cost. In a world of generally booming markets for oil they did not find such expansion too difficult, even though, of course, their expansion was partly at the expense of business that might otherwise have gone to the major companies. More recently, however, the growth of markets for oil in Western Europe and Japan has begun to slow down and has thus introduced a more difficult period for these new companies in the international business. Many of them, in fact, have been taken over by the 'majors', which became unwilling to risk the loss of any further percentage of the total markets available.

Neither have many of these new companies indicated much ability or willingness to get involved with refining and marketing in Asia, Africa and Latin America where conditions of doing business are perhaps too different from what they have been used to in the U.S.A. or Western Europe. They have thus not chosen particularly to take advantage of the increasingly strong reaction in the developing world against the control effectively exercised over the whole of the oil business in these parts of the world by the seven major international companies, which through the subsidiary companies they established in most countries of Latin America, Asia and Africa sought to market crude oil and products from their larger-scale operations in the major oil-producing areas.

The reaction against the international oil companies arose from an enhanced degree of economic and political nationalism in a period in which colonialism in any guise or form has been highly suspect. Many countries thus viewed the control over their own oil industries by one or more of the major international companies very much as a form of economic colonialism incompatible with the status of a sovereign nation. The result has been an increasing tendency for such nations to exercise their authority over the companies concerned through import quotas, price controls, insistence on the employment of nationals rather than expatriates, the imposition of unfavourable taxes and other regulations, etc. Some countries even established and encouraged alternative systems for securing their supplies of oil from overseas and it was in such cases that new entities and companies could find opportunities for development. E.N.I. and the French state-sponsored entities did so to some extent in Africa and Asia, but the American 'independents' (that is, U.S. companies other than the five American majors) only followed suit to a limited degree before deciding that they also were not particularly welcome in most developing nations.

Oil and World Power: Background to the Oil Crisis

This nationalist reaction against the major companies arose first amongst the larger Latin American nations, which, after a century or so of political independence, sought also their economic independence from what they considered to be an aspect of American imperialism. Thus, countries such as Chile, Brazil and Argentina gradually restrained the freedom of action of these companies to operate within their territories. The companies were, for example, refused permission to expand their activities beyond those existing at a certain date, or obliged to integrate their own operations into a framework established by state control and direction. Moreover, to supplement and intensify these measures the countries concerned often created state-owned oil entities which were then given the overriding responsibility for ensuring the provision of the countries' needs for petroleum. Today, only Paraguay and recently independent Guyana of the thirteen nations of South America are without their state oil companies. This trend was also quickly taken up by many of the more recently independent countries in Asia and Africa, and today nearly thirty countries in these two continents have state-owned oil entities with responsibilities extending from exploration to final marketing. This trend towards state control and/or ownership appears to be likely to continue amongst the developing nations, where suspicions about the wisdom of permitting the international companies to look after the oil sector are still increasing, especially in the light of the changed relationships since 1971 between the oil companies and the oil-producing countries. Direct relationships with the latter are becoming much more attractive.

Except for oil exploration and production, it is, however, in the countries of Europe, together with Japan, that the principal post-war expansion of the international oil companies has occurred. Even in these areas the question of allowing the companies freely to supply, refine and market the oil required was increasingly raised even before the oil crisis of 1973–4 and countries such as Finland, France, Italy, Austria, Spain and Portugal have all decided to place oil partly, at least, in the public sector through the establishment of a state-owned oil enterprise. And where state companies have not been established, other European governments have, almost without exception, involved themselves in attempts to persuade the companies concerned to pursue policies, as regards refining, price of products, etc., which accord with what the country considers nationally desirable. It is perhaps Japan, as will be shown in detail in Chapter 6, which has taken this degree of persuasion through supervision and control further than any other country. There, through the powerful Ministry of Trade and Industry, national control is exercised at all significant points over the activities and decisions of the international companies selling oil to or in Japan.

Thus, the post-war period, particularly the 1960s, has been one of severe limitations on the freedom of the international oil companies to take decisions solely in the light of their own corporate interests and to follow up opportunities for expanding their activities in refining and marketing oil. They have moved ahead less rapidly than would otherwise have been the case and have thus had their degree of dominance in these activities somewhat curtailed, though, even so, in the changed oil world of the 1970s they have remained powerful enough to restrain oil supplies and to secure major increases in oil prices. At the same time they also faced limitations on their ability to do as they would commercially and corporately like to do in the main areas of oil production. In the first place all major producing countries insisted on a larger share of the profits from oil production. Then they also began to insist in some cases that the companies' operations should either be made part of a joint venture with a state-owned entity, or brought much more directly under the general overall control of a Ministry of Petroleum or similar official body. And often other non-major companies were invited into a country to participate in, or even to initiate, an oil-development programme all to the detriment of the major companies' share of total production.

Producing countries took these lines of action against the companies working concessions in their territories, in the light of what they saw their economic and political interests to be. In the early post-war period of rapidly increasing demand for oil, at price levels much in excess of supply prices, the governments were usually able to secure their objectives because, no matter what they demanded, the business remained very profitable for the companies, which could increase prices more than sufficiently to offset the additional payments and so increase their profit levels at the same time. However, from the late

1950s to 1970 this situation, highly favourable to the producing countries, deteriorated under the impact of a world surplus of oil-producing capacity and consequent price weakness in many markets. Producing countries soon found that the international companies, with the flexibility given to them by their operations in a number of major producing areas, were able to concentrate their activities in areas where there was least interference from the governments concerned. This flexibility was a factor in the enthusiastic development of new oil resources in Libya and Nigeria in the 1950s and early 1960s and in Australia, Alaska and the North Sea in more recent years. The companies thought that developments in new areas would enable them to withstand unwelcome pressures from the governments of the longer-established producing areas. The producing countries were made painfully aware of this danger in the late 1950s when potential oil surplus and the need to stimulate demand persuaded the companies to announce significant overall reductions in the prices they 'posted' for crude oils. Such reductions decreased the revenues which host governments received from the oil industry for, in most cases, such revenues were calculated on the basis of the posted prices. The result of this shock was the formation in 1960 of the Organization of Petroleum Exporting Countries (O.P.E.C.), whereby the oil producers sought collectively to enhance their bargaining power by standing together in order to prevent the companies from playing one country off against another. O.P.E.C. grew in stature quite quickly in the short period of its existence and at first succeeded in preventing further reductions in posted price levels, so ensuring the maintenance of government revenues per barrel of oil produced. It then also successfully negotiated technical changes in the methods whereby company profits are calculated, and as a result government revenues per barrel have even been increased by a few cents. Up to 1970, however, O.P.E.C. had not succeeded in introducing a mechanism for controlling and regulating the output of oil in member countries. And in the absence of such controls there still existed a potential danger of further reductions in crude oil prices. Paradoxically, it was the earlier encouragement that the producing countries had given to companies other than the 'majors' to participate in oil exploration and development that stood as the major hurdle in the achievement of this objective. If the countries concerned had only had the seven major international companies to negotiate with, then some form of regulation of oil output, acceptable to both sides, would probably have been achieved sooner. However, the 'majors' were forced to battle for markets with the 'independents' and the competition became so acute, even amongst themselves, that the prospect of the international prorationing of oil production – whereby production levels could be tied in to estimated demand levels at a given price (which is the sort of system that is worked within the major producing areas of the U.S.A.) – became more remote than it was at the time of O.P.E.C.'s formation! Only in December 1970 did the producing countries manage to achieve a consensus for collective action which immediately enabled the downward trend in prices to be reversed. Thereafter, there were soon major increases in 'posted' prices for crude oil – and thus in government revenues per barrel. And just a little later – in 1973 – the producing countries started to exercise control over how much oil should be produced, so leading to the oil crisis and the reality of fundamental changes in the international oil system.

Thus, today, the international oil industry – the part of the world's oil industry with which most of this book will be mainly concerned (the exceptions are the chapters on the U.S.A. and the U.S.S.R.) – consists of a number of interacting elements. There are not only the major international companies, such as Shell and Esso, which formerly ran the industry much as they pleased, but also a range of additional companies also interested in producing oil and selling it on the markets of the world, together with the oil interests of over a hundred national governments throughout Europe, the Middle East and the developing world. The large companies continue to dominate both the stage and the play as the producers, refiners and sellers of most of the world's oil, and they are brought into virtually daily contact with the governments of those countries in which they both choose and are allowed to have interests. To some degree these companies also have to act as intermediaries between the conflicting oil interests of producing countries on the one hand and consuming countries on the other. Thus they operate not only as commercial enterprises attempting to maximize their profits but also as diplomatic channels attempting to keep the oil flowing around the world. Their function in this latter respect may, however, now be a short-lived one, for, if state interests and direct involvement in oil continue to expand at the rate at which they have expanded in the post-war period, then in another decade or so it seems more than likely that the oil companies will no longer be required as intermediaries. The economic and political negotiations needed to get oil from the points at which it is produced to the points at which it is to be consumed will then be undertaken by the governments of the countries directly concerned. This possibility is examined in more detail in later chapters.

When this happens, the 'international oil industry' will be international in a very real sense, with all that this implies. On the one hand there are the dangers that such a situation will pose as a result of the confrontation of conflicting national interests, but on the other hand, there are also the opportunities that such a situation will present for the effective internationalization of this most important, internationally traded commodity. This could conceivably be under an agency responsible for the production, refining, transporting and marketing of the oil within the framework of the most rational system that it is humanly possible to conceive: a system whose basis already exists and which could, therefore, emerge out of the increasingly sophisticated logistical systems that are currently being developed by the separate international companies, not only for the sake of their own profitability but also because their managers are responding to the intellectual challenge of such approaches to the organization of the world's largest industry.

2: The U.S.A. and World Oil

The U.S.A. has always been (except for a few years in the latter part of the nineteenth century), and still remains, the world's largest oil producing, refining and consuming nation. Moreover, the American oilman – and many of his fellow countrymen – look upon the oil industry as an American 'invention' and continue to express scepticism as to the ability of any other nationality to deal successfully with oil and to the possibilities of organizing the industry in any way other than that tested and tried in the U.S.A.! These attitudes emerge, of course, from the early rise to importance of the U.S. domestic oil industry and the growing overseas interests of the largest American firms, which, as we have seen, have dominated the international oil business ever since its earliest days. Until recently, only Anglo-Dutch Shell and the British Anglo-Iranian (now B.P.) provided effective competition; and even one of these – Shell – has very important American interests in the form of the U.S. Shell Oil Company and its subsidiaries (60 per cent owned by Shell International). This company is so large that it contributes approximately one-third to the total world-wide Shell Group's revenues and well over one-third of the Group's profits. Moreover, its expertise in all branches of the industry is utilized in the international activities of Shell in a variety of operations – a process which culminated in 1967 with the appointment of the president of Shell Oil to a managing directorship of the Shell Group. On the other hand, for non-American Group employees, periods of service in the U.S. company appear to be a prerequisite for 'getting to the top'. All the managing directors of the Shell Group have been sent to work in the U.S.A. at various parts of their careers. Technically and organizationally then, and also from the point of view of equipment and contractual expertise, the industry remains American-orientated – and, as we shall see in the chapters dealing with the developing countries, this situation often leads to charges of economic imperialism or colonialism. But from the U.S. standpoint the same situation is interpreted as a willingness to make American expertise available overseas, through investment by U.S. oil companies, to all nations that care to make use of it. And the U.S. government does, of course, consider it a national responsibility to offer protection to this investment and reacts quite predictably to any apparent 'threat' against it by foreign governments. Such an attitude in its turn confirms in others the 'economic imperialism' interpretation of American oil interests overseas. The official U.S. attitude is well expressed in the following description by the U.S. State Department's former Director of the Office of Fuels and Energy:

The U.S.'s government exercises virtually no power of control over the operations abroad of American oil companies. Its concern with them is of another kind. Our companies work abroad in close relationship with host governments. In countries where crude oil is produced the relationship is that of a partnership between company and government, with the company providing the capital and taking the risks inherent to exploration and development in return for a grant by a government of a right to use the re-source. In consuming countries oil companies provide the services of refining and distributing petroleum products. Companies obtain profits from these operations commensurate with the large amounts of capital required and the risks assumed. Governments in turn receive an agreed share of profits in return for the rights they have awarded for the resource itself, or revenues by way of taxes accruing from the refining and distribution of petroleum products. These relationships are mutually beneficial to companies and governments, and each is dependent upon the other in organizing a system for the production and distribution of petroleum which is economic, efficient and insures a fair return to both, for what they have contributed to the enterprise. The U.S. government is greatly concerned that American oil companies abroad should be able to continue their operations overseas within a framework of mutually agreed relationships with host governments, serving the public efficiently wherever they are, and earning whatever is properly theirs because of the capital, skill and good fortune that have accompanied their operations.

Thus, the organization of a large part of the international oil industry is part and parcel of the U.S.A.'s world-wide interests in which the investments of U.S. private companies in virtually every country of the non-communist world are linked to and supported by official U.S. government policy. Assets of over £5,000 million are invested in oil abroad by U.S. companies – accounting for about one-third of total U.S. foreign investment – and, as the State Department Director of Fuels and Energy says, 'the loss of a significant part of them would be a serious matter to the nation as well as severely inequitable to the private owner'. The potential loss from a national point of view arises partly from the contribution that oil companies' operations overseas make to the U.S. balance of payments. For 1972 it was estimated that oil industry earnings abroad sent back to the U.S.A. exceeded $2,000 million. This, in turn, exceeded by some $500 million the sum of the total cost of the country's oil imports and the outflow of money to finance the continual development of the oil industry overseas. The importance of this to a country with persistent balance of payments problems arising from its military and aid commitments overseas is, of course, self-evident. But apart from this narrowly commercial consideration there are wider issues involved, for the U.S. government is also concerned with the security of oil supplies for itself and its allies, with the economic strength of all nations not unfriendly to it and with 'selling' its own way of doing things for ideological reasons.

The question of the security of oil supplies from overseas will be dealt with later in the chapter when we look at the U.S. position in world oil trade. It is sufficient at this point to indicate the official U.S. view that security of supply must, in the words of the previously quoted state department official, be based 'on the maintenance of a type of relationship between foreign companies and local governments similar in its general framework to that which exists today' – meaning, of course, quite simply a belief that only American companies operating overseas can ensure the continuity of supplies to the United States! Given this view then U.S. foreign policy in areas where crude oil production is important has had to be concentrated on maintaining the *status quo* with any threat to this met with appropriate diplomacy. The way in which this works has been seen in the case of the United States' relations with Venezuela over the last twenty-five years.

Venezuela has been the major source of foreign oil imported into the United States throughout the period in which the U.S.A. has been a

23

net oil importer – since 1948. Its exports to the U.S.A. grew rapidly from 1940 until the imposition of U.S. import quotas in 1959. Even since then they have continued to grow slowly – although more recently they have also had to compete with oil imported from the Middle East, Libya and Nigeria. Venezuela's oil development has thus been directed more closely to meet U.S. requirements than that of any other country; and more U.S. oil capital has gone to Venezuela than to any other country. Most of this investment took place between 1940 and 1957 when, except for a short period of political difficulty in 1948 (see p. 68), the investment climate was exceedingly favourable. Although changes were made from time to time in taxation regulations and in various other aspects of the concession arrangements, there was no question throughout this period of the nature of the arrangements being fundamentally altered. In fact, in 1956–7 Pérez Jiménez chose to auction off extensive new areas to foreign companies on similar conditions to those under which the existing companies were already operating.

In 1958, however, following the overthrow of Pérez Jiménez, the Venezuelans elected to office a left-wing party, Acción Democrática, which had pledged, while in opposition in exile, the nationalization of the country's oil resources and industry. Its leader, and later the country's new President following the overthrow of Pérez Jiménez, was Romulo Betancourt, whose book, *Venezuela: Política y Petróleo* (F.C.E., Mexico, 1956), had made out the case for this line of action against the country's most important and most powerful economic sector. The companies, as in 1948 at the time of the first and very short-lived Acción Democrática government, immediately saw their fundamental interests at stake and it seemed as though they might react to protect them by seeking to intervene in Venezuela's affairs – if necessary, by supporting any attempt to overthrow the government by force. In doing so, they might, under normal conditions, have expected the backing of the U.S. government, acting to protect American oil investment and the nation's oil supplies in line with their declared policy. The U.S. government undoubtedly made it quite clear in private to both government and companies that action along these lines would be the ultimate sanction and that the government would protect U.S. investment and the flow of oil supplies to the

United States by force, if necessary. Such intervention would certainly not have been out of keeping with the U.S.A.'s normal practice in the Caribbean area – and in this case with somewhat more justification than in a whole series of other Caribbean interventions. The oil companies, however – all American with the single exception of Shell – received immediate advice (tantamount, of course, almost to instructions) to work for a *modus vivendi* with the left-wing government. At the same time the latter was persuaded to take no action – such as expropriation of the companies' assets – which would bring the situation to a head. Thus a crisis was averted, much to the relief of the U.S.A., faced by this time with the difficulties in the Caribbean area caused by the defection of Cuba to the communist camp.

It was the Cuban situation which so exercised the U.S.A. at this time and, in the light of it, Venezuela was seen as the key to political stability in the whole region as well as a test case for the ability of a left-wing, but reformist, government to survive the economic, social and political pressures of opposition from extremists. A crisis in Venezuela had thus to be avoided, and under the guidance of the U.S.A. both government and companies pulled back from the brink and eventually evolved a working relationship which gave the government high, guaranteed and gradually increasing revenues from oil, such that it could not only finance its programme of economic and social reform, but also have some to spare so as to be able to afford to keep potential power groups, such as the army officers, from trying to achieve power. At the same time, the companies retained ownership of their considerable assets and the ability to continue to make profits on their Venezuelan operations. For the U.S.A. this represented success indeed, not only because it left the reformist government of Venezuela with a chance of succeeding but also because it secured the single most important source of its oil imports and maintained the essential framework of relationships between the Venezuelan government and its own oil companies. (Chapter 4 discusses this issue from Venezuela's point of view.)

Such U.S. political intervention in respect of oil has certainly not been restricted to the Western hemisphere, but elsewhere it is very difficult to disentangle the role of oil from other considerations. Collectively U.S. investment in oil in the Middle East exceeds that in

Venezuela, and the Middle East also increased rapidly in importance as a supplier of crude oil to the United States from the beginning of the 1960s. In the light of these facts it was not surprising that U.S. strategy towards the area aimed at the creation of a collective defence organization against any possible interest from the Soviet Union, which, of course, has a common frontier with one of the main oil-producing nations of the area – Iran. United States diplomacy thus worked hard for the formation of the Central Treaty Organization – CENTO – which had as its objective the protection of U.S.A.-dominated oil-producing areas in the Middle East against external intervention. This diplomatic effort eventually succeeded in bringing Turkey and Pakistan together with Iran as the local member nations of the Organization. Though with its formation in 1955 the U.S.A. undoubtedly breathed a little more freely than hitherto, it should not escape notice that all the main oil-producing nations, with the single exception of Iran, declined to join, basically because at the time they felt their quarrel to be more with the existing economic and political interests of the U.S.A. than with hypothetical dangers from the U.S.S.R. which, given its own rapidly developing oil production, had no apparent motivation to become involved in the region.

Nevertheless at that time – and, indeed, until very recently – the U.S.A. has been powerful enough to back up its interests with sufficient military force – or potential force – to ensure that no fundamental change in the situation occurred. U.S. backing for the British presence in the Middle East, particularly in the Persian Gulf; a supply of arms to favoured rulers; and intervention with force, when necessary, as in the case of the landing of U.S. troops in Syria and Lebanon when there seemed a real threat to the important pipelines coming through these countries on their way from Saudi Arabia and Iraq to the Mediterranean – these were amongst the devices used to implement the policy of safe-guarding the oil investment and of denying the oil to a possible adversary.

U.S. policy towards Middle Eastern oil in the post-war period has thus essentially been an intensification of its policy between the wars, when governmental support and backing of many kinds were used to carve out commercial oil interests for the U.S.A. in an area previously dominated by Britain and France – the successor powers to the pre-

1918 Turkish domination of the area. At that time U.S. pressure was sufficiently strong to force Britain and France to concede ground, so that U.S. companies secured undivided control over oil resources in Saudi Arabia and partial control over exploration rights in all other territories on the western side of the Persian Gulf. Only in Iran did the U.S.A. fail to secure a share of the oil rights in the pre-Second World War period, but even this was an omission which it was able to make good after the war in the agreement following the dispute between Iran and the Anglo-Iranian oil company. In this dispute, which began in 1951, all the company's installations were expropriated by the Iranian government and for three years virtually no oil, other than that required for domestic use, was produced or refined. It was U.S. mediation which eventually, in 1954, produced a formula whereby the dispute was ended. As part of this formula, a consortium of companies was established to work the Iranian oilfields and the Abadan refinery on behalf of the National Iranian Oil Company. In the light of a more than twenty-year-old American interest in securing dominance over Middle Eastern oil it is perhaps hardly surprising that U.S. companies gained a somewhat better than 25 per cent interest in the consortium and thus brought the U.S.A. into the one area in the Middle East from which it had previously been excluded.

American successes in expanding and intensifying its oil interests in the Middle East and in keeping out the Soviet Union by means of collective defence agreements and military strength have, however, been tempered by setbacks arising from change within the area itself – change which the U.S.A. has had to struggle to slow down, let alone stop. In part this has arisen from increasing nationalistic resentment against the strength and dominance of the American oil companies in the region; and in part it emerges from Arab suspicions of the role of the U.S.A. in supporting Israel. The latter consideration has caused some continuing difficulties, such as Arab unwillingness for the Iraq Petroleum Company's pipelines from the Northern Iraq fields to Haifa to be used (see Map 4), and Arab insistence that Israel be denied oil supplies by any company wishing to continue to operate in Arab countries. The more serious repercussions, however, have come intermittently with the Arab–Israeli wars of 1956, 1967 and 1973. On each occasion U.S. involvement on the Israeli side was suspected by the Arab states and counter-action was thus taken against the United States and/or the American oil companies. In 1956 the partly American-owned pipelines across Syria from the Northern Iraq oil fields were blown up and severe restraints were placed on American oil companies' commercial freedom to sell oil to whom they pleased. It took many months before the situation reverted to the *status quo ante bellum*.

In 1967 the threat to U.S. oil interests seemed to be even worse, with a possibility at an early stage of widespread government intervention or even expropriation. The enormity of the repercussions of such action on the oil-producing countries' revenues was, however, quickly appreciated and the Arab nations contented themselves by declaring that Arab oil should not move to the U.S.A. – decisions which lasted little more than a few days as far as most major producers were concerned and no more than a few weeks for the rest. In the meantime, of course, the U.S. oil companies working out of Arab countries continued to supply oil to the non-embargoed destinations, most of which were, of course, also served by U.S. oil interests, while Iran took over responsibility for replacement supplies back to the U.S.A. itself. The disturbance thus turned out to be a relatively limited one as far as the United States itself was concerned – and even the closure of the Suez Canal (as in 1956) did not much affect the flow of supplies to the United States, but did permit the U.S. oil companies to earn higher profits as a result of the increase in the rates they could charge for their tankers!

By 1973 the United States had already significantly increased its reliance on oil imports from the Middle East and, as shown below, was expecting to continue to become increasingly dependent on such oil. The Arab oil-producing nations interpreted this as implying a greater ability on their part to bring pressure to bear on the U.S. continuing pro-Israeli policy and thus, following the renewal of hostilities, announced the complete embargo on all oil sales to the United States. Again the blow was softened by the ability of the international oil companies to switch other oil to the United States (in exchange for more Arab oil to the non-embargoed countries), but on this occasion, given the greater dependence of the U.S.A. on oil imports as compared with the earlier period, it did lead to supply difficulties in certain parts of the United States and a need for voluntary – and a little compulsory – constraint on oil use in the winter of 1973–4. A much more important result of this experience, however, was an American decision to reverse completely its earlier acceptance of the idea that it could rely at least to some degree on energy from the outside world. Within a few weeks of the Arab nations' action President Nixon announced 'Project Energy Independence 1980' and was soon backed by the Congressional support for the finance needed in the effort to become completely self-sufficient in energy by the end of the decade, an effort which by 1974 was already well under way. In the meantime United States' support for Israel remained as strong as it had always been. Yet it was U.S. intervention, rather than that of Western Europe (the latter, given its greater dependence on the continued flow of Arab oil, sought to appease the Arab nations by moderating its views on Israel), which brought the first real move towards *rapprochement* between the conflicting parties and the possibility of a long-term settlement in the region.

The other changes within the Middle East itself have had a serious effect on U.S. interests established through the oil concession system. Some of the early oil concession agreements, and even some drawn up in the post-Second World War period, virtually gave the U.S. oil companies sovereignty over the territories concerned. They gave the companies the right to explore without let or hindrance any part of the national territory concerned. Then, if they discovered oil resources, the right to determine unilaterally whether to exploit them or not and, if they decided to exploit them, then the extent to which they would do so. And all this was originally in return for a small royalty payment and some share of the profits, the determination of which was in any case a function of the ways in which the companies organized their accounts. In the changing post-war political climate – and in light of changes in U.S. oil-company/host-government relations that had already taken place or were in the process of taking place in Mexico, Venezuela and Indonesia for example – the U.S. government could not achieve a continuation of such relationships on its companies' behalf no matter how satisfactory it might have found the existing situation.

The first major potential crisis occurred as early as 1949 when Saudia Arabia claimed, as part of a revision of its concession arrangement with the Arabian-American Oil Company, 50 per cent of the company's *net* profits from selling Saudi Arabian crude oil. Further discussion on the background to this dispute is contained in Chapter 4, but here it should be noted that it was an unwelcome development from the point of view of the U.S.A., anxious both to maintain stability in the Middle East – and thus needing to assuage the demands of the Saudi Arabian government – and also to ensure the continued profitability of one of its main overseas oil companies. The company and the Saudi Arabian government were obviously in line for a showdown when, in order to protect its underlying interests, the U.S. government offered a formula whereby the company agreed to pay the Saudi Arabian government the 50 per cent of its net profits as demanded, but was then, in effect, reimbursed by being allowed to offset these tax payments against its tax obligations in the U.S.A. itself. The Saudi Arabian government thus gained its objective of significantly higher revenues. Net company profits for Aramco remained the same; but the U.S. taxpayer had to forgo the share of the company's profits that he had previously enjoyed. In other words, the U.S.A. considered its interest in the area's oil industry and the way in which it was organized so vital that it was prepared to forgo, on behalf of its taxpayers, the large amount of taxes it had formerly been paid by the company. This formula was thereafter applied to all other American oil operations overseas. Companies involved in such operations thus secured zero tax obligations at home on profits earned from these operations, and have since continued to enjoy this favourable situation.

While the U.S. taxpayer can presumably be said to have been consulted 'retrospectively' over 'his' decision to subsidize oil-company/oil-producing nations (in that the original decision has not been reversed following elections in which the politicians responsible put themselves at risk), the same cannot be said for the oil consumers and taxpayers of other nations who have indirectly been adversely affected by the decision. Moreover, adverse effects on these unconsulted individuals add up, of course, to produce adverse effects on the economies of other nations, and thus the U.S. government's action, emerging from collusion with the two other parties concerned – the oil companies and the oil-producing governments – produced a swing in the geo-political relationships of nations. For consumers in other nations, the short-term effect arose from the consequential impact which the change had on the stabilization of the price structure – or more particularly the posted price structure on which the eventual price of oil products to the majority of consumers was, at that time, firmly based. Thus the introduction of a more flexible and, from the consumers' point of view, a more favourable pricing system was delayed. And as far as taxpayers in other countries were concerned, the agreement ensured that the companies chose to show their profits in the producing operations, where they could offset domestic taxes, and so produced a situation in which they apparently made few or even no profits on their local refining and/or marketing operations. Thus, other taxpayers in these countries had to be more heavily taxed in order to make up for the taxes which the oil companies might otherwise have paid. Thus, for oil-consuming countries of the developing world particularly, consequent high oil-import prices combined with the absence of revenues from the local operations of the international oil companies produced an economically disadvantageous position – one example of the way in which U.S. policy decisions adversely affect nations which then have to be given aid in order to make them economically viable – so that the American taxpayer pays twice over.

The effect of the U.S. tax concession (later extended by the U.K. government to the British-based international companies) in the Middle East and other major oil-producing areas did, of course, have the desired effect as far as American interests in the international oil industry were concerned – that of avoiding a showdown between the companies and the governments. A potential major cause of political unrest in the Middle East was thus eliminated and any long-term interruption of international oil supplies, on which, as already indicated, the U.S. was becoming increasingly dependent, was made much more remote.

Thus until the beginning of the 1970s, through a combination of luck, judgement, appropriate diplomatic pressure, military threats and displays of force when necessary, and a realization by all parties (U.S. government, U.S. companies and governments of oil-producing countries) that everyone's interests were being reasonably well served, at least in the short term, by keeping the oil flowing freely,

U.S. companies were able to continue to expand their oil-producing activities in practically all parts of the world. These activities, moreover, came to be generated not only by the large international companies mentioned at the beginning of this chapter but also by a dozen or so others, which had hitherto been largely confined to domestic U.S. operations until the middle or late 1950s.

The motives for the corporate decisions by these companies to expand their operations beyond their familiar territory of the U.S.A. – and sometimes Canada – arose in the first instance from the opportunities which they saw for highly profitable operations in a post-war world short of energy and in which high prices were willingly being paid for low-cost oil from Venezuela and the Middle East. By the early 1950s this motivation was supplemented by a realization that with American oil production being kept in check both by physical and institutional factors (the most important of the latter were the very rigid controls over production exercised by the regulatory bodies such as the Texas Railroad Commission), growth in the U.S. oil market itself was likely to be met increasingly by supplies from overseas, where the immediate flush of post-war exploration and development had quickly revealed a supply which, in terms of the world's total requirements at that stage, could only be described as limitless. The domestic companies thus evaluated the alternatives either of importing part of their U.S. crude-oil requirements through the old-established international groups or of going out to seek concessions overseas for themselves. They decided, in the main, as it was likely that oil would be available under the first alternative only at prices well above the costs of producing and shipping the oil to the U.S.A., that the second procedure was likely to produce more advantageous results, in anything but the very short term, from their own corporate points of view, particularly in respect of profits.

Thus first Venezuela, then the Middle East and, most recently and most significantly, North Africa have been searched for possible concession areas by such companies. Many of them were quickly very successful in discovering new oil reserves. For example, one of the first companies to take the overseas plunge – Sun Oil of Philadelphia – quickly achieved success in concessions in Venezuela and found fields capable of producing over five million tons of oil a year. More recently

Occidental Oil of Texas found, without much difficulty, one of the largest fields in Libya and attempted to achieve an annual production capacity of 50 million tons. (An attempt which was frustrated first in 1971 by Libyan controls over the level of production and, in 1973, by Libya's expropriation of the company's operations.) Not all the efforts of the former U.S. domestic companies achieved such great successes, but almost all of them found some oil (or gas) and many of them started to ship it back to the U.S. – import quotas permitting – as quickly as possible.

It became apparent, even before the end of the 1940s, that the combination of oil-producing restrictions in the U.S.A., the rapidly growing supply potential in Venezuela and the Middle East and the successes of U.S. oil companies in finding oil overseas was undermining the position of the U.S.A. as an oil producer and exporter. U.S. exports dwindled rapidly in the post-war period, reflecting both increased pressure of demand at home on a controlled supply and the availability of lower-cost oil from elsewhere which could be substituted for American oil in overseas markets. At the same time, oil imports into those parts of the U.S.A. most remote from the indigenous producing areas – notably California and the north-east coast – started to grow. By 1948 imports exceeded exports and for the first time in the history of the oil industry, the U.S.A. became an oil-deficit nation. Thereafter imports continued to grow and, with them, concern for 'security of supply' – the most potent argument in the armoury of weapons used by the domestic oil producers, whose protests in the face of overseas competition became increasingly vehement.

As this phenomenon of an increasing dependence on oil imports coincided with the political difficulties of the Cold War and a feeling in the U.S.A. that much of the world was hostile to its power and influence, politicians quickly played up the security-of-supply argument in their pleading for restrictions on imports of oil. As the pressure mounted the Eisenhower administration was forced to take action. In 1954 and again in 1958 it called for voluntary restraint on the part of importing companies. The larger companies heeded the warning, but there was legally nothing to stop other companies, and particularly those bringing new fields into production, from taking advantage of such voluntary restraint on the part of others – thus carving out larger markets for themselves.

As a result the 'more patriotic' companies now joined forces with the other pressure groups to get something more than voluntary restraint, which was apparently having no overall effect on controlling the rate of growth of imports. So in 1959 President Eisenhower introduced mandatory quotas on both crude oil and oil products and effectively closed the U.S. market to the free entry of oil from the rest of the world (except for Canada and Mexico, whose oil was excluded from the restrictions on the grounds that imports from these countries were not at risk as they did not depend on ocean transportation). The quotas were related to the U.S.A.'s total use of oil and were set at roughly the level of imports' percentage contribution to U.S. oil supplies in 1959 – approximately one-eighth. This meant that the amount of oil imported could grow, but no more quickly than the overall growth of U.S. consumption, which was approximately 3 per cent per annum compared with a 15 per cent annual rate of growth in oil imports over the previous ten years. Thus domestic oil interests were not only guaranteed almost 90 per cent of the existing market but also almost 90 per cent of all incremental demand, while external sources, which by 1959 were sending over 50 million tons to the U.S.A., could look to no more than a very modest rate of increase in this market compared with the high rate of growth that they had enjoyed over the previous decade.

The economic effects of this decision by the U.S. government have had far-reaching consequences both inside and outside the country. Inside the U.S.A. it gave a high degree of protection to domestic oil interests, whose output was maintained at a level far higher than it would have been with continued unrestricted foreign competition. It has, in fact, been estimated that during the 1960s, between one-third and one-half of domestic oil production would have been closed down, particularly production from the coastal or near coastal fields, which lacked the protection given by the cost of inland transportation in getting foreign oil to the interior of the very extensive land mass. This estimate was based on a comparison of the market opportunities for imported oil, which during this period could be landed at U.S. east coast refineries at a price of $1.50 per barrel, with the cost of producing and shipping U.S.-produced oil to the country's markets. Domestic production levels of over 500 million tons per annum were achieved only with a well-head price level averaging more than $3.00 per barrel, such that if the price customers needed to pay to obtain their oil requirements had fallen to as little as half this figure one can see that the production of much expensive domestic oil would have been eliminated.

This cost of the mandatory oil quotas policy obviously kept up the price of oil to the consumer, and in end-uses where there were no possibilities of substitution the consumer had to pay the additional cost without any choice. In many end-uses, however, other sources of energy were substituted for oil and as the oil import policy kept oil prices up, so many consumers elected to use other forms of energy. Natural gas – whose price in the U.S.A. was, in contrast, kept down by government intervention – has benefited particularly in home heating and similar markets. In addition American coal has also enjoyed a significant boom at the expense of foreign oil and has been able to retain and even increase its markets in thermal electricity generating plants not only in the areas of coal production themselves but also in the east-coast megalopolis, which could otherwise have provided outlets in bulk for cheap foreign oil. Internally, therefore, a large number of powerful pressure groups were well pleased with the mandatory oil quotas, as were those oil refiners who were eligible for 'tickets' giving them the right to import specified quantities of foreign oil. These rights became negotiable currency, for with a price differential between domestic and foreign oil of about $1.50 per barrel until 1970 it was obviously more profitable to pay, say, $1.00 for a 'ticket' which gave the right to import a barrel of the foreign product. The overall cost to the refinery needing crude oil was still 50 cents less than if the domestic product were used.

Thus, a single act of government (and amendments to the quota system up to 1972 only relaxed the restrictions to a degree) ensured that the U.S.A. remained the world's largest producer of petroleum. Without the quota system it would, during the 1960s, have been overtaken certainly by the U.S.S.R., probably by Venezuela and possibly by one or more Middle Eastern producing nations as well. It also encouraged the continued search for new petroleum resources within the U.S.A. by increasing the profitability of the oil industry at home, so providing the incentive for exploration and development. The discovery of the Alaskan oilfields can be said to be mainly the result of import quotas, for as Alaskan production would naturally have had free access to the rest of the U.S. market, there was every incentive to develop it in spite of the state's physical separation from the rest of the country and the difficult working conditions there.

This act of government, however, also produced a situation in which U.S. oil and coal reserves ran down faster than would have been the case if unlimited foreign oil had been allowed into the country. Excluding Alaskan potential – as yet of an uncertain magnitude – the U.S. domestic oil industry has had a struggle to maintain reserves sufficient to sustain the higher production levels required to meet growing demand. It was argued that, if reliance on foreign oil is to be considered a security risk, then the best policy to pursue is one which encourages imports in the short term – while they remain readily available, that is – so as to conserve U.S. domestic resources for the time when the potential risk becomes an actual one.

This argument was never effectively answered, suggesting that protection of domestic interests rather than concern for the security of overseas supplies was the more important element in American attitudes. As events have turned out, however, the post-1970 development of a temporary energy shortage in the U.S.A. (largely as a result of low-priced natural gas inhibiting the proving of reserves sufficient to sustain an unexpectedly high rate of demand arising out of the electrification of the economy) has necessitated a reappraisal of U.S. policy towards oil imports. In mid-1973 import controls were lifted except for a small remaining tariff to give protection to some domestic producers. However, given the strong upward movement in world oil prices between 1971 and 1973 it became unlikely even then that this degree of protection was needed to keep the U.S. oil producers in business. Its more important function was, indeed, to raise the profitability of the oil producers so that their interest in finding and producing new oil in the U.S.A. would be stimulated – not only in terms of oil from the remote Alaskan fields but also for oil from the high-cost smaller on-shore potential oil-bearing structures and for possible oil reserves lying off-shore on the Atlantic continental shelf of the United States.

More domestic oil will be produced, however, given the financial and other inducements from a U.S. administration which is determined, like most of its predecessors, to minimize the country's dependence on imported energy. (This has become particularly true in the light of the 1973/4 experience of the Arab oil-producing nations' embargo on oil supplies to the U.S.A. as a means of bringing political pressure to bear on it to change its policy in the Middle East.) This in part will be from the large Alaskan discoveries (following the rapid defeat, after the embargo on Arab oil to the U.S., of the environmental protection interests which earlier held up their development for so long). In part it will be achieved by technical developments such as the use of underground nuclear explosions, designed to release quantities of oil which cannot otherwise be extracted from certain oil-bearing formations because of particular geological and other physical conditions (the first experimental blasts have been announced as apparent successes). Similarly, decisions have also been taken to go ahead with the extraction of oil from the tar sands and oil shales which are quarriable in virtually limitless amounts in several states of the Union, giving oil at a cost well below the price of oil in international trade in 1974. So the rapid development of this new industry can now be expected as a result of the United States' continued wish to be as self-sufficient as possible in oil – the same motivation, in fact, which originally lay behind the introduction of the mandatory quotas on oil imports. 'Project Energy Independence 1980' will ensure the resources required to achieve this aim.

In overall terms, then, the short-term losses for the American economy, which arose from higher energy prices to consumers than they would have had to pay without oil quotas, can be offset to some degree against the technological and other developments in energy production that have been encouraged and which now promise in the longer term to help the U.S.A. to maintain its economic lead over the rest of the world. It is particularly ironic that the imposition of quotas and other elements in a generally autarkic energy policy should have produced the completely unforeseen possibility of development of oil export potential from Alaska, whose oil resources could, indeed, now be fully exploited with a view to serving not only the U.S. market but also markets in other parts of the world. It is conceivable that Alaskan exports – particularly to Japan and other parts of the Far East – could, within a decade, offset any remaining need for U.S. oil imports from other parts of the world unless, to be entirely logical in its argument for ensuring future oil supplies, the government forbids the export of this oil to other countries!

But if the results of the mandatory quotas and autarky have not been entirely disadvantageous for the U.S.A. itself, the same cannot be said for certain other parts of the world. These, of course, are the ones which produce oil for export. It has been shown earlier in this chapter how many U.S. companies eagerly sought concessions to search for oil abroad and, in many cases, quickly achieved success, thereby raising the hopes of the host countries for important new sources of revenue and employment and for other economic advantages. These companies had entered into these expensive commitments in order to find, produce and export oil back to the U.S.A. The mandatory quotas thwarted these plans – even more effectively than would perhaps at first appear in the light of the way in which the quota system worked.

The quotas were not allocated on a percentage basis to all who requested them but were given to those companies which were 'traditional' importers of oil and oil products (that is, those companies which had been importing oil during the earliest post-war period). Thus, newcomers to the international oil business have been virtually excluded from the U.S. market unless, of course, they have been prepared to purchase a 'ticket to import' from one of the 'traditional' importers that thus stood to make profits much more easily out of selling their rights to import than out of continuing to trade in foreign oil. This has happened to some extent, but, by and large, the American companies which had discovered oil abroad with the intention of selling it in the U.S.A. have been forced either to sit tight on their discoveries or to seek markets elsewhere. It has been estimated, as previously indicated, that the quotas led to some 150 million tons more oil per annum being produced in the U.S.A. than would otherwise have been the case, and so overseas producers have 'lost' an equivalent amount. In addition, higher oil prices in the U.S.A. in the

1960s arising from quotas could well have reduced consumption to a figure 100 million tons lower than what it would have been with cheaper foreign oil available. Thus, in total, the major oil-producing nations have been denied the right to produce each year some 250 million tons of oil, which would have produced revenues for the governments concerned of at least $1,000 million together with other income generated as a result of the physical activities in the production and export of the oil.

Yet this is not the end of the story, as the U.S. decision to quota imports led, as indicated above, to some companies deciding to search for markets in other parts of the world so that they could obtain some income to offset their exploration and development expenditure. This, in turn, proved to be the single most important factor in upsetting the price equilibrium which had been established, outside North America and the communist countries, by the contrived orderly marketing arrangements of the seven large international companies which had hitherto controlled the great majority of producing operations and marketing outlets.

In order to break into this orderly market, the new companies with crude oil available at first offered it to independent refiners at prices below those formerly posted by the international majors; they then started to build refineries themselves and thus enhanced their marketing opportunities by making available a variety of products for as many customers as could handle them. The international companies reacted by reducing their prices where necessary to keep business, and, at a later stage, were forced to reduce prices even to their own subsidiaries in order to enable the latter to compete and remain profitable in the local markets with which they were concerned and which were being subjected to competition from the independents.

Thus, the oil that became available on the world market as a result of import quotas in the U.S.A. acted as the catalyst upsetting the earlier post-war norm of orderly marketing. As prices in the market place fell away so this was reflected back in efforts by the companies to contain and even reduce their payments on each barrel of oil to the host governments, which as a result saw their revenues and economic livelihood being threatened. Out of this, as we saw in Chapter 1, emerged O.P.E.C. – the Organization of Petroleum Exporting

Countries – and a subsequent battle to try to ensure that the producing countries did not lose revenues by virtue of price weakness. The collective strength of O.P.E.C. inhibited further royalty and other tax reductions which the companies would otherwise have achieved, but, on the other hand, the market weakness certainly eliminated a large part of the ability of the countries concerned to secure the larger unit returns from oil exports that could have been achieved, had the action of the U.S. government in limiting oil imports not upset the delicate equilibrium of the world market.

U.S. government action thus rebounded unfavourably as far as the oil-producing nations in general were concerned. In particular, however, it proved seriously disadvantageous to Venezuela, which, in the face of the increasing production of lower-cost oil from the Middle East, had gradually lost its markets in Western Europe and became dependent largely on United States markets. U.S. quotas virtually eliminated Venezuela's only significant growth market overnight, and the oil economy of the country suffered for over a decade. The government of the country thus made repeated efforts to secure some form of preferential treatment based on its particular geo-political relationships with the U.S.A. and within the framework of Western hemisphere treaty arrangements. In economic terms Venezuela considered the U.S.A. to be its 'natural' market. Though such a concept has little economic validity in a situation of different production costs at different locations, and of falling ocean freight rates which eliminate the competitive transport advantage of the nearer supplier, the Venezuelans continued to make use of it and the idea has thus achieved reality in political terms. In geo-political terms, moreover, Venezuela occupied the key position in the Caribbean area following the defection of Cuba to the communist alliance. Venezuela used these facts, coupled with a constant reiteration of the U.S.A.'s original concept of 'hemispheric solidarity', to try to persuade the U.S.A. to make an exception for Venezuelan (and other Latin American) oil similar to that granted to Canada and Mexico. Venezuela even stressed that it would not take undue advantage of its exemption from the quota system and would be prepared to negotiate reasonable marketing opportunities in the same way that Canada has voluntarily limited its exports to the U.S.A. Alternatively Venezuela argued that its oil (or Latin American oil in general) should be given a privileged position within the quota system, possibly by guaranteeing it a specified share of the total and of the annual incremental tonnage permitted under the system.

These were powerful arguments, and the U.S. administration was several times on the brink of accepting Venezuela's pleas in one way or another. But each time it withdrew from the brink and refused special treatment to Venezuela except over questions such as freeing from quota the Puerto Rican market for petrochemical feedstocks – a market which Venezuela was particularly well placed to serve and for which it also had appropriate types of crude oil and products readily available – and over freeing imports of residual fuel oil in general, which happened to be to Venezuela's advantage. The U.S.A.'s refusal to take specific action to help Venezuela – a refusal used in Latin America as another example of the way in which it fails in its duties to the continent to whose support it gives a great deal of lip service – was based in public on a declared anathema to government interference in the right of private oil importers to buy their oil where they choose and in private on an unwillingness to upset oil-producing nations in the politically unreliable Middle East. The public reasoning rang very hollow in the light of the fact that the imposition of quotas was in itself a much greater interference with the right of private enterprise to choose its own supply sources. The private reasoning, on the other hand, was not without some foundation, although Venezuela said that its fellow member countries of O.P.E.C. indicated that they would not have been very upset by a decision of the U.S.A. to accede to Venezuela's pleas. Their 'indications' might have been made, however, in a pretty certain knowledge that their sincerity would not be put to the test by the U.S.A. Thus, though many other factors combined to produce difficulties for the Venezuelan oil industry in the 1960s (these are considered in Chapter 4), the decision of the U.S.A. to restrict its imports of overseas oil was certainly one of the most important.

But if Venezuela's loss as a result of the U.S. import quota system in terms of government revenues, jobs and new expenditure by overseas oil companies in the country can be estimated at many hundreds of millions of dollars each year between 1959 and 1973, the same quota system produced economic gains for other nations in other parts of the world – notably Western Europe and Japan, whose energy consumers steadily benefited from the reduced oil prices arising out of the 'surplus' created by the quota system. Though this 'help' to Europe and Japan on the part of the U.S.A. was quite inadvertent, it seems not impossible that its importance to the economies of Western Europe was as great as the effects of the Marshall Plan for European recovery. Moreover, while the Marshall Plan had a time limit and a U.S. Congress which examined its expenditure very critically each year, the beneficial effects to Western Europe of these low oil prices went on for year after year without the inquisition of a Congress which, for other reasons, was unlikely to do anything to end the system. The U.S.A. had energy cost advantages over the rest of the manufacturing world from at least the beginning of this century. This advantage was eliminated – or all but eliminated – after 1959 by the availability of very low cost oil to Europe and Japan. One can perhaps offer this as one of the reasons why the U.S. found the economic going so difficult in the 1960s and only managed to achieve growth rates significantly below those of most other industrialized nations.

Thus, though the oil industry might still be considered an American invention and an American-dominated one in the main, some parts of the rest of the world learned not only to live with this but to take such an economic advantage of it that their gains from it over this period of nearly fifteen years probably exceeded the advantages gained by the U.S.A. Both oil-producing and oil-consuming countries increasingly 'called the tune' in the system of the international oil industry – and the U.S. companies involved jumped to it when called; and then had the U.S. taxpayer bail them out when the going got too tough. The cry of 'U.S. domination of international oil' began to have a somewhat ironic ring to it. At the beginning of the 1970s the situation seemed to be getting even more ironic – as it appeared that the U.S. would have to compete on the world oil market for increasingly large supplies of energy which, at least temporarily, could not be produced in the U.S. itself. Even having successfully bought the oil, it still had to face difficulties in transporting it to the U.S.A. and in refining it along the east coast – given the success of the environmentalists in preventing the construction of terminals for mammoth tankers and of new refineries to run on the foreign crude oil. However, American influence in oil matters has quickly reasserted itself. Following the Arab–Israeli war of 1973, and the resulting embargo on oil to the United States plus the traumatic rise in international oil prices as the oil-producing countries have, working together, chosen to exercise their power, the United States is already benefiting in two ways.

Firstly, it is benefiting from the greatly enhanced profitability of the international oil companies, most of which are, as shown in Chapter 1, American by ownership and control – their flow of profits is certainly helping the U.S. balance of trade position. Secondly, given the limited extent to which the U.S. economy depends on oil imports, it has been able to divorce its energy pricing system from that set by international oil. In doing so it is ensuring its consumers a very significant energy cost advantage (of 50 per cent or more) over their rivals in other parts of the industrialized world. This is particularly true, of course, in Western Europe and Japan which, as shown in Chapters 5 and 6, allowed their economies to become very largely dependent on foreign oil. Now, in the radically changed oil power situation of the 1970s, they find themselves in difficulties over both the supply and price of the commodity flowing in a system which has become so much more favourable to the United States since 1972: though how long this will last depends on the way the major oil producing and exporting countries choose to exercise their greatly increased powers.

3: Soviet Oil Development

Amongst Soviet claims to have led the world in the field of technical developments is one which attributes the world's first oil well to the Soviet Union. The validity, or otherwise, of this claim is not relevant to the task in hand, but the fact that it can be made at all does indicate the early date of the exploitation of oil resources in Russia. The expansion of this early initial exploitation into an industry of world significance in the late nineteenth century was a function of European trading interests. They sought and obtained concessions there in order to provide Europe with alternative oil supplies and thus break the near monopoly which Rockefeller's Standard Oil had achieved with American oil products. The shallowness of the deposits and other attractive geological conditions in the vicinity of Baku and the completion in the 1880s of good transport facilities to the Black Sea coast encouraged the growth of Russian oil production, while the proximity of the oil to potential markets, particularly those in Europe, compared with the alternative supply points in the U.S.A., made these early Russian ventures financially interesting. A little later, the rapidly emerging Shell group also bought Russian oil to break the monopoly of Standard Oil east of Suez, but success in this direction depended on an ability to deliver the oil in bulk rather than in tins and drums whose shipment through the Suez Canal necessitated expensive safety precautions. Success was achieved in 1892, with the entry into service of an ocean-going tanker which was given safety clearance by the Canal authorities. Thus, Russia's oil development was given another boost and in the period before the First World War it was second only to the U.S.A. in its total oil production. In fact, Russia was for a few years even ahead of the U.S.A. in annual production. Physical conditions for oil production remained attractive, the markets of Western Europe continued to grow and foreign capital continued to be drawn to this important producing area. Thus, the prospects were good for the rapid and continued development of the country's oil resources. This typical nineteenth-century and early twentieth-century approach to the development of a country's mineral resources by foreign companies, mainly from the United States and the United Kingdom, was, however, upset by the First World War and then terminated abruptly by the Soviet Revolution in 1917.

As a result of the revolution the oil industry in Russia, like every other sector of the economy, passed into the ownership of the state. In the chaos of the immediate post-revolutionary period, Soviet oil production declined markedly and its export trade in the commodity virtually disappeared. However, as the Soviet authorities gradually gained effective control over the country's economic life, the Baku oilfields were reactivated under the stimuli of a domestic need for oil and the possibility of reviving exports, whereby the Soviet Union could earn some of the hard foreign currency so desperately needed for its economic development. Production from Baku, therefore, gradually edged upwards and ultimately by the late 1920s the Soviet Union was producing more oil per annum than had ever been produced in the pre-revolutionary period. This success must, however, be put in perspective, for it took place at a time when world oil production was increasing even more rapidly under the stimulus of a big growth in demand by motor transport and by the industries of North America and of Western Europe. The Soviet Union's production efforts did not in this period keep up with the general rate of world increase. But they did, nevertheless, produce enough oil to meet requirements in the U.S.S.R. itself – requirements limited by the deliberate choice of the U.S.S.R.'s policy makers not to expand its motor industry or to encourage the use of motor transport. Elsewhere in the Soviet Union the growing number of factories, springing up under forced industrialization, could be fueled by coal and lignite available in closer proximity to the main industrial areas of Moscow and Leningrad or from the major hydro-electric schemes being developed on some of the country's important rivers.

Soviet oil was, however, increasingly successful in foreign markets, and to encourage this desirable development the Soviet government invested in tankers, oil depots and distribution facilities in many countries of Western Europe including the U.K., where products were sold under the trade name R.O.P. – Russian Oil Products. As a result of a relatively aggressive sales policy in the chosen markets of Western Europe the Soviet Union achieved about a 15 per cent share of the total market available. Although this share fluctuated in the 1930s, largely because increasing home demand created pressure from time to time on the country's limited producing facilities, this general level of penetration of Russian oil into Western European markets still existed at the outbreak of the Second World War in 1939.

During the Second World War most of the Soviet Union's existing oil-producing facilities were overrun by German armed forces. This gave a great incentive for the Soviet Union to seek oil in other parts of the country, much of which was of a sedimentary character and hence at least potentially petroliferous. However, wartime difficulties and other conditions made exploration and development almost impossible and for most of the war much of the Soviet Union's war effort depended upon the success of the convoys of oil tankers and other ships moving around the coast of northern Europe to the north Russian ports of Archangel and Murmansk, and on some overland movement of oil by rail from Iran to the southern parts of the U.S.S.R.

At the end of the war the Soviet Union initiated a massive reconstruction of its economy and one of its earlier efforts was a plan for the rapid expansion of the country's oil and gas resources. Wartime oil exploration had indicated the existence of large fields in the area between the Volga and the Urals, and these were rapidly developed, so that they could immediately supplement the output of the rehabilitated fields of the Baku area. Within a few years, however, their size enabled them to dominate the pattern of Soviet oil output and the new area of production became known as the 'Second Baku'. Although the Soviet economy was still essentially based upon the use of coal and other solid fuels, and although preference in capital investment programmes tended to be given to the development and expansion of hydro-electric resources, oil and gas started to increase their share in the total energy requirements of the expanding economy. Since the early 1950s, increases in oil and gas production and an increasing contribution of these two fuels to the total energy economy has continued apace and by 1973 they were responsible for over 60 per cent of the total amount of energy used in the Soviet Union. By 1980 their share is expected to be over 75 per cent.

The location of Soviet oil and gas production is shown in Map 1. As this map shows, production from the Caucasus region and from the Volga–Urals fields is now being supplemented by new developments in Soviet Central Asia and in western Siberia – with the latter tentatively termed the 'Third Baku'. Moreover, the pace of exploration continues and the search has been taken into central and eastern Siberia, where the potential for oil and gas production is considered very high indeed and where important discoveries have already been made. The old and new areas together are expected to yield over 640 million tons per annum by 1980, when the country's oil production could well be the world's largest (Soviet oil production overtook that of Venezuela in 1961 to make it second only to the U.S.A. and it seems likely to exceed the latter's some time in the mid-1970s, unless Alaska proves to be very prolific very quickly).

This success of the Soviet Union in developing its own oil resources has minimized, if not entirely eliminated, what was considered to be a potential threat to the Middle East in the earlier part of the post-war period. As the Soviet economy expanded in the 1950s many observers argued that its need for oil would lead the Soviet Union to cast covetous eyes on the productive capacity of neighbouring countries such as Iran and adjacent Middle East countries like Iraq and those of the Persian Gulf. The great successes achieved in expanding domestic production now make this argument appear less important and unlikely to re-assert itself (this issue is discussed in greater depth in Chapter 8). Paradoxically, however, in recent years Iran has considered it to be in its own national interests to reach a commercial agreement with the Soviet Union whereby it supplies adjacent areas of the U.S.S.R. with some of the natural gas produced from its southern fields as a joint product with their oil production. This gas has no other markets – except local industrial ones that are slow to develop – and a massive natural gas line, the capacity of which is to be increased by over 50 per cent by 1975, runs from these fields across the country into the Soviet Union, where it links up with an existing Soviet natural gas pipeline system. The agreement between Iran and the Soviet Union is certainly in the national interest of the former

Map I. Soviet Oil and Gas Production and Export Facilities

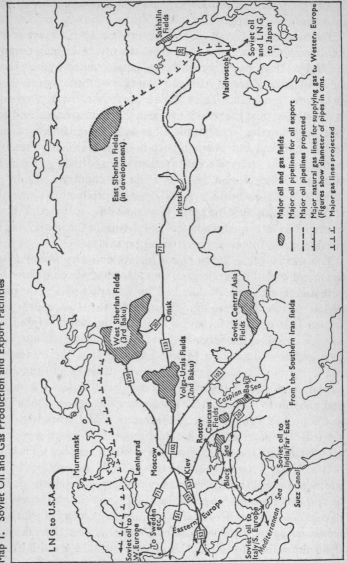

– with no other immediately foreseeable large market for its gas production – and is important for the latter in that it represents a new willingness to consider importing energy in order to save the considerable amounts of capital which would otherwise be required in making indigenous energy available to the areas concerned, whilst at the same time releasing gas from favourably located Soviet fields for export to Western Europe. The agreement between Iran and the Soviet Union can, therefore, be interpreted quite satisfactorily solely in economic terms and its political overtones appear minimal.

This and a similar agreement to import small quantities of gas from a field just over the border in Afghanistan are the only significant ventures of the Soviet Union into an oil and gas import policy. Otherwise the basis of its policy is one of energy self-sufficiency no matter what the cost, and although certain parts of its territory – particularly the far east and the far north – could probably have imported their energy requirements at lower cost to the Soviet economy than that involved in taking domestic energy to these areas, there has been no question of the Soviet Union responding to offers from time to time in this direction by various oil companies and other traders in the Western world. A national pipeline system and local distribution networks have been built to ensure that most parts of the Soviet Union – including all those with a significant degree of industrialization – can be supplied from the country's producing areas. Since production is being continually increased in the light of anticipated future growth of energy consumption it now seems unlikely that there could be any fundamental change in the Soviet attitude of more or less complete autarky in its energy sector.

Soviet interests in international movements of oil and gas have, in fact, been in the opposite direction, for since the mid-1950s the U.S.S.R. has reverted to its pre-war policies of seeking export markets for them. There seem to have been two distinct motives behind the Soviet Union's search for markets overseas – the first wholly economic, and the second economic to some degree but with political overtones. In the first place, it has sought export opportunities for its oil in all countries where the oil could earn 'hard' foreign currencies and where it could be used in barter-type arrangements for goods the U.S.S.R. requires in its development programme. For this type of

49

trade crude oil and petroleum products are virtually ideal exports in that the purchasers will know exactly what they are getting, because there is an internationally agreed specification which has to be met. Oil exports are thus less likely to be technically or otherwise suspect than other products of the Soviet Union's relatively recent industrialization, many of which have not been subjected to the rigours of Western-style consumer evaluation.

Thus, Soviet oil exports constitute desired and acceptable goods competing in most respects with similar products from elsewhere, as far as much of Western Europe and Japan are concerned. This view, however, has only gradually been accepted, and its acceptance is in large part a function of the retreat from the Cold War attitudes still prevailing when the Soviet Union initiated its major oil export campaign in the mid-1950s. Its attempts to sell oil in Western Europe at that time were interpreted in political terms by the U.S. State Department and some of the major American oil companies. Western European nations were 'warned' of the great economic risks involved in relying on an energy source which, it was argued, could be turned off at the whim of the U.S.S.R. policy makers. These opponents of Soviet oil made more than full use of the one occasion on which the U.S.S.R. had declined to honour an oil supply agreement as a result of changed political circumstances. However, as this was the special case of a Soviet refusal to go on supplying Israel in 1957, after it had been declared an aggressor nation by the United Nations for its invasion of Egypt, it was difficult to accept it as a valid precedent. In fact, the European nations which became interested in Russian oil were able to turn such arguments back on to their instigators when they showed just how dependent the American companies were on Middle Eastern Arab countries for their oil supplies, while these countries argued that their willingness to continue supplying oil depended on the recipient's willingness not to help Israel in its battle against the Arab nations. Britain and France, of course, suffered the political whim of the Arab oil-exporting countries in this respect in the months after their collusion with Israel in the 1956–7 Suez crisis, as did the Netherlands specifically and Western Europe generally in the aftermath of the 1973 conflict in the Middle East.

In that there are underlying political factors which involve almost all of the world oil industry in one way or another, most European nations were somewhat sceptical, to say the least, of American efforts to 'knock' Russian oil in this way. Thus, the arguments were largely ignored and Soviet oil has gradually found markets in the countries of Western Europe, as both state entities and private refiners and marketers have found Soviet offers increasingly acceptable. Of course, as a new entrant to the market at a time when most outlets were controlled by the major international companies, the U.S.S.R. could only succeed in its exports attempts by offering oil at cut prices. But there is no evidence to suggest that prices were ever cut more than the commercial expertise of the Russians indicated that they should be, in order that, as some people suggested, the Soviet Union could undermine the economies of Western Europe! Indeed the evidence available points to Soviet unwillingness to sell their oil at the very depressed prices which have obtained from time to time in some Western European markets like Switzerland, where in the 1960s oil was available from a very large number of companies for the non-tied outlets. Supporters of the view that Soviet oil is being 'dumped' in Western Europe, and/or sold to secure some political or strategic advantage, point to the wide discrepancy between the prices of Soviet oil in Western Europe and the much higher prices which are charged to Eastern European countries. What such observers are in effect pointing out, however, is a good example of the great disadvantage of being a captive customer in a time of 'over-supply'. The high oil prices paid by the East Europeans, lacking freedom both from political causes and within the framework of their long-term bilateral trading treaties with the U.S.S.R. to negotiate their oil supplies from elsewhere, were not the only ones existing in the world of oil at that time: there were also the much more widespread and even higher prices paid by associated companies of the international majors, which were simultaneously selling crude oil and products much more cheaply to non-associated companies and state entities for whose business they had to compete.

To a large degree, however, the particular motivations which lay behind the Soviet oil export drive in Western Europe did little more than provide a subject for academic debate; a topic for discussion in international bodies such as NATO and the Council of Europe under pressure from its oil company-owning members; and a convenient excuse for some oil companies to explain away their own high prices in a situation where Soviet oil was available at much lower prices. But while the debate and discussion were raging individual countries tested Soviet oil, found its specifications to be acceptable, and proceeded to take advantage of it in the interests of their own economic development.

Sweden was in the forefront of the partial switch to Soviet oil, the importation of which it quite deliberately built up to some 15 per cent of its total oil import requirements. Significantly it was Sweden – unencumbered by membership of NATO and the pressures that were brought on its members from its oil-company-owning nations – which first indicated that the usual security-of-supply arguments against Soviet oil could, in fact, be reversed. It was pointed out that Sweden's oil-based economy depended upon political stability in the Middle East and the willingness of countries there to continue to supply oil. Such a situation not only implied security dangers but had already given rise to difficulties both in the early 1950s as a result of Iranian nationalization and in the later 1950s as a result of the Suez War. In such circumstances, oil from the Soviet Union – imported as part of a bilateral trading arrangement in which Russia obtained goods that it really needed from Sweden – reduced the security risk. Sweden also pointed out that transport of Soviet oil would be less liable to interruption than that of oil from other sources once the proposed pipeline from Soviet oilfields to the Baltic was completed. Only in the event of a major war involving the great powers would Soviet oil be at risk, and in that case it would be unlikely that many nations of the world would be very worried for very long about their oil imports.

The significance of Sweden's early success in its oil dealings with the U.S.S.R. was not lost on other European nations, which one by one have accepted the validity of the economic arguments and discounted the alleged security-of-supply risks as argued officially by NATO under extreme American pressure. Even Western Germany has been willing to negotiate large supplies of Soviet oil in exchange for Russian markets for its iron and steel production and for export openings for other manufactured goods. France and Belgium have similarly encouraged Soviet oil trade – though neither to the same degree as Italy, which has deliberately set out to take the maximum possible economic advantage of large-scale Soviet oil availability. This attitude has stemmed from Italy's evaluation of oil as a source of energy which would help to eliminate the country's long-standing resource and locational disadvantages in the field of fuel and power in comparison with the more favourably blessed countries of north-west Europe. Low-cost imported oil promised much in this direction, but Italy soon found that access to such oil was largely denied to her through the organization of the international petroleum industry working within the framework of a system of posted prices which kept them high. Italy's immediate reaction was to give more or less *carte blanche* to E.N.I., the state oil entity, to seek oil abroad. Its first efforts lay in finding and developing oil resources abroad, but it quickly became obvious that success in this direction would take too long to achieve and, in the meantime, the Soviet Union had appeared on the scene as a large-scale supplier at prices well below those that Italy could obtain elsewhere. Soviet oil thus served both the political and commercial interests of E.N.I. and the economic interests of the nation and, from small beginnings in the mid-1950s, E.N.I. steadily built up its dependence on Soviet supplies. To encourage this development the Soviet Union responded by offering preferential outlets for Italian goods, and the two nations eventually signed a massive bilateral agreement in 1963. This involved a total of 25 million tons of crude oil to be delivered over five years, with the timing of supplies such that by 1968 the Soviet Union would be supplying Italy with about 16 per cent of its total need at price levels which appeared to give discounts of some 30 per cent off posted prices. From Italy's point of view the bargain was even more favourable in that it also secured guaranteed export markets for massive quantities of Italian steel pipes and automobile factories, amongst other goods. Italy came under severe pressure from fellow members of NATO to modify the arrangement but refused to do so and has gradually increased its use of Soviet oil to 12 million tons per year, to which must now be added the equivalent of another 5 million tons of oil per year in the form of Soviet natural gas. This will be discussed further later in this chapter.

Only Britain and the Netherlands amongst the principal Western European oil-consuming nations continued to refuse to accept the advantages of Soviet oil – the latter because of its ownership of the larger part of the Royal Dutch/Shell Group; the former partly because of its interest in the ownership of two of the international major oil companies but more because of its unwillingness to act against a NATO policy strongly supported by the United States. Britain finally reversed its policy in 1971 – when NATO ceased to argue along its traditional lines and some years after Shell itself had got reinvolved in the Eastern European oil trade – and the Soviet Union re-established its marketing outlets in Britain.

Soviet oil exports to Western Europe thus steadily increased from only 3 million tons in 1955 to over 40 million tons in 1969 and about the same quantity each year since then. In response to this success and to ensure its continuing success in the future, the Soviet Union steadily improved its arrangements for delivering the oil to Western Europe (see Map 1).

At first the oil was moved from interior fields to the Black Sea ports by a combination of different modes of transport, including pipeline where possible, and barges and rail as alternatives, where necessary (see Map 1). Then the Soviet Union chartered tankers as required to ship the oil to Europe. In these early days any 'profit' on exports to Western European countries must have disappeared in these expensive transport arrangements and in others which were even more expensive, such as the rail-haul of fuel oils and even crudes from the end of the pipeline system in European Russia to the Baltic ports of both the U.S.S.R. and Eastern European countries for transshipment to markets in Scandinavia. The increasing Western European export-requirements were, however, made part of the oil-transport expansion programme under development for the U.S.S.R. and Comecon (the Soviet Union-Eastern European Organisation for Economic Co-operation) and they did, in fact, help to justify the more rapid development of a pipeline system which now takes oil down to the Black Sea to ocean-going tankers and also directly across European Russia into Poland, East Germany and other communist countries of Eastern Europe and so to the Baltic, where loading terminals for exports to Scandinavia and other Western markets have been constructed. The demand for exports, over and above the demand for crude oil in Eastern Europe, justified the construction of this crude-oil line which, with a diameter of some 48 inches, is the world's biggest. Since the completion of these delivery facilities Soviet oil has had a more secure transport system than oil from any other part of the world. The completion of the pipelines has also reduced the supply price of Russian oil to Western European markets and hence assisted its market penetration.

However, Soviet oil remains an alternative for Western European countries to oil from other sources and their purchases can be switched as contracts run out in the light of changed economic conditions and new political attitudes. Such uncertainty is not, of course, very satisfactory from the Soviet Union's long-term planning point of view and recently, therefore, it has been making efforts to secure outlets on a much longer term – in fact, almost on a permanent basis. One effort has been directed at persuading appropriately placed countries of Western Europe to allow extensions of the Soviet Union–East European pipeline system to be built to supply directly refineries in Western Germany, Austria, Switzerland and even eastern France. With such direct deliveries, security of outlets is very much greater, but so far these efforts have been unsuccessful, though in 1969 only the intervention of the Federal West German government, under severe pressure from the U.S.A., thwarted an agreement between the Soviet Union and the Bavarian state government. Had this agreement gone through, the Soviet Union would have been in a very strong position to put in branch pipelines to the other countries noted above. More recently, however, in light of the 1973 *rapprochement* between East and West Germany, there has been a revival of interest in the possibilities of extending the Soviet–Comecon pipeline system to Western Europe. It now seems likely that the first stage in such a development will be in connection with a refinery to be built in West Berlin and designed to run on Soviet crude oil brought in by an extension of the line running to East German refineries.

Along with the negotiations for extensions of its pipeline system to Western Europe, the Soviet Union also decided to obtain security of outlets by buying or building refineries and distribution facilities in Western European countries. The Soviet oil export agency thus entered the market for petrol stations in the United Kingdom and is in the process of building up its distribution system fed by refined products exported to Britain from refineries on the Baltic and the Black Sea. Across the North Sea, in Belgium, the same agency has successfully negotiated an interest in a refinery at Antwerp, to which Soviet crude oil will be fed by tankers from Soviet crude-oil export ports and out of which will emerge products for distribution in Western Europe. It is now thus obvious that the Soviet Union plans a long-term future for its oil exports to Western Europe and in order to secure this is pursuing commercial policies which are not dissimilar to those followed previously by American oil companies which wished to break into these markets.

Soviet oil exports to Western Europe have been made possible by the rapidly increasing production of oil in Russia and by the growing availability of natural gas as a primary source of energy in national end-uses which would otherwise have required oil. The deliberately planned substitution of oil by gas has ensured an enhanced export potential of oil. Since 1969 it has also become evident that the Soviet Union has a surplus of natural gas after filling its own needs and is now in the process of seeking export openings for this too. As with oil, only low additional transport costs are involved in getting this gas to Western Europe, for it can be moved through lines already constructed to take gas from the producing areas of the Soviet Union to the consuming areas in the west of the country and to consumers in Eastern European countries. This is the main reason why Soviet gas – originating in fields up to 2,000 miles away – had, by the end of 1972, achieved export markets in Austria, Italy, West Germany and even France in competition with gas from the huge Groningen field of the Netherlands, which, in this geographical context, virtually constitutes local production.

The first agreement was reached with Austria in 1968 for the delivery of upwards of 100 million cubic feet daily (mcfd) – the energy equivalent of about 1 million tons of oil per annum – and in 1969 first Western Germany agreed to take 250 mcfd and then Italy opted for 600 mcfd for a contract period of 20 years – making it the largest international gas contract ever signed. Negotiations with other West European countries have continued and were successful with Finland early in 1971. Agreement with France was reached in 1972 and at the same time West Germany signed even larger contracts for Soviet gas to be delivered for 20 years from 1976. These Soviet successes in exporting natural gas to Western Europe were initially a function of the policy pursued by the Dutch natural gas export concern – NAM – which aimed to maximize its short-term financial returns rather than the quantities of gas sold. It thus fixed an export price which was far above the long-term supply price of the gas from the Groningen field and, in the absence of competition, aimed to secure considerable monopoly profits. However, after 1971, partly as a result of competition from Soviet gas, Dutch pricing policy changed in order to meet the competition from the Soviet Union and made the latter's task of marketing gas in Western Europe more difficult than had previously been envisaged. Natural gas is some three times more expensive to transport by pipeline than the equivalent amount of energy in the form of oil and so the much nearer Dutch sources of gas have a significant advantage over Soviet supplies. However, to set against this transport cost disadvantage, one should note that much of the Soviet Union's natural gas is a 'by-product' of oil production so that the costs of the producing operation can be set against the oil produced in the joint operation (as has traditionally been the case in the United States for much of its natural gas production). Even more recently, of course, since 1972 – with the change in world oil markets – gas from any source has become a commodity with a very ready market in Western Europe.

Moreover, the Soviet Union has also secured access to very low-cost gas from Iran, whose gas output from its main oilfields has hitherto been mainly flared at well-head. A large 40-inch line has been constructed from the Iranian oilfields across the country to the border with the Soviet Union (see Map 1). Over 1,000 million cubic feet daily is now being delivered through the line at a price to the Soviet Union at the border of only 1·86 U.S. cents per therm. With such a low purchase price and with only marginal transport costs to allocate to the gas moving to Western Europe (as fixed costs can be recovered from domestic and East European sales) and with even larger quantities available in the foreseeable future, Western Europe may well find gas originating from, or coming through, the Soviet Union an even more attractive proposition, particularly in light of the greatly increased post-1973 doubts over the security of Arab oil. Overall, from the point of view of the total energy economy the prospects for the next decade seem to be for much closer links between the Soviet Union and Eastern Europe on the one hand, and Western Europe on the other. Though this possibility of such long-distance overland energy flows may appear surprising, it should be noted that the distances involved are not so much greater than those involved in the transfer of oil and gas from south-west U.S.A. to the important consuming industrialized parts of the U.S.A. away to the north and north-east, or in the planned movement of Alaskan and Northern Canadian gas to the United States.

Thus, from all angles except the now largely discounted political one recommending minimum east–west contact, Soviet oil and gas links with Western Europe make good sense for both seller and buyer. Had the Soviet Union confined its oil-exporting activities to this area suspicions about its motives might have been quickly dispelled. As it has turned out, however, the Soviet Union either deliberately sought – or had thrust upon it – sales of oil in other parts of the world. Its success in selling to Japan – and the even greater success which will follow the completion of a major pipeline all the way across Siberia to an export terminal on the Pacific coast of the Soviet Union (see Map 1) – need not delay us very long. The motivations and the pattern of development, including the expansion of transport facilities, parallel what has happened between the Soviet Union and Western Europe and make as much economic sense from both parties' point of view – perhaps even more from the Soviet Union's, for sales of oil to Japan are buying, in return, the goods, capital and expertise needed for the economic development of Siberia and nearby Soviet territories. The significance of this should not, moreover, be interpreted merely in economic terms, for the development and consequent populating of these eastern territories could be as much connected with the need to strengthen the area's links with the rest of the Soviet Union, in the light of a possible future policy of expansion by China, as with economic growth pure and simple. Indirectly then, the Soviet Union is strengthening its defences *vis-à-vis* China partly on the basis of oil exports to Japan. This appears to give even greater justification for viewing Soviet interest in oil exports to Japan as essentially long-term, though from the Japanese point of view it does now raise difficulties given its alternative of seeking its required oil from the rapidly expanding and potentially very large production in China (this point will be discussed at greater length in Chapter 6).

In addition, over the last fifteen years Soviet oil has been moving to parts of the 'Third World' – to countries whose economic relationships with the Soviet Union can certainly not be interpreted in anything like the same way as those of Western Europe and Japan (see Map 2). Most interpretations of the Soviet Union's willingness to send oil to countries like India, Guinea and Brazil (to give but one example from each of the three continents constituting the Third World) give pre-eminence to political motives. In Soviet eyes such countries are in a position of economic subservience to the major capitalist powers such as the United States and the United Kingdom, and it is therefore a Soviet responsibility to help to break these bonds and thus realign the countries concerned with the socialist world. Offers of oil at prices lower than the countries can obtain within the framework of their neo-colonialist existence provides an excellent means of attaining this aim at a very low real cost to the Soviet Union. In the short term, the relatively small quantities of oil required can be provided at little more than the cost of transport – a cost more likely than not to be easily recoverable in an acceptable currency from the country to which the oil is being sent. The validity of such argument is unchallengeable; and in fact, as will be demonstrated in a later chapter, the developing countries did, in the main, find that they could get 'capitalist' oil only at prices far above supply prices as a result of the control exercised over transport, refining and distribution by a small group of international companies which had no incentive to break the 'unwritten code' covering the price at which oil was sold to such countries. To this degree Soviet oil sales to developing countries have been part of the conflict between the political systems of West and East. The more outstanding example of this arose in the case of Cuba following Fidel Castro's successful take-over of power in 1959.

Cuba produced practically none of its own energy requirements up to the time Castro took control and they were instead imported in the form of crude oil and oil products from Venezuela by three of the major international oil companies. The new government began to question the validity of the import prices they were charged for they

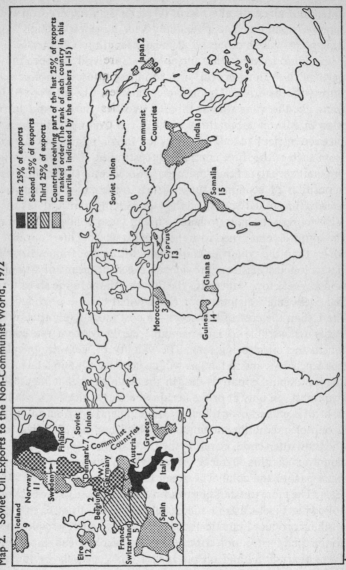

Map 2. Soviet Oil Exports to the Non-Communist World, 1972

■ First 25% of exports
▨ Second 25% of exports
▧ Third 25% of exports
▨ Countries receiving part of the last 25% of exports in ranked order (The rank of each country in this quartile is indicated by the numbers 1–15)

amounted on average to almost $3 per barrel, in spite of the very short sea distance from Venezuela where, at that time, crude oil was available at the export terminals at under $2 per barrel. But Castro's government found itself unable to secure alternative lower-cost supplies in the absence of any importing and/or refining facilities outside the control of the major companies, which claimed the absolute right to deny the use of their facilities to oil from any source other than their own affiliated companies overseas. This legally enforceable right prevented Cuba from diversifying its sources of supply and thus from reducing the cost of its oil imports within the framework of the existing system. This adverse position for Cuba was confirmed when the companies refused to refine crude oil which the Soviet Union had agreed to sell to Cuba at a delivered price of $2.10 per barrel. Cuba's reaction was to interpret the refusal within the framework of its rapidly deteriorating relations with the U.S.A., the government of which gave the companies concerned a guarantee of its support for their refusal to handle Soviet oil and, indeed, may well have encouraged their action in order to bring the difficulties with Cuba to a head over a matter on which the 'law' was quite clear. The Cuban government refused to accept the refusal and countered by 'intervening' the refineries (that is, placing them under direct government control) and gave instructions for the importation and refining of Soviet oil to the extent of the trade agreement – enough to cover approximately one-third of the country's total requirements. The companies in their turn declined to have anything more to do with Cuba and withdrew their staff and terminated their supplies. The Eastern political system retaliated by agreeing to supply the whole of Cuba's needs – the catalyst which finally transformed Cuba into a member state of the Eastern system and led to the establishment of the largest single flow of Soviet oil to any country outside Eastern Europe.

It would obviously be nonsense to deny the existence of basic political motivations in the Soviet Union's decision to sell oil to Cuba (in the same way that it is impossible to exclude political considerations from the U.S.A.'s attitude towards oil sales there), and although the situation has nowhere else moved to the same extreme position, there are other cases where much the same elements were involved. But in these other cases somewhat different reactions by the parties involved have inhibited such extremism. Sometimes the major oil companies concerned have agreed to handle Soviet oil through their refineries. In other cases governments have decided to provide their own facilities either by buying them from the companies concerned or by building new ones. And in yet other cases – most 'notably India, potentially one of the world's greatest oil markets – the 'threat' of Soviet oil as a replacement for oil imported by the international companies was sufficient to make the latter agree to significant price concessions.

It is, however, somewhat too facile to interpret this growing Soviet interest in the developing countries merely as part of the communist world's efforts to subvert the capitalist world's system. Such an interpretation mistakenly equates the best interests of the developing countries necessarily and inevitably with continued trading relations in oil via the major international oil companies. In that these countries have virtually been held to ransom over such trade because of their own weaknesses in both economic and political terms and by lack of effective competition between the supplying companies, it is possible to argue that their economic interests are better served as a result of the increasing availability of Soviet oil. The solely political interpretation also ignores the real Soviet economic interest in expanding its trade with developing countries. In spite of the great range of the Soviet Union's resources in foodstuffs, agricultural raw materials and minerals there are some of these commodities that it cannot produce for itself in sufficiently large quantities – for example, copper, rubber, wool – and whose import has, therefore, to be financed through exports. Oil is a good 'line' to offer, both because of the quantities in which it is available and the comparative advantage which the Soviet Union has in its trade and also because of its acceptability to developing nations as a substitute for supplies from other sources. Most other Soviet goods have specifications of unknown quality and in the case of machinery, motors and electrical equipment, etc., are probably not compatible with existing stocks which originate from North America and Western Europe.

The Soviet Union has yet a further economic incentive to increase its trade with developing countries. This arises from the ability of many of these countries to supply tropical and sub-tropical products such as cocoa, rice, coffee and fruits, the domestic production of which the

Soviet Union's physical environment severely limits. Until very recently such commodities were considered luxuries which neither the Soviet Union as a country nor most of its citizens could afford. Increasing affluence, however, is creating a vast potential demand for such products, some part of which could be effectively met as a result of bilateral trading developments arising out of oil exports. Thus, even as far as the developing countries are concerned, there are some strong economic factors at work encouraging the export of Soviet oil, and the trade can be expected to continue to grow. The fact that so many developing countries are securing a higher degree of independence in their oil sector by obtaining control over refining and distribution facilities (this is dealt with at greater length in Chapter 7) will enhance the prospects of growth. In this respect it is worth noting specifically that the Soviet Union and its allies in Eastern Europe are helping to create this degree of independence by giving aid to the oil industries of the developing countries. Soviet statements have indicated time and time again the importance that is attached to such aid. When one notes that almost 25 per cent of the finance for the oil sector in India's third five-year development plan was provided by Soviet or allied sources, and that the Soviet Union has agreed to provide experts and finance for the exploitation of Brazil's oil shale and tar-sand resources, and that more than a dozen other developing countries have accepted Soviet assistance for oil developments of one kind or another, then it is clear that the Soviet Union's ability in this direction should not be understated.

Some years ago, W. E. Pratt, a leading petroleum geologist and engineer and formerly Vice-President of the Standard Oil Company of New Jersey, claimed that 'American freedom of enterprise appears to be indispensable to the task of finding oil in the earth'. He went on to say that 'Russia has vast territories ideal in their promise for new oil-fields', and that 'situated in the United States and explored by those American methods, the same territories would pour out a veritable flood of oil'. Yet within a few years the Soviet Union has achieved that 'veritable flood' without the 'benefits' of American men, methods or capital and is well on its way to achieving targets for the 1980s which were considered unlikely, if not impossible, by American experts only a few short years ago.

It should be noted, moreover, that cooperation in the field of oil and gas between the U.S. and the U.S.S.R. seems likely to be one of the first and most important results of the political *détente* achieved by the two super-powers in the period between 1971 and 1973. Agreements in principle for the use of American capital and technology in the rapid exploitation of known but as yet undeveloped fields in Siberia were signed in June 1973 and their implementation is only a matter of the time required for working out the details and for an evaluation of the position by the United States, following its decision in November 1973 to pursue a policy of self-sufficiency in energy. There still seems a good chance that the agreement for the U.S.S.R. to supply energy to the United States will be excluded from this self-sufficiency aim. Trade in liquefied natural gas, if not in oil as well, from the Soviet Union to the United States seems highly probable before the end of the 1970s – a very far cry from the quite recent American opposition to Soviet exports to Western Europe and Europe's sale of oil-industry hardware to the U.S.S.R., and a splendid example of the way in which oil and gas policies are inextricably interwoven with general political and economic issues.

The next decade now seems more likely than ever to see the Soviet Union ahead of the U.S.A. in oil and gas production, satisfying not only its national and its allies' demands but also market openings for Soviet oil in many parts of the world. If during this same period the U.S.S.R. also decides to involve itself in oil and gas production in the Middle East – as now seems likely, given the recent agreement with Iran and an even more recent arrangement with Iraq – then such involvement will emerge out of growing Soviet expertise in this field – of both a technical and commercial character – rather than out of political interference for its own sake. The Soviet Union has demonstrated that an oil industry working on other than capitalist lines can be successful, and it will wish to demonstrate this in other parts of the world including the Middle East in much the same way that American companies, proud of their heritage, have exported their way of doing things. Commercially, the Soviet Union could thus gain access to oil on which it can make a 'profit' when selling in the world's markets. Here again, its behaviour is in line with good American oil company practice.

4: The Major Oil-Exporting Countries

The main area of interest of the international oil industry lies outside the U.S.A., the U.S.S.R. and the world's other communist countries. This area comprises two sets of nation states. The larger set consists of the hundred and more nations in the world's increasingly complex political framework whose interests in oil, and whose attractions for the international oil companies, lie in their functions as oil-consuming nations. These countries' oil problems, and their associated geo-political implications, will be considered in later chapters. Meanwhile, in this chapter we are concerned with the much smaller set of nation states – a handful of countries producing oil in great quantity not primarily for their own use but for exporting, in crude or refined form, to other parts of the world. These nations are picked out in Map 3, which shows those countries in which oil production exceeds oil consumption by four times or more.

Not only are there few of these – only fifteen in all – but as the map shows they exhibit a marked geographical concentration. For both these reasons whenever oil is in the press headlines it is highly likely to be the result of some geo-political problem or other arising out of the relationships of these countries with the oil companies concerned. The interests of the oil-producing countries are clear and easily recognized, especially as, in almost every case, the oil industry forms the dominant element in their economies. The negotiations between host country and oil companies that take place from time to time therefore affect the fundamental national interests of the countries concerned and thus raise great issues which have to be aired at considerable length – a phenomenon that has never been more clearly marked than in the period since October 1973 when the oil-exporting countries began to exercise their potential influence on world politics and economics for the first time. Without oil these countries would

Map 3. The World's Oil Exporting and Importing Countries 1974

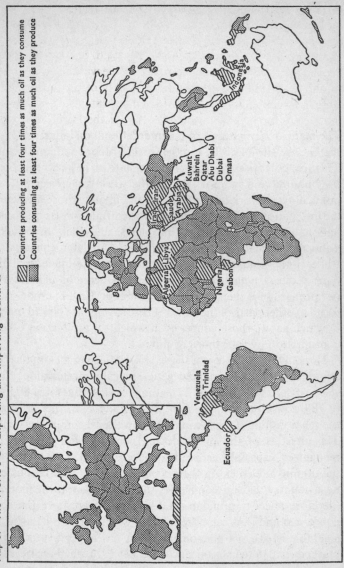

Countries producing at least four times as much oil as they consume

Countries consuming at least four times as much oil as they produce

Kuwait
Bahrein
Qatar
Abu Dhabi
Dubai
Oman

Iraq Iran
Saudi
Arabia

Algeria Libya

Nigeria
Gabon

Indonesia

Venezuela
Trinidad

Ecuador

certainly be of significantly less importance on the world stage and far less attention would be paid to the Middle East – the area in which they are mainly concentrated. However, their relatively recent rise to importance in this respect should be noted. It is essentially a post-Second World War phenomenon. Before the war they were concerned to only a very limited degree in the supply of oil to the rest of the world – which, in any case, was much less interested in oil owing to the greater importance of other fuels and the lower all-round consumption of energy due to a lesser degree of economic development. Before the war the world's single most important supplying nation was the U.S.A., with the U.S.S.R. and Mexico not far behind. Today, their functions as overseas suppliers of oil are very limited, and instead Venezuela, countries in the Middle East – especially around the Persian Gulf – and one or two other countries have become those very limited parts of the world from which not only have rapidly increasing amounts of oil been obtained but also, until very recently, an increasing share of the world's total energy requirements. Today, excluding North America and the communist world, the nations we are concerned with in this chapter account for over 90 per cent of total production and no less than 95 per cent of all oil moving in international trade.

The first nation to undergo a meteoric rise to significance as a major producer and exporter was Venezuela in the 1940s. After twenty years of somewhat desultory exploration there, the companies concerned were finally galvanized into an urgent flurry of activity by their expropriation and expulsion from Mexico, where the oil industry was brought under national ownership in 1938. For twenty-eight years a succession of revolutionary governments in Mexico had always seen such action as the ultimate outcome of the conflict between state and companies, but since it had been avoided for so long, the companies had come to believe it would never happen. When it did the promising prospects for oil exploitation in the Maracaibo Basin and in other parts of Venezuela benefited from the companies' needs to find oil quickly to replace the 15 million tons or so per annum they had been lifting from their Mexican fields mainly for sale overseas. This important stimulus to Venezuelan oil development was, moreover, soon supplemented by a second, even more important one: the petroleum needs of a rapidly expanding wartime U.S. economy. These wartime demands proved too great a strain on the U.S. domestic oil industry and gave companies still greater incentives to seek new resources in Venezuela. Because it was the nearest possible alternative supply point for the United States, supplies from Venezuela were at minimum possible risk from enemy action at sea. As a result, oil production there rose rapidly from only 20 million tons in 1937 to some 30 million tons in 1941, and to over 90 million tons by 1946, by which time the country was the world's most important petroleum-producing nation outside the United States. Since almost all the oil was exported, in contrast with the mainly domestic use of American oil, Venezuela became the world's most important oil exporter (a position which it just held on to until 1970 but which it then lost to Iran and Saudi Arabia).

In the post-war world, in which there was an energy shortage as a result of dislocations in many of the most important coal-producing areas, the demand for energy from other possible supply points grew rapidly. The Venezuelan politico-economic environment at the same time was also highly favourable to foreign investment in oil because the dictatorial régime there welcomed such investment as a means of amassing private fortunes for those individuals close to the régime. These two factors ensured the continuation of the growth of Venezuelan oil production throughout the rest of the 1940s and up to 1957.

This twenty-year period of growth was marked by only one short interlude of restraint – the few months in 1948 when a government came to power under the leadership of a political party, Acción Democrática, whose electoral manifesto called for the nationalization of the country's oil resources and whose leaders in exile had lived mainly in Mexico, where oil was already nationalized. The reaction of the oil companies to this new government was immediate and very blatant. Investment virtually ceased, development came to a halt and production was stabilized, while the managers of the companies concerned attempted to decide how far they were prepared and able to work within the framework of the policies likely to be adopted by the new régime. As it turned out their fears were shortlived for, after a short period of democratic rule, the country reverted to a military dictatorship – a reversion which was almost certainly only made possible so quickly with the active help of at least some of the oil companies concerned!

The new dictatorship of Pérez Jiménez soon regained the confidence of the oil companies, and oil production was once more established on its strong upward trend. Companies like Shell and Esso, long established in Venezuela, and also other companies new to the country but anxious to participate in the bonanza, fell over each other in their efforts to secure concessions in the large, promising areas of Venezuela still unexplored. In the mid-1950s Pérez Jiménez organized what amounted to a 'grand auction' of some of these areas. The successful bidders paid some $1,500 million for the exploration and development rights and started work immediately to prove that Venezuelan production could be pushed beyond the annual level of over 150 million tons already achieved. But no sooner had this work got under way when dictatorship in Venezuela was again overthrown and, after a short period of provisional rule, Acción Democrática again achieved power in 1958. Predictably, the reaction of the oil companies developed in much the same way as it had on the earlier occasion in 1948, and once again investments and development plans were curtailed or abandoned and oil offtake limited, as clarification was sought of the possible oil programme of the new government – which, this time, was not shortlived. In fact it achieved what no other elected government in Venezuela had ever achieved – its full term of office and its succession by another elected government.

Nevertheless, in 1958, conflict between the government and the companies seemed almost inevitable, as Acción Democrática still had proposals for the nationalization of the industry in its manifesto and, moreover, took action early in its period of control to increase taxes on the industry steeply. It also gave its support to the oil union's pressure for greatly increased wages and fringe benefits, so seeming to indicate that a head-on clash was but a matter of time. But after 1958 Acción Democrática did not treat its nationalization commitment seriously and certainly made no move in this direction. In fact, by this later date Venezuela was so completely dependent economically on the oil industry that no government – and certainly not one as anxious as Acción Democrática to achieve its country's economic progress – could afford to think of action which would essentially close down the oil sector of the economy. No other sector could avoid repercussions from such action, and the consequent unemployment and distress would certainly undermine the government's political strength. The government's freedom of action in economic terms was thus heavily constrained, and even in political terms there was little to be said for action which, no matter how immediately 'popular', seemed likely to create such stresses and strains in the system that the instigators of it were unlikely to survive.

But if by 1958 the government's ability to act out its basic philosophical beliefs was constrained, then so was that of the oil companies. By this time, as explained previously (see pp. 124–5), they were under pressure from the U.S. State Department to achieve a *rapprochement* with the Venezuelan government which was believed by the United States to be the government which provided the key to the stability of the whole Caribbean area. But stability in Venezuela – particularly in the period following Fidel Castro's success in Cuba – demanded an expanding economy. This, in turn, depended upon the continuing development of the country's oil industry, which accounted for something like 25 per cent of the country's gross national product, provided the government with over 60 per cent of all its revenues and accounted for over 90 per cent of the nation's total exports. The companies, therefore, though powerful in the Venezuelan context, had to reorientate their attitudes and policies to the even more powerful force of the foreign policy of the U.S.A., which required that the oil industry make it possible for Venezuela to achieve its objectives of continued economic advance. This demanded their willing cooperation with a government which they certainly disliked and probably distrusted, but for which there was no acceptable alternative and which therefore they could certainly not think of overthrowing as they had in 1948. Economic and political necessity, therefore, as interpreted by the U.S.A., produced a situation in which the international oil companies, dedicated to the idea of as little government intervention in industry as possible, and a government, devoted in theory at least to socialist planning, had to work together. This development – unusual for its time – has since been paralleled in both oil-producing and oil-consuming nations as the companies have been obliged to recognize the validity and permanence of governmental concern over oil and oil policies. Some other cases of this kind are presented in later chapters.

The expansion in Venezuelan oil production since 1958 has by no means been as rapid as in the earlier post-war period, but advances have taken place and some investment has continued. Government revenues from oil have been increased. All in spite of the fact that in the period between 1958 and 1972 Venezuelan oil became increasingly uncompetitive in many markets of the world as a result of rapidly expanding, lower-cost oil output from countries in the Middle East and, more recently, in North and West Africa. Moreover, falling unit costs of transporting oil across the oceans – as larger and larger tankers were brought into use – helped to eliminate Venezuela's competitive edge on markets in closer geographical proximity to it than to other main producing areas. This was particularly important with respect to the U.S. market, which had hitherto been considered the particular preserve of Venezuelan oil but in which Middle Eastern and other oil now became competitive.

However, it is necessary to stress that Venezuela's slower rate of growth was not only a result of its deteriorating competitive position in overseas markets. The new government of the country did not accept the need for as rapid an expansion of the oil industry as had its predecessors. Two arguments were advanced in support of this belief. First, Acción Democrática considered that Venezuela had become too dependent on oil and that the situation was one of danger for the well-being of the country in the long-term. It therefore deliberately took action to reduce the oil industry's share of the total economy by encouraging diversification into other fields. Secondly, the government argued that rapid expansion of oil production and sales was at the expense of the price obtained for each barrel of oil. By restricting output, price levels could be maintained and Venezuela's oil thus conserved to provide the means of economic development in the future. This 'conservationist' view depended for its validity on several assumptions: firstly, that there existed a very limited amount of oil for the world's future use; secondly, that oil would not be replaced to any large degree by other forms of energy in the future for which the oil was being 'conserved'. It also assumed that no use could be made of the wealth created by oil sales in the short-term. Because none of these assumptions were valid the government's argument about conservation proved to be very weak, particularly as any strength it might have had was negatived by an unwillingness on the part of Venezuela's overseas competitors for more than a decade to accept the restraint on production levels that it implies. In other words, Venezuela's efforts to protect price levels through the pursuit of a conservationist policy were meaningless whilst other countries moved in to supply oil that Venezuela might have otherwise supplied – so that the deterioration in prices continued after all. Venezuela's enthusiasm for the Organization of Petroleum Exporting Countries (O.P.E.C.) stemmed from this situation and its formation and work will be discussed later in the chapter.

From the interplay of all these economic and political forces, Venezuela, between 1958 and 1972, achieved an average annual growth rate in oil production of rather less than 3 per cent – compared with the 10 per cent per annum it achieved over the previous fifteen years, and a world annual growth rate in the same period of 7 per cent. In 1958 Venezuela's production of 142 million tons accounted for 17 per cent of world total; its 1972 production of 182 million tons was only 7 per cent of the total – in spite of the fact that the closure of the Suez Canal since mid-1967 gave Venezuelan oil a 'temporary' boost in markets west of Suez, particularly in the United States: a boost which may be further strengthened by the 1973/4 Arab embargo on oil supplies to the United States, in which situation Venezuela has been able to reassert its ability to charge relatively higher prices for its oil exports.

Though the Cuban crisis and resultant pressures by the U.S. State Department can be seen as the main factors which saved the Venezuelan oil industry from a serious absolute decline in the 1960s, one must also note the impact of the growing professionalism of the Venezuelan government in dealing with the companies. In earlier days the expertise was all on the side of the oil companies, which had to respond only to the political pressure of the government. Since 1958 the Ministry of Mines and Hydro-carbons in Venezuela has built up a team able to argue in technical and economic terms with the industry's representatives and, as a result, it has been able to offer advice as to exactly how much pressure should be put on the companies to make concessions – particularly as regards taxation arrangements. Thus, the government has been able to increase its share of total profits on several occasions; to collect taxes in arrears, the liability for which the companies challenged; and, more recently, to change the basis on which total profits were calculated by having the companies write in to their calculations a notional tax-reference selling price invariably higher than the actual selling price of oil out of Venezuela. All this had the effect of increasing the revenues which the country collected on every barrel of oil exported, and by 1970 this amounted to more than $1 per barrel, compared with less than half this amount when Acción Democrática came to power, and in spite of the generally weak market for Venezuelan oil throughout the period. By virtue of these actions government revenues from oil continued to grow at a rate high enough to finance the requirements of the economic and social development programme – the main short-term aim of the government in its oil policy.

Limitations on the continued success of this approach were, however, becoming very obvious. Government revenues per barrel could only be pushed to a much higher level without eliminating all the profits to the companies concerned, so that they would no longer have any incentive to continue to produce oil in Venezuela, if the prices at which Venezuelan oil was sold overseas rose. This development did in fact take place, beginning in the later part of 1973, as part of the success of O.P.E.C. in limiting the total oil supply. This will be dealt with later in the chapter. In the absence of this factor increases in government revenues depended upon an expanding output – which was something that could not be achieved through the existing concession system, even if the government wanted it to happen, because of oil companies' unwillingness to invest the necessary money in Venezuela when many better opportunities existed elsewhere. But, in any case, the government did not accept the idea of the concession system as a means of producing the nation's natural resources, except as a short-term expedient for ensuring the continued flow of oil and, in the light of external pressures, to allow the existing concessionaires to work their agreed areas. Since 1958, therefore, there have been no new concessions – and, as a result, Venezuela's proven oil reserves stand to be used up in about thirteen years at the current rate of production. If this situation does not change then Venezuelan oil output must soon inevitably start to decline, in spite of the higher prices and taxes from the end of 1973, and by the time the concessions are legally relinquished in 1983 (unless, in fact, as now seems likely, they are nationalized before then), it seems probable that Venezuela could become little more than a relatively minor producer.

In line with its political philosophy, Acción Democrática has sought to resolve this issue through the establishment of a state oil company – C.V.P. – which has been given responsibilities for working any concession areas which might be relinquished by private companies and for negotiating joint arrangements to work as yet unexplored areas of Venezuela with oil potential. It has made a start in a small way as far as the former are concerned (and now has producing capacity amounting to about 9 million tons per year) and in 1969 accepted offers from a dozen or so petroleum companies for joint operations in the southern part of Lake Maracaibo. The work in this area is being carried out and financed by the companies, but the ownership of any oil discovered will be vested in the state entity, which will pay a fee to the successful companies for their efforts. C.V.P. may also give these companies the opportunity to market the oil if they so wish – though with C.V.P. involved in important decisions such as those of export prices. Alternatively C.V.P. may sell the oil itself, and whether it does or not will obviously depend upon the state of the international market.

This contractual system does, of course, give the Venezuelans a much greater degree of control over their oil resources. Although many companies always felt justified in seeking to participate in it, and have now been joined by many others – particularly in respect of the enormous potential for oil from tar-sands that exists in Venezuela – it still remains to be seen, in the light of changes since 1973 in the opportunities for securing oil concessions in other parts of the oil-producing world, how quickly, if at all, it can add to Venezuela's proven reserves of oil and/or to its annual output. At best, at the moment one can see it as a device which will prevent an early and possibly catastrophic decline in production levels, thus safeguarding government revenues for a few more years. Whether it will enable Venezuela to exercise more influence in the development of the world oil market is doubtful, unless consuming countries also decide to put the oil industry under national control and then conduct their negotiations for supplies directly with other state entities in producing countries. The extent to which consuming countries are developing their policies in this direction emerges in Chapters 5, 6 and 7. In the meantime our attention must turn to the interests and policies of the world's other major oil-producing region – the Middle East.

Middle Eastern oil production dates back well over fifty years. As early as 1913 the importance of oil from Persia for Britain, in particular, was demonstrated in the decision of the British government to finance the continuation of exploration there at a time when private interests were considering giving up their efforts. This action created the Anglo-Persian Oil Company, in which the British government held a 51 per cent interest – an interest which has been virtually maintained ever since (it is now just under 50 per cent), though the designation of the company has changed twice – first to Anglo-Iranian in 1935 and then, in the early 1950s, to British Petroleum. As a result of the close tie between Britain and Persia (Iran), Persia became the major oil-producing nation in the Middle East in the inter-war period and held this position until the 'nationalization' dispute of 1950. By 1939 it was already producing about 10 million tons per year – twice as much as was produced at that time in all the other Middle Eastern countries put together. Disagreement between Britain, France and the U.S.A. over the political control and the development of the oil resources of other parts of the Middle East delayed the expansion of production in countries such as Kuwait and Iraq (see Chapter 8 for a discussion of this situation), but when an agreement between these nations was finally signed in 1935 the scene was set for the exploitation of these countries' known oil resources. In the few years remaining until the outbreak of the Second World War development went ahead quickly in Iraq, so that the country's output increased to about 4 million tons in 1939. Anglo-Persian and Gulf Oil, which had between them (on a 50:50 basis) secured the concession to the oil resources of the Sheikdom of Kuwait, soon discovered an oilfield which promised to be of major significance, but the outbreak of war in 1939 brought the development to a halt and Kuwait's entry as an oil producer was delayed for almost a decade. During the war, production was maintained as far as possible in those fields that had already been developed, in order to serve the needs of the Allied forces east of Suez as well as civilian markets in areas around the Indian Ocean. But such a limited demand acted as a restraint on the growth of the area's oil industry during this period, and in 1944 – the last full year of the war in Europe and the Middle East – the whole of the Middle East produced only 20 million tons – little more than it had in 1939 – and by this time had fallen way behind Venezuela as a major producing region.

The immediate post-war period brought rapid changes. The seven international companies quickly started exploration and development work throughout the Middle East under the same stimulus that had encouraged them (with the exception of B.P.) to pursue their active efforts in Venezuela – that is, a world short of energy and hence a willingness to pay high prices for any oil that could be won out of the Middle East. Moreover, oil out of the Middle East could still be sold at a delivered price which not only reflected the higher costs of producing oil in the U.S.A. but which, for most customers, also included a transport component calculated as if the oil originated in the Gulf of Mexico. For many markets of the world to which Middle East oil was delivered this meant that higher freight charges could be levied than were necessary to cover the costs of the voyage from the Middle East. This commercial advantage was further enhanced by the companies' knowledge that the area's political stability was still guaranteed by the presence of Britain both in political and military guises throughout the region. Thus in the early post-war years the companies had no hesitation in committing many hundreds of millions of dollars to the exploitation of the Middle East's oil resources.

The two main oil-producing countries of the region – Persia and Iraq – quickly benefited, as output from the existing oilfields was brought up to the maximum possible by expenditure on the pipelines and other facilities needed to get the oil from the fields to the markets (see Map 4). The pre-war oil discoveries in Kuwait were speedily developed and even the earlier very optimistic evaluations of its fields were quickly shown to be much too low. In Kuwait, it seemed, the companies could hardly put a drill in the wrong place, for almost every 'wildcat' and development well that was sunk proved to be a producer of an enormous size, with many wells capable of producing up to

10,000 barrels per day – an energy equivalent of about three-quarters of a million tons of coal per year. The two companies with shares in this bonanza very soon became embarrassed by the size of the resources with which they had to cope. Neither Anglo-Iranian nor Gulf Oil had the necessary markets for these quantities of oil within their own control (unless it was merely to replace production from elsewhere – Iran in the case of Anglo-Iranian and the U.S.A. in the case of Gulf). They therefore both made long-term arrangements to sell large quantities of Kuwaiti oil to other major companies which had immediate access to markets with a rapidly growing demand able to absorb this production. Under the stimulus of these bulk sales Gulf and Anglo-Iranian were able to continue to expand their output in Kuwait. In Saudi Arabia a consortium of American companies only was formed under the name of Aramco, with concession rights to discover and exploit the oil resources of practically all that vast country. Again, success was quick and cheap and the fields of Saudi Arabia were brought into production as soon as the physical facilities were available to move the oil to the coast for tanker transportation to the markets of Western Europe – and, in growing quantities by the late 1940s, to the U.S.A.

Since this early post-war period, production in these four Middle Eastern countries has leapt ahead and in 1973 they produced over 750 million tons – or some 50 per cent more than the total production of the U.S.A. in the same year. Their increases in output, however, have not been in a continuous and smooth upward curve, as the world's total production and consumption have. Output from year to year in each country (see Map 4) has depended upon the interaction of a series of factors, each of which has influenced company decisions on how much oil should or could be lifted from a particular country or field. The central element (though much modified by other factors, as we shall show later) in decision-making has been the consideration of costs to the companies in delivering oils to their various markets at any given moment with the various permutations of producing and transport facilities available to them. Except in the early post-war period, when, as already shown, the pressure of market demand necessitated maximum output from all producing units, the amount of oil producible in the Middle East from the facilities available has

Map 4. The Oil Industry in the Middle East and North Africa

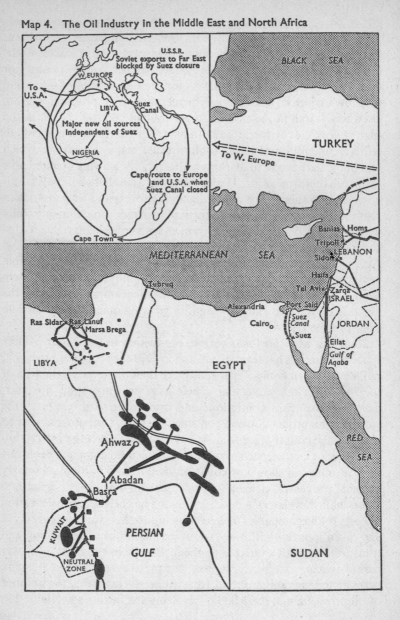

U.S.S.R.
Soviet exports to Far East blocked by Suez closure

BLACK SEA

W. EUROPE

To U.S.A.

LIBYA

Suez Canal

Major new oil sources Independent of Suez

NIGERIA

Cape route to Europe and U.S.A. when Suez Canal closed

Cape Town

TURKEY

To W. Europe

Banias Homs
Tripoli
Sidon LEBANON
Haifa
Tel Aviv Zarqa
ISRAEL

MEDITERRANEAN SEA

Tubruq

Ras Sidar Ras Lanuf
Marsa Brega

LIBYA

Alexandria

Cairo

Port Said
Suez Canal
Suez

JORDAN

Eilat
Gulf of Aqaba

EGYPT

RED SEA

Ahwaz

Abadan

Basra

KUWAIT

NEUTRAL ZONE

PERSIAN GULF

SUDAN

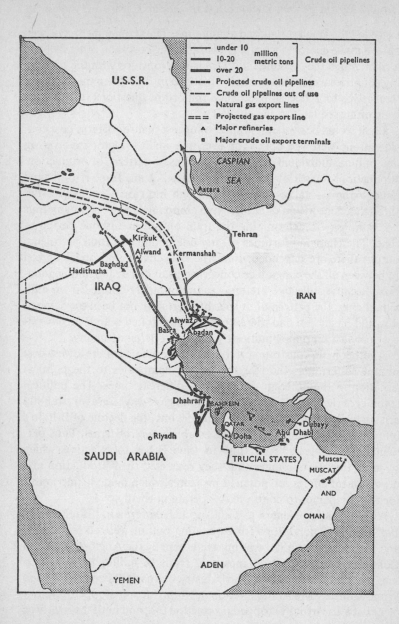

exceeded the amount required at any time. Thus companies have been able to make choices according to contrasting costs and other factors: a right which they retained until their relationships with the producing countries were fundamentally changed in 1973 when the countries themselves took decisions on such important questions (this will be fully discussed later in the chapter).

But it would be oversimplifying to suggest that short-term cost considerations were the only – or even the main – factor involved in determining individual companies' choices of patterns of production. Production in each of the four countries – Iran, Iraq, Kuwait and Saudi Arabia – takes place not through individual companies but through a consortium of at least two companies. Each company thus had some say in determining the total output in any one period of time. The changing fortunes of any one country in total petroleum output therefore depended upon the collective compromise agreed to between all the companies concerned after discussion and negotiation. Because collective preferences undoubtedly differed from individual ones, the pattern of output has certainly not been the same as it would have been had there been an uninhibited search for lowest-cost production opportunities by each producing company.

Another main constraint on the automatic choice of the lowest-cost output pattern was the reaction by the companies to the political situation in the different countries at different times. The political stability of the early post-war period soon gave way to grave instability arising from the growth of nationalist feeling, the decline of Britain's influence and the conflict over the establishment of Israel. Thus particular governments from time to time either took action which so upset the oil companies that they restricted their production and development efforts, or pursued measures which made it impossible for the companies to continue to operate normally.

An outstanding event of this kind occurred in Iran in 1951. Between 1945 and 1950 conditions for expanding output were so favourable and so much new capital was invested there by the Anglo-Iranian Oil Company that production increased from 16 million to 32 million tons per year. Then, in 1951, the industry was nationalized by the then Prime Minister, Musaddiq. Nationalization not only stopped development but also virtually stopped production too, and until the issue was resolved by negotiation three years later the production of oil from the Iranian fields was limited to the million or so tons required annually for domestic consumption. The nationalized Iranian oil industry lacked the legal right to sell abroad the oil produced from freely and willingly negotiated concessions made previously between government and company and recognized by customary international law. The Anglo-Iranian Oil Company's threat to take legal action against any entity 'buying' and using its oil was sufficient in the circumstances of the time to ensure that over this period no Iranian oil moved on to world markets.

By 1954 the oil that could have been produced from Iran was flowing from Kuwait, Iraq and Saudi Arabia. But agreement between the oil companies and Iran was reached in 1954 and a new type of relationship between government and companies established. The former retained ownership of the oil but permitted the latter to work it and to sell it as contractors to the National Iranian Oil Company. With the agreement, which brought in companies other than the Anglo-Iranian which had previously had sole concessionary rights, oil quickly started to flow again from the existing fields and the new consortium of contracting companies moved in to explore for fields in the other parts of the country that they were permitted to work. This arrangement was highly successful and both old and new fields repeatedly established production records. In 1971 overall production topped 200 million tons for the first time. Iran has largely achieved political stability in the last decade and has also remained unaffected by the troubles with Israel, in contrast with the Arab Middle East. These advantages, coupled with the low cost of much of Iran's productive capacity and its proximity to the coast and new off-shore tanker terminals that give a low transport cost component in the free-on-board cost at point of export, led to the country easily achieving the highest rates of oil production growth amongst the Middle Eastern countries in the 1960s.

But even rates of increase in output averaging nearly 15 per cent per annum – nearly twice the growth in world demand for oil – have not been accepted as satisfactory by the Iranian government, and in the latter part of 1966 there appeared to be a danger of a major upheaval in government/company relationships. The Iranians sought to establish the principle that what the oil companies did in various countries by way of exploration, development and production should be related to the development needs of those countries, particularly in terms of the total populations that had to be sustained and provided for out of oil revenues. Iran, with over 30 million people, claimed that a 15 per cent rate of growth in annual oil production was far too low to meet the needs of the country for development capital. In 1967 the government insisted that the rate of growth should be at least of the order of 17 per cent – a rate of increase which they claimed was physically possible from the known characteristics of the oilfields. The companies concerned did not seriously challenge the validity of this claim, for their searches had been enormously, and somewhat unexpectedly, successful. But, if they agreed to increase their rate of offtake in Iran to this degree, they faced trouble elsewhere, for it would mean eliminating much of the growth from other producing areas in the Middle East. The other countries concerned could not be expected to see eye to eye with Iran over the question of relating oil offtake to the development needs of the local population. The oil companies also estimated that so concentrating their development efforts on Iran would be more expensive overall than they could reasonably expect their alternative strategies to be. At first, therefore, they fought Iran's proposal with a great deal of vigour, but ultimately they were more or less obliged to acquiesce under the threat of what amounted to the cancellation of their contractual rights to work in Iran and the prospect of 'their' oil being sold on world markets through the assistance of the Soviet Union and of companies in the Western world not associated with the consortium. The changed government/company relationship arising out of the 1954 agreement had removed the legal ability of the companies concerned to claim ownership of the oil on world markets. They were now only contractors working under licence from the Iranian national company, and thus the outcome of the dispute was in marked contrast to the outcome of the earlier 'nationalization' dispute which closed down production. It gave a first clear indication of the rising significance and power of the producing nations in the post-war oil industry, not simply in terms of their ability to win an increasing share of the profits, but in terms of decisions on levels of production and their rates of increase – a development in their power which was to be fully achieved within a few years.

Similarly, in other parts of the Middle East the 'oil fortunes' of individual countries have varied according to changing political circumstances. In Iraq, changes in government have on several occasions in the 1950s and the 1960s caused the Iraq Petroleum Company (a consortium in which five of the international majors have an interest) to cut back on production levels and/or investment plans, with the result that the increase in oil output has been in a series of fits and starts. In 1965–6 greatly increased port dues on Iraqi oil shipped out via the Shatt al Arab made the oil cost more than alternative supplies from other parts of the Middle East, with the result that the southern Iraq fields were partly closed down. Moreover, the country's northern fields have had their output affected from time to time by other difficulties over transport, in this case arising from circumstances outside the control of the Iraq government. This is because these northern fields depend on crude-oil pipelines that run to the Mediterranean coast for their outlet to markets (see Map 4, pp. 78–9).

In the early post-war period a problem arose because these lines passed through territory which came to form part of the state of Israel in 1947. Arab opposition to the formation of Israel meant that these lines could no longer be used, and northern Iraqi oil production had to await the completion of new arms of these lines to new export terminals in Lebanon. But the new lines also passed through Syria, whose extremism in the Suez crisis of 1956–7 caused their sabotage and closure, so that Iraq's northern fields again had to be shut for a period of several months. And more recently, oil production had to cease for a third time as a result of disagreement between the Syrian government and the pipeline company over the royalties to be paid by the latter for the right to transport the oil across Syrian territory. After a long period of unsuccessful bargaining, in December 1966 the Syrian government formally took over the pipeline installations as a means of bringing pressure to bear on the company to increase its payments. The Iraq Petroleum Company reacted, however, by diverting tankers normally calling at the Mediterranean coast terminals to other loading points. Thus, the storage capacity at Banias and Homs was quickly filled, the flow of oil through the pipelines was brought to an end and oil production in the northern Iraq fields had to be stopped. Agreement on the royalty transit rates was eventually reached in March 1967, but in the meantime Iraq lost the royalties and other revenues which would have accrued from four months' oil production, with consequent damage to its economy.

Iraq's government thus took steps towards establishing another outlet from the northern fields – albeit a somewhat more expensive one for serving markets west of Suez – viz. a pipeline direct to the Iraqi ports on the Persian Gulf. Though this would have eliminated one cause of the fluctuations in Iraq's production, the continuing difficulties arising between the Iraq government and the Iraq Petroleum Company, which, with its wholly owned subsidiaries, was still responsible for Iraq's total oil production, continued for some time to affect output. In 1967 the Iraq government unilaterally took back about 99 per cent of the acreage of the country conceded to the I.P.C. for petroleum exploration and development, claiming the need to make use as quickly as possible of any resources in these areas, which, so it argued, the I.P.C. had effectively sterilized as its member companies preferred to make their explorations elsewhere in the world. The I.P.C. denied this allegation and claimed that it was giving as much attention to developing Iraq's resources as all the difficulties would allow. This dispute continued through to 1971 and led the I.P.C. to do little more than mark time in its production schedules. In the meantime the government offered some of the former I.P.C. acreage to other companies and also made agreements to work some of the reserves itself with the help of the Soviet Union, which in return for loans at low rates of interest and for technical help was to be reimbursed out of any eventual crude-oil production.

Only the unexpected agreement in 1973 between Iraq and the I.P.C. – following the general agreement on a *modus vivendi* between the oil-exporting countries and the major international companies in 1971–3 – prevented what could otherwise have been a battle royal between the parties concerned. Iraq would most certainly have been supported actively by the forces of Arab nationalism, by other petroleum-exporting countries, by the Soviet Union and probably also by some commercial as well as political interests in the West (for instance, the French and Italian state oil entities backed by their respective governments) – anxious to see the power of the international majors curbed still further. The I.P.C., on its part, could normally have expected the unflinching support of the U.S., British and Dutch governments but, given some obvious validity in the Iraqi claims against the I.P.C. and, more important, the changed geo-political conditions in the Middle East in particular and the oil world in general, they probably threw their influence behind getting the I.P.C. to concede the very considerable amount of ground needed to reach an agreement favourable to Iraq. It still remained to be seen, however, whether I.P.C.'s reaction to this defeat would have been to put Iraq low on their list of priorities for investment in oil exploration and production facilities and, on the other side, whether or not Iraq's new partners in some of the acreage given up by the company – especially the Soviet Union – would have been willing and/or able to help in developing new production facilities as quickly as Iraq might wish. Even these questions, however, became irrelevant in the new-style arrangements between the oil-producing nations and the oil companies following the late 1973–early 1974 establishment of the former's unilateral rights to take whatever decisions they liked on ownership, production and price without reference to the oil companies.

In Kuwait and Saudi Arabia the growth of oil production has suffered less serious fluctuations, and those there have been have arisen from quite different circumstances. Both countries have been capable of producing much more oil than they have actually produced for most of the period since 1950, though how much more is difficult to say, because the companies operating in Kuwait and Saudi Arabia never had any obligation to publish their producing capacity or reserves figures. In part, therefore, production levels in these countries have been able to respond readily and immediately to situations elsewhere. For example, when Iran closed down in 1951 Kuwaiti production was stepped up considerably virtually overnight to make up the total supplies required. More recently, Kuwait and Saudi Arabia have 'suffered' from the rise in Libyan output, which increased to 150 million tons by 1969, for without this development they could have expected to be responsible for much of the tonnage involved. In part also, production has had to be orientated to the markets available to the producing companies. This has been especially significant in the case of Kuwait, where until very recently all production was the responsibility of the Kuwait Oil Company, in which only B.P. and Gulf Oil had interests. The total market outlets of these two companies always remained too limited for them to exploit Kuwaiti reserves to the maximum, even after finding additional outlets through long-term sales contracts with other major companies (for example Gulf Oil with Shell) and even after seeking, very aggressively, the opportunity to provide crude oil to independent refiners in many different parts of the world.

Nevertheless, Kuwait and Saudi Arabia both had continually rising production levels for the whole of the post-war period up to and including 1972. It is not accidental that this has occurred in countries in which there has been an absence of radical political change, and in which outside powers – Britain and the U.S.A. – retained considerable political control in the case of the former and considerable influence in the case of the latter. However, neither country has been content with this situation, and as they have both sought greater independence of Britain and the U.S.A. so they have sought to eliminate the monopoly control exercised in each case by a single consortium over their oil sector. Both have formed local oil companies to participate in refining, transport and local marketing of oil and these companies are now building up their experience, expertise and investments in chemical plant and tankers etc. in order to participate more widely in the future. Both countries, by agreement with the consortiums concerned, limited the areas under concession to them. The areas relinquished have been or will be offered to other parties, and thus oil production in each country could ultimately become the responsibility of several groups, rather than just one, so reducing the risks to the maintenance of production levels. Moreover the new agreements, such as those reached between Kuwait and Japan in 1968, carry stringent requirements concerning the size and speed of the exploration and development efforts which the companies are to undertake. They also oblige the companies to maintain appropriate production levels once oil reserves have been proved. This measure was first designed to overcome the problem that Kuwait already experienced with B.P. and Gulf, in the period when they 'sat on' discovered resources to the detriment of Kuwait's revenues, but more recently it has been used to enable the government of Kuwait to put an upper limit on the amount of oil produced, given the country's new interest in maintaining upward pressure on the price of oil and its need to reassure itself about the ability of its discovered resources to sustain high production sales in the long-term.

Venezuela and the four countries of the Middle East already considered in this chapter have since 1945 produced over 90 per cent of all oil traded internationally and are thus quite obviously the dominant elements in any examination of the interests of the producing countries. But two further aspects of these interests must be briefly surveyed – first, the interests of minor and/or newer producers; and second, the significance of the formation of a producers' association – the Organization of Petroleum Exporting Countries (O.P.E.C.).

One noticeable feature of the post-war period is the disappearance as 'oil powers' of countries which had considerable influence as producers and exporters up to 1939. Mexico is one example. For a short time in the early 1920s Mexico was even the world's leading producer outside the U.S.A. and it continued as an exporting nation of some significance (contributing about 10 per cent of oil entering world trade) right up to 1938. Nationalization of the oil industry in that year, however, cut off exports immediately, as the dispossessed companies threatened legal action against anyone 'purchasing' oil from the new state entity, Petróleos Mexicanos (PEMEX). (This was identical to the action taken over the nationalization of Iranian oil in 1951 – see p. 80.) The differences between the Mexican government and the companies were eventually resolved when the former agreed to pay and the latter agreed to receive compensation over a period of twenty-five years. This made it possible for Mexican oil to enter world markets free of legal restraints, but exports have in fact never been resumed on anything more than a minor and intermittent scale as PEMEX has had more than enough to do since its foundation to ensure that it could meet the rapidly growing requirements of the Mexican national market. More recently it was prevented from offering crude oil for sale overseas by a decision of the Mexican government which argued that the country should itself secure the economic advantages to be gained from refining the unprocessed raw material into more 'valuable' products. Unfortunately, the markets of the world were not very anxious to accept Mexican oil products in preference to supplies of crude oil from elsewhere, and no significant export trade has been built up. Today, therefore, Mexico is a self-sufficient rather than an oil-exporting nation, except for a little border trade with the U.S.A. (Mexican oil is not subject to U.S. quotas), and for small-scale and intermittent sales to importers in Western Europe.

On the other side of the world, Indonesia – formerly the Dutch East Indies – was an important supplier of oil in the pre-war period, not only to markets in Asia and the Far East but even to Western Europe. The Japanese occupation and the destruction of the producing and other facilities during the war eliminated Indonesia as an oil-exporting nation in the early post-war period. Reinvestment by the companies concerned immediately after the war, following re-establishment of Dutch rule, soon reactivated the oilfields and export terminals, etc., and made possible a production of some 10 million tons by 1948. Most of this went to Japan, Australia and other relatively close markets to which Indonesian oil had a transport cost advantage over Middle East supplies. But the possibility of increasing production above that level was soon thwarted by fundamental disagreements between the oil companies and the new independent Indonesian government. In spite of long negotiations and various attempts to set up new arrangements for exploration and development which would satisfy not only the national aspirations of the newly independent country but also be acceptable to the companies, little additional output was achieved and until the late 1960s Indonesia remained a small contributor to international trade in oil – even within the Far East, whose markets were, in the main, supplied from the Middle East. In the last few years, however, Japan has taken an increasing interest in Indonesia with a view to reducing its dependence on the Middle East, and important new agreements have been concluded for Japanese exploration of Indonesian oil areas (see also Chapter 6). The initial results have been promising – so much so, in fact, that companies from other countries have also sought and secured acreage, particularly in off-shore waters, and it now seems certain that Indonesia's steadily expanding role since 1970 in providing oil in international trade will expand very markedly in the next few years. Its proximity to the world's largest and most rapidly growing single national market for imported oil – Japan – is acting as a powerful stimulus in this direction, particularly since the Japanese government indicated its intentions of diversifying the country's imports away from its more than 80 per cent dependence on the Middle East (see Chapter 6). These intentions were given a powerful additional motivation by the oil-supply crisis in late 1973, following the Arab cutbacks in oil exports as a reaction to the war with Israel.

Another Far Eastern country, Burma, figured in the pre-war world as an oil-exporting nation of some importance, but now it is a country producing only just sufficient for its domestic use. Oil-industry development there has been prevented by difficulties between the government and companies which formerly operated the concessions. Now the Burmese oil industry, like the Mexican, is wholly within state hands, though with some help from foreign companies as contractors, and there appears to be no interest in reviving an export trade.

Thus, there are countries which have considered the ideology of political nationalism more important than the opportunity to expand oil production and exports by allowing foreign companies suitable concessionary agreements. Other countries, on the other hand, saw the opportunities provided by oil for enhancing government revenues and solving balance of payments problems as more important in determining their attitudes towards foreign oil companies. Most significant amongst those with this kind of attitude were two in Africa – Nigeria and Libya.

Exploration for oil in Nigeria started as long ago as 1938, but war-time disruption and then an immediate post-war interest in other parts of the world by the two companies concerned, Shell and B.P., prevented serious attention being paid to Nigeria until the late 1950s. Exports from Nigeria were only initiated in 1962, but from then until the outbreak of the civil war between the Federal government and the break-away state of Biafra – in whose territory many of the oilfields were located – production and exports went ahead very rapidly. Shell and B.P. were roused to greater activity when concessions were granted to other companies whose initial exploration efforts proved to be very successful, in spite of the great physical difficulties (climatic and physiographic) of looking for oil in the Nigerian coastal region. In 1966 exports exceeded 25 million tons and the plans and projects then announced indicated a possible export level of 50 million tons by 1970 or 1971. The rapid expansion took place under the great stimulus of a very favourable petroleum law, which amongst its provisions regulating oil development included one which had the effect of limiting the percentage of profits taken by the government to only about 35 per cent of the total profits. This figure was little more than half that taken by the major exporting nations (a situation which has now changed as Nigerian tax rates were raised after 1970 to the general level set by member countries of O.P.E.C. – which Nigeria in fact joined in that year). This certainly encouraged companies to press on quickly with their developments, as did Nigeria's favourable location with respect to the Western European and North American markets – with no Suez Canal problem to worry about and a much shorter haul than from the Middle East. Unfortunately, progress was temporarily restrained by the civil war and exports in 1968 were virtually nil. With the end of the civil war and the re-establishment of order, however, Nigeria's advantages in the oil-exporting business quickly led to the renewal of the strongly upward trend in the country's contribution to the world oil trade – a development already apparent by the end of 1969 following the Federal forces' recapture of the main oil-producing areas and export terminals. The restoration of peace in 1970 led to a full resumption of oil activities in what had been Biafra, and the successful development of new oilfields well to the west of the areas affected by the war. This enabled 53 million tons to be produced from Nigeria in 1970 and over 70 million in 1971, since when it has increased to over 100 million tons per annum to make Nigeria the world's fifth largest oil-exporting country in 1974 – unhindered, of course, by the 1973–4 limitations on exports engendered by the Arab–Israeli war. Oil company efforts have, of course, since 1967 been greatly stimulated by the country's favourable location for European and North American markets (see top-left inset, Map 4) and more recently by Nigeria's non-involvement with the political problems of the Middle East.

Nigeria's rapid development in the late 1950s and the 1960s was influenced by a favourable petroleum code. The same happened in Libya. Exploration there dates only from 1961, when interest in North Africa was stimulated by major oil and gas discoveries by French state enterprise in neighbouring Algeria. Thereafter, its favourable petroleum law attracted many companies to join in the search, for the costs of possible failure were not inflated by large payments which had to be made to the government irrespective of what the exploration produced, as was the case for new concessions in some older producing countries. As it turned out, many of the eagerly participating companies quickly achieved success – to such a degree, in fact, that exports from Libya began in 1962 only 18 months or so after the initial exploration effort. By 1969 they had reached a level of 150 million tons, putting the country into third position in the world league table of petroleum-exporting countries.

The annual rates of increase in production in Libya over the early period of development greatly exceeded those of other producing nations, as companies took advantage of the favourable taxes. But the introduction of a new, comprehensive oil law in 1966 appeared to threaten this situation. From the point of view of the companies, the most disadvantageous provision of the law was Libya's claim to a share of the profits from production equal to the share claimed by the 'traditional' oil-producing countries. As this had the effect of reducing the companies' profits by at least 25 U.S. cents per barrel (that is by almost one-third), some of the companies rethought their expansion programme in the light of the availability of oil elsewhere and turned back, in part at least, to other areas for the incremental tonnage they required to serve their expanding markets. There was thus a danger that the rate of increase in production would fall away, although there was no doubt that some increase would continue as new companies achieved production for the first time and as pipelines and terminals were completed to move the oil away to world markets. One of the main reasons for Libya's rapid development as an oil power lay, in fact, in the multi-company nature of its exploitation, for eight groups of companies, embracing fourteen companies in all, quickly achieved production or made significant discoveries – in marked contrast with the single company or consortium development in the major Middle Eastern oil powers.

However, just as the established producers were preparing to con-solidate their positions, rather than planning for further rapid ex-pansion, they were presented with the clearest possible demonstration of the important geographical advantage which Libya has, even more than Nigeria, over the Middle Eastern countries in respect of the transport of oil to markets in Europe and North America. To the advantage of the shorter distance to these markets was added that of being situated on the 'market side' of a closed Suez Canal. So, when the Suez Canal was blocked as a result of the Middle East war in June 1967, the companies threw out their plans for merely consoli-dating their positions in Libya and turned to the alternative strategy of rapid expansion in order to achieve the savings in tanker capacity and in transport costs made possible by shipping oil from the Mediterranean to Western Europe and North America, instead of round the Cape of Good Hope from the Persian Gulf (see Map 4, pp. 78–9). Thus Libyan oil was eagerly sought and physical facilities expanded to make greatly increased production and export possible. In 1968 the companies achieved a 50 per cent increase in production and exports over 1967, and in 1969 work continued to increase pro-duction and pipeline capacities to a level almost another 50 per cent higher than that for 1968. With the continued closure of the Suez Canal, Libya could, within a year or two, have become the world's third largest oil producer (behind only the U.S.A. and the U.S.S.R.) and the largest oil exporter, overtaking even Venezuela, which has held this position since the end of the war, and Iran, whose produc-tion was, as shown previously, being increased more quickly than in most other countries as a result of its need for development funds. This development, however, required that Libya remained interested in its production being increased!

After the middle of 1970, in fact, Libya joined Venezuela in arguing for higher prices – and limited some companies' output in order to bring pressure to bear. As Libya, with its small population, has little immediate need for additional revenues from oil exports this pressure has steadily built up with a consequential near-stabilizing effect on the country's total production. Then in 1973 the likelihood of reduced production levels was introduced by the nationalization of some of the important producing operations – with no immediate plans for alternative ways of exploiting and selling the oil. Thus Libya was already set on a course for the limitation of production when, later in 1973, this became a general policy aim of the Arab oil-exporting nations. Libyan production in 1974 seems likely to be little more than 50 per cent of that in the peak production year of 1970.

Finally, we must examine briefly the Organization of Petroleum Exporting Countries (O.P.E.C.). Unlike nations concerned with the production of other primary goods, the world's major oil-producing countries have enjoyed throughout the post-war period the benefits of a rapid and continuing increase in demand for oil. They have not suffered from the fluctuations in demand and price levels that have, for example, afflicted the countries that produce metals such as copper and tin or agricultural raw materials such as cotton and wool. They have, therefore, become used to the idea of each new year being better than the previous one as regards oil industry activities and government revenues from the industry. The existence of a small number of very large international companies working informally together through the late 1940s and most of the 1950s to control most of the world's markets for oil guaranteed this situation. But by 1959 these companies were under some pressure in the market place – from each other as well as from outsiders – and they decided to reduce their tax commitments to the producing countries by reducing the posted prices for crude oil, which in the case of most countries determined the level of payments to governments. This decision caused an unexpectedly strong reaction in the countries concerned. The very short-term result was that the companies had to restore some of the price cuts. A somewhat longer-term result was the formation of O.P.E.C., as the Middle Eastern oil-producing countries were finally persuaded by Venezuela that such an international producers' organization was essential to curb the freedom of action of the international companies in their dealings with them.

As has been explained earlier in the chapter, Venezuela had very strong economic motivations to secure such a collective agreement, but the reaction in the first instance of the Middle Eastern countries in favour of such an organization was essentially political, for their reserves and production potential was such as to ensure rising total revenues even with reduced revenues per barrel. However, the validity and importance of such political motivations should not be understated and it is in this political direction, rather than in an economic sense, that O.P.E.C. had its main significance, at least until 1971. Politically, it demonstrated the potential power of a group of developing nations against the international companies, which had hitherto been able to 'play off' any one of the countries against the others. It also gave the group of nations experience in working together in analysing problems which they had, in part, in common. But economically its success was limited in the first ten years of its existence, because, from this point of view, the interests of its member nations differed too much. Thus, while they were collectively able to agree on and successfully work for the implementation of 'royalty expensing' (a technical change in the formula for agreeing gross profits so that the countries' share was increased by a few percentage points), the organization failed entirely over the critically important economic issues such as the prorationing of output to agreed levels. Such control of output – in order to maintain prices – was really only in the interests of Venezuela, Indonesia and possibly Iraq; for the others, the more oil they produced from their apparently near-inexhaustible reserves, the better. However, it would have been far too much to expect agreement quickly on such fundamental economic issues. The most surprising thing about O.P.E.C. by 1969 was that it continued to exist ten years after its formation and was, indeed, becoming increasingly aware of the realities of world oil power! Certainly the oil companies at first expected it to be nothing more than a very short-term phenomenon but its continued presence through the 1960s at least persuaded them that they could no longer take unilateral decisions to reduce posted prices and they soon came to regard it as having a nuisance value in hindering their efforts to organize the world oil industry.

O.P.E.C. thus came to represent an important element in the growing sophistication of the oil-producing world and then, with its collective agreement made in Caracas, Venezuela, in December 1970 to present a joint demand to the producing companies for increased royalties and taxes on oil, it not only secured an immediate significant increase in oil prices but also demonstrated clearly that the balance of power in the oil world was moving away from the oil companies and in favour of the nations with oil resources. This success of O.P.E.C. clearly demonstrated to its members the advantages of collective action and since then it has come to operate as a kind of producers' cartel which, by mid-1973, had already secured two further sets of increases on posted prices and government revenues and forced oil-company recognition of the validity of producing country 'participation' in the producing operations. It thus became quite clear that the international oil companies had indeed come to recognize the strength and significance of O.P.E.C. as a new power centre in the world of oil. So much so, in fact, that they now recognized that their own immediate best interests (that is, the maximization of their short-term levels of profitability) lay in willing cooperation with the oil-producing countries. O.P.E.C.'s collective action in raising revenues from oil could be used as an argument to secure significant price increases in oil products in the consuming countries. This cooperation between the producing countries – working through O.P.E.C. – and the international companies, also working jointly together, was a development of immense importance in the distribution of world oil power, the immediate impact of which was strongly felt in oil price rises and oil shortages in many consuming countries.

At this stage O.P.E.C. may well have become counter-productive for the oil-producing nations' interests, for its success, in cooperation with the already somewhat suspiciously-viewed international oil companies, was beginning to convince the oil-consuming nations of the existence of a 'plot' to increase the costs of their most important imported commodity. Thus there could well have been the formation of an O.P.I.C. – an Organization of Petroleum Importing Countries: a development which proved to be unnecessary in the period when O.P.E.C. had failed to have any significant effect on the price of crude oil. The new inability – and unwillingness – of the oil companies to absorb the additional costs created by the success of O.P.E.C., coupled with the post-1970 inability of the consuming nations to take any further measures to reduce the cost of their oil imports (until 1970 such measures had been possible and will be discussed in later chapters), seemed likely eventually to generate the motivation and the collective will for action against O.P.E.C. and the international oil companies. This action might ensure some constraint on the degree to which increasing revenues and profits could be earned from the export of cheaply produced oil.

Many of the oil importing and consuming nations, including Japan and Western Europe, as well as some of the nations of the Third World in Latin America, Africa, and Asia, were already beginning to make alternative provision for their energy needs – particularly by the local development of oil and gas and the more rapid expansion of nuclear power. Given time, the expansion of these energy powers would have diminished the rates of increase in oil output in the major producing and exporting countries. Should the rates of increase have fallen below the hitherto 'accepted' level, the producing nations would then have suffered harm as a result of lower earnings from oil exports, and had to face up to the same kinds of economic problems that they alone in the countries outside the industrial world had not had to face in the period since 1945.

This possible scenario has, however, since mid-1973 been completely undermined. The most important consuming countries failed to note the change in the world oil power structure which had occurred since 1971 and ignored the need to constrain the demand for oil in order to take the pressure off the constrained supply. Worse than this, the threat of a massive increase in U.S. imports came to be seen as a net addition to the accepted rate of increase in oil imports by Western Europe and Japan. And further to this powerful set of economic circumstances in which potential demand for O.P.E.C. oil clearly outpaced the potential supply (in the short to medium term), there were political circumstances which gave most of the O.P.E.C. countries – the Arab ones, that is – the immediate incentive to cut back on their deliveries of oil to the pro-Israeli, Western world. And out of this economically and politically engendered scarcity, monitored and indeed controlled by O.P.E.C., there arose the opportunity for the price of oil to be raised to whatever levels the exporting countries chose to ask, giving rise to the traumatic four-fold price increases in the posted prices of crude oil between October and December 1973. This was accompanied by the perhaps even more significant notification of the O.P.E.C. countries' intentions to disregard the agreements they had previously reached with the oil companies in respect of all essential decisions over the supply and price of oil, and, furthermore, to 'participate' in the oil companies' operations in the producing countries over a very much shorter time than had also previously been agreed with them. These few months in the latter part of 1973 took the oil world into a fundamentally new position as far as the distribution of power is concerned – with O.P.E.C. and the oil-producing nations very firmly in control. This fundamental change in the world of oil power from 1974 onwards is discussed in Chapter 9.

5: Oil Policies in Western Europe

Before the war the economy of Western Europe was, in the main, based upon the use of coal as its primary source of energy, with very little of the diversification into oil and gas that occurred in the U.S.A. (see Chapter 2). Between 1939 and 1945, however, the European coal industry was very badly hit by wartime dislocation and destruction and much of the productive capacity in countries such as West Germany, Belgium and France was out of action because of difficulties either in the mining areas themselves or in associated transport facilities. Even in places which were not directly affected by land fighting or intense bombing – for example most of Britain's coal-mining areas – the coal-mining industries were, nevertheless, affected by the running-down of facilities, the lack of capital investment and the difficulties in obtaining labour. Thus, in 1946 coal output in Western Europe totalled only 340 million tons (with Britain contributing nearly 60 per cent) and the prospects for a rapid growth of production were anything but bright. Most of the industrialized countries were thus brought face to face with a probable serious deficiency in the total energy supply required for post-war reconstruction.

In such a situation the possibility of obtaining oil supplies from overseas appeared to offer a sure and almost immediate solution to the impending energy crisis, and increasing quantities of petroleum products started to move to Western Europe from the U.S.A., the Caribbean and the Middle East. In this early post-war period, oil imports had to be largely in the form of immediately usable products, as most of the limited amount of refining equipment that had been built in Europe before the war had, along with the coal mines and the railways, suffered physical damage and could thus only be brought back into production as rebuilding took place. Moreover, rebuilding was, in any case, only going to solve part of the problem. The pre-war refining capacity of Western Europe had been small, as the economic advantage then lay in refining oil at source and in shipping the products to their markets in Europe. Not even relatively undamaged Britain could offer refining facilities to meet Europe's needs and it too had to import products from the U.S.A. and elsewhere.

This dependence of Europe on imported petroleum products – paid for in part by U.S. aid – did not persist for more than a few years. First the larger countries and then the smaller ones began to investigate the possibilities of curtailing the impact of growing oil imports on their balance of payments, as most of the oil available came either from dollar areas or through American companies and hence produced a serious drain on Europe's very limited dollar resources. The initial investigations concentrated on ways of encouraging the development of large oil refineries, so that the import of oil products could be substituted by the import of crude oil and its processing in Europe. This would ensure a reduction in the unit foreign exchange costs of Europe's oil requirements, even allowing for the dollar cost of much of the equipment required in the new oil refineries. Thus governments used both the carrot and the stick to persuade the oil-supplying companies to go along with them in the implementation of this policy. The companies were, for example, given loans at less than the then current rates of interest for financing the construction of refineries and they were guaranteed the availability of foreign exchange to import the necessary equipment. But at the same time they were told that once the refineries had been established preference would be given through tariff or quota arrangements to crude-oil imports over product imports, with the result that companies which failed to build could well find themselves forced or priced out of the markets.

As it turned out, however, the companies needed little encouragement to follow this official policy. Development in transport and refining technology coupled with the rapid growth in European demands for oil persuaded them that the establishment of refineries in Western Europe offered a lower-cost and more profitable way of meeting these demands than the traditional importation of oil products. The growth in the size of crude-oil tankers brought down the unit cost of crude-oil transportation very considerably, and the size of demand in the industrialized parts of Western Europe now meant that larger refineries could be constructed, thus ensuring the achievement of significant economies of scale in the new projects. And as oil moved in to take up markets in those areas of Europe which had formerly depended almost exclusively upon coal, so the rise in demand for fuel oil outstripped that of all other products. In fact, it increased sufficiently to ensure the local use of all the fuel oil that the new refineries could make. In contrast, the pre-war demand for fuel oil had been so small (it had been unable to compete with indigenous coal) that even the small refineries had been obliged to re-export some of this product. This had meant higher transport costs on the whole operation, which made it more expensive than the alternative of manufacturing the products near the source of the crude oil.

So from the point of view both of Western European governments and of the large international oil companies there were, in the years immediately after the war, strong economic motives for the construction of large oil refineries. By 1950 the first of the post-war constructions – for example, at Fawley in the U.K., Pernis in the Netherlands and Marseilles in France – were already successfully operating, mainly on crude oil imported from the rapidly expanding fields of the Middle East (see Chapter 4). Very soon afterwards the economic arguments for refinery construction in Europe were reinforced by strategic and political ones. Before the war, the major oil-producing areas had been securely under British and French control, but now the Middle East was entering on a period of extreme nationalism in which the influence of Britain and France declined very markedly (this is described and explained in Chapter 8). The consequent political instability, both of the region in general and of individual oil-producing countries in particular, persuaded both the importing nations and the large international companies against additional investment in refineries in such places. It became clear that it would be better to limit investment in the oil-exporting areas to that required in the oil-producing operations, and to spread the risk by building the refineries in countries where the degree of political stability and the guarantees against expropriation seemed greater than they were in the Middle East. Various events emphatically demonstrated the political and strategic considerations involved. These included the closure of the pipeline from Iraq to Haifa and the consequent closure of the refinery at Haifa because, as a result of the formation of the state of Israel in 1948, the Arab nations refused to make crude oil available to it. Shortly afterwards, in 1951, the Anglo-Iranian oil company was nationalized and the country's oil-producing facilities and the world's largest refinery, at Abadan, were closed down for a period of more than three years. As oil became more important in the economies of the Western European countries so the degree of risk that they were prepared to accept over oil supplies became smaller and was accompanied by an escalating interest in the development of local refineries. Thus, by the mid-1950s Western Europe was, by and large, self-sufficient in refinery capacity, and the continent's main estuaries and other favourable locations were dotted with refineries (see Map 6). The pattern of European trade in oil had now changed from one in which the main imports were oil products to one in which the crude oil requirements for the continent's new refineries were imported. By this time the annual saving of foreign exchange achieved by the development of a European refining industry was of the order of £50 million.

But Western Europe was not satisfied merely with the successful establishment of a refining industry. There was also serious concern over the international companies' controlled system of oil pricing, for this placed Europe under an unnecessarily high burden of foreign exchange costs for its growing requirements. In the post-war period there still persisted an element of the international oil cartel established by the major oil companies in the early 1930s as a result of the world depression. This had achieved a pricing system which kept prices higher than they need to have been in certain markets. It had also restricted the development of low-cost sources of oil because of the effect that the system had on equalizing the delivered price of oil to Western Europe no matter what its source.

The system worked in roughly the following way. Posted prices for crude oil and oil products were established at U.S. Gulf ports and freight rates were established for the transportation of oil from these ports to the ports of Western Europe. Oil from the growing producing nations of Venezuela and the Middle East was only made available by the international companies at the same prices on a grade-for-grade basis. The delivered price of this oil in Western Europe was then calculated by the companies concerned, as though it was shipped from the Gulf of Mexico, rather than at a price reflecting the cost of the actual movement involved. Thus, the prices of oil in Western Europe were not only tied to prices which reflected the relatively high cost of the regulated production of oil within the U.S.A., no matter what the costs of production were in the Middle East or in Venezuela, whence most of Europe's supplies originated, but they reflected also higher than necessary transport charges.

Western Europe was paying, on an average, about $4 for each barrel of crude oil imported and even higher prices for imports of oil products. As might well be imagined, the governments of Western Europe were not at all happy with this situation. In 1950, as a result of pressure by these governments and by the U.S. authorities responsible for the Marshall Plan, by means of which some of Europe's oil imports were being financed, the first break in this system occurred when the companies agreed to post separate prices for oil produced in Venezuela and in the Middle East. Though these posted prices were at first not much lower than those of the equivalent grades at the Gulf ports of the U.S.A., they quickly became so as price levels in the U.S.A. rose in the post-war inflationary situation. The eventual effect of this was, of course, a more favourable situation for Western European importing nations. In addition, separate freight rates reflecting the use of larger, lower-cost tankers were established for direct movements from the Caribbean and from the Middle East. As a result of these important changes the average delivered price of oil per barrel in Western Europe came down to under $3.50.

Even this general price level was well over the supply price – that is, the lowest price at which companies concerned in oil exploration and production would need to sell in order to achieve an adequate return on their investments, including due allowance for the degree of risk involved in the enterprise. The existence of such a favourable general price level made the oil industry a highly profitable one and thus encouraged the entry of new producers in many parts of the world. The potential producers looked particularly to the marketing opportunities in Western Europe, where, with rapidly expanding economies and the increasing substitution of oil for coal, the consumption of oil was increasing at a rate of some 15 per cent per annum. New companies – both American and European – started to ship oil to Western Europe, with the result that the posted-price system and the freight-rate system, which together had fixed an 'appropriate' price for the delivery of any grade of oil to any port in Europe, came under such pressure that they eventually broke. Marketing companies and refineries not tied to the major international oil companies which 'organized' the systems started to shop around for their supplies and increasingly found them at prices well below those quoted officially on the basis of posted prices and agreed freight rates. At first the activities of such companies usually affected only the fringes of the national markets, but as their business started to boom the international companies themselves were forced to respond in order to keep their own local companies competitive and able to make profits on their local operations. They were obliged to lower the prices at which they transferred oil to their affiliates in European countries, with the result that practically the whole of the market and not just the fringe business started to enjoy lower prices – which has naturally led to even greater growth in oil consumption. In the period between the late 1950s and 1970 oil in Europe went ahead at a more rapid rate than ever before and steadily forced coal into a position where it made a relatively small contribution to Western European energy. Oil replaced coal as the most important source of Western Europe's energy in 1966 and by 1970 had achieved this position in every individual Western European country – excluding Britain, whose coal industry 'held out' the longest against competition from oil.

Thus, in the main, Western European countries achieved their immediate post-war objectives of increasing the size of their own refining industries and of securing their oil imports at prices more closely related to the cost of production in the areas from which most of Europe's oil originates – the Middle East and, more recently, North Africa. There have, of course, been country-to-country variations in the implementation of these policy objectives. Italy, Scandinavia and Western Germany possibly pushed the policies to their ultimate conclusion, whereas Britain and France tended to remain relatively isolated from this main stream of development as a result of their own particular interests in other aspects of the international oil industry. France gave preference to oil from the franc zone, notably Algeria, and maintained prices at a level which made this possible. The French government exercised strict control over the oil industry throughout the post-war period, as indeed it was already doing before 1939, in order to ensure that national policies were respected by the companies concerned. Britain, the headquarters of two of the international oil companies, tended to view itself as having a national interest in the maintenance of prices on an international level and this, coupled with the dominant 90 per cent share of the international companies in the British domestic market, ensured, at least until 1965, that the country's import prices remained well above the levels applying throughout most of the rest of Europe. In 1965 the average import price per barrel of oil into Britain remained some 25 per cent above the average import price into the rest of Western Europe – to the detriment of the country's balance of payments and a continuing factor in explaining Britain's economic difficulties. However, competition came even to Britain and, as new companies moved in to take advantage of its highly profitable oil market, the established companies were obliged to shave their prices in order to meet it. In the late 1960s the oil market within Britain was probably not much less competitive than that in most other European countries, although Britain still failed to enjoy the balance of payments advantage of reduced import prices of crude oil to the same degree as Germany, Italy and Scandinavia.

But there is another aspect of the energy situation in Western Europe that affects attitudes to oil – the impact of oil on the continent's indigenous energy supplies. This, of course, is limited to those countries where coal has been important. As we have already shown, the difficulties over indigenous coal in the early post-war period led to oil being welcomed enthusiastically as a means of overcoming the energy shortage. But the coal industries of Britain, West Germany, Belgium and, on a smaller scale, those of France and the Netherlands steadily overcame these difficulties. Recapitalization of the mines enabled mechanization and later automation to be introduced so that production and labour productivity increased and the continent's demand for coal could easily be met. By this time, however – the later 1950s – the demand for coal was already declining steeply as a result of its substitution by oil in many end-uses. By 1958 the pattern of post-war energy shortage – a pattern in which every ton of coal that could be won from the ground was more or less assured of a market at a price which was government controlled in order to prevent it rising too high – had changed.

From then until 1973 the European coal industry had to face up to the prospect of decline occasioned by its inability to compete with oil in a wide variety of uses – in domestic home-heating, in electric-power generation and in basic industries such as iron and steel, etc. Coal from the higher-cost mines of the continent proved impossible to sell and thus every major coal-producing nation had a programme of mine closures, usually accompanied by measures designed to prevent social distress in the mining areas. But the programme of closures in almost every case moved too slowly to keep the relationship between supply and demand in equilibrium, and other measures had to be used in order to prevent the situation getting out of hand. Thus, most coal-producing nations were obliged to give protection to their coal industries either through subsidies on coal production or by the imposition of taxes on oil products competing with coal in end-uses other than transport.

For example, in Britain a policy of rationalization on the part of the N.C.B., whereby many mines have been closed down and production reduced from its post-war peak of 227 million tons in 1957 to only 130 million tons by 1973, was insufficient to produce equilibrium between the oil and coal industries. In the early 1960s the government was obliged to put a tax of 0.83p per gallon on all oil used for heating purposes. This tax – since raised by stages to just over 1p – may seem to be insignificant compared with the tax of 22p on each gallon of petrol used for motoring, but even so it represented a purchase tax on the ex-refinery price of fuel oil of up to 50 per cent. According to estimates made by the Ministry of Power in the middle 1960s the tax maintained the output of coal at a level some 18 million tons per annum higher that it would otherwise have been. Such taxation measures – common to all the major coal-producing nations of Western Europe – have sometimes been accompanied by other measures designed to force 'captive customers', such as government departments and other state-owned entities, to burn coal even when oil was cheaper. But all this did no more than ameliorate the adverse situation for coal, whose economic viability was seriously undermined by the growth of oil.

Thus, at the beginning of the 1970s, no more than 80 to 100 million tons of Britain's coal output remained competitive with oil without protection. This situation was paralleled throughout the continent, with the prospect of the virtual close-down of the French and the Dutch coal industries, over two-thirds of the coal industry of Belgium and some 60 per cent of the West German industry, in the absence of governmental measures designed to help coal in the energy marketplace. By 1973 oil provided over 64 per cent of Europe's total consumption of energy and by this date Western Europe could, therefore, no longer be termed a coal-based economy. It had become an economy based on the availability of two sources of fuel and power, with the competitive position remaining strongly in favour of oil throughout almost the whole of the continent.

During the post-war period the growing use of oil in an increasing number and variety of end-uses, technical developments in refining and inland transportation, and changes in the political structure of Western Europe, such as the establishment of the European Common Market, all combined to produce a fundamentally changed geography of the oil industry within the continent. Before the war the pattern was a simple one. Oil products were distributed in relatively small quantities by road and rail to the centres of inland demand from the coastal import terminals or from the small refineries at ports such as Hamburg and Marseilles. The immediate post-war development confirmed this general pattern, but the oil was now, of course, moving mainly from the expanded refining centres which were being established at convenient points of crude-oil import around the coasts of Europe (see Map 5). The quantities involved in some cases grew sufficiently quickly to justify the construction of product pipelines to take the oil from the refineries to the major internal cities. Important examples of this development were the oil-product lines laid from refineries at the mouth of the Seine to Paris and, in the U.K., the lines from refineries on the Thames and the Mersey to distribution centres in the Midlands.

At a later stage, however, it became clear that this method of supplying oil products was not the cheapest way of reaching some inland centres, with their growing requirements of fuel oil which cannot, for technical reasons, be pipelined over long distances. Thus, possibilities were investigated of establishing inland refining centres from where local distribution could take place and which would be supplied with crude oil through pipelines running from import terminals on the coasts. As a result, refineries were built in the Ruhr, fed by crude-oil pipelines from the Rotterdam area and northern Germany. Even more recently, since the mid-1960s, refining centres have been established in Bavaria, eastern France and Switzerland, dependent upon crude-oil supplies coming in by pipeline from the southern European ports of Marseilles, Genoa and Trieste. Their use as crude-oil import terminals to serve the refineries in the centre of Western Europe does, of course, markedly reduce the amount of ocean transportation needed – the oil has only to be brought the short distance from the originating source of the crude oil in the Persian Gulf/Eastern Mediterranean or North Africa to the southern Mediterranean ports of Europe. In the evolution of this pattern the tankers are saved a return journey of over 4,500 miles around the coasts of Western Europe to the ports of northern France, the Netherlands and Germany (see Map 5). With the continued development in pipeline technology it could well have been that even northern Europe (for example the northern parts of Germany and Scandinavia) would also have been fed by pipelines coming up from the Mediterranean rather than by tankers bringing the crude oil in to nearby deep-water ports. This possibility, however, now appears to have been thwarted by the likely availability of large quantities of oil from the North Sea fields by the second half of the 1970s – a development which will greatly reduce northern Europe's dependence on imported oil. Though the growth of these new patterns has depended largely upon the developing technology of pipelining and refining, some of the change has undoubtedly arisen from the movements towards economic and political integration in Western Europe whereby the barriers against the movement of goods between the nations of the Common Market have been largely eliminated. In this situation the geo-political problems associated with frontier crossings which might have arisen with the international movement of oil within Western Europe were greatly reduced and the international oil companies were able to plan optional refining and distribution patterns in the continent as a whole.

But this interrelationship between European integration and the oil industry, though important in contributing to lower costs for the industry and thus to the possibility of lower prices to consumers – which is the sort of favourable effect that customs unions are 'supposed' to have – has not provided the main topic for discussion between European 'oilmen' and the politicians and administrators. At the time of the formation of the Common Market, oil was still relatively unimportant. Its predecessor, the European Coal and Steel Community, while being made responsible for the development of a European coal policy, was given no such authority over the oil industry, which at that time was probably considered to be of too little importance to justify such governmental interest. But since the oil industry's rise to importance in the mid-1950s, many complicated and long-lasting discussions have taken place on the establishment of an overall energy policy, including oil, for the Common Market countries. However, because of the basic disagreements which arose between the interests of those members of the European Economic Community with no indigenous energy supply industries to protect and those which have, energy policy has remained one of the unresolved and difficult sectors in the pathway towards European economic integration. There can be little doubt that an agreed energy policy for the whole of the area will ultimately emerge. When it does the political changes generated will eventually have repercussions on attitudes towards oil within the community with a trend in the direction of more effective and more comprehensive government control. French experience in this respect, dating back some thirty years, perhaps gives the best idea of what will happen.

Thus, a common energy policy for the E.E.C. will involve some degree of protection for the remaining domestic energy industries. Whilst the oil industry will continue to be run by individual companies – both public and private – it will have to be along lines which are either laid down or subject to supervision by European civil servants. Such control – which is reflected in similar advancing measures of government control among the non-members of the Common

Market – should not even be too upsetting to U.S. firms which are used to effective and comprehensive government intervention at home. It will, moreover, produce a situation within which they can be certain of securing an adequate return on their investments, and take away much of the normal commercial risk to which they would otherwise be subjected. This will apply particularly in the case of 'Community' companies – that is, companies whose parent company 'belongs' to a member nation, as opposed to foreign-owned companies – for they are likely to be accorded preferential treatment on both political and strategic grounds.

The development of comprehensive energy policies in the Common Market and in other countries of Western Europe has in general, however, been opposed by the oil companies, which have seen them as a means of restricting their growth and freedom of action. But in the 1970s such policies could well become a means whereby the interests of the greatly expanded oil industry – now with an established position to defend – are given some protection against more recent developments in the energy economy of Western Europe, which will otherwise threaten not only their growth prospects but also their future overall profitability. The first development is the recently discovered availability of large quantities of natural gas within Western Europe itself (see Map 6). This primary energy source has been available throughout most of the post-war period in northern Italy and southern France, but the quantities involved have been relatively small and capable only of providing a limited amount of the energy required in the two countries in a period in which energy demand was moving ahead very rapidly. Thus, the oil companies hardly felt the effect of the competition at all. But the gas field of Groningen in the northernmost part of the Netherlands is a very different matter. This field was not discovered until 1959, and only slowly evaluated, but is now known to be the world's largest exploitable gas field outside the Soviet Union, exceeding in size even the largest fields in Texas. It has already been shown capable of producing up to 10,000 million cubic feet of natural gas daily, or the equivalent of over 80 million tons of oil per annum. As the premium or high-price markets for this gas in the Netherlands and nearby parts of France, Belgium and West Germany are satisfied, it is increasingly being made available for use in processes and amongst

Map 5. The Oil Industry in Western Europe

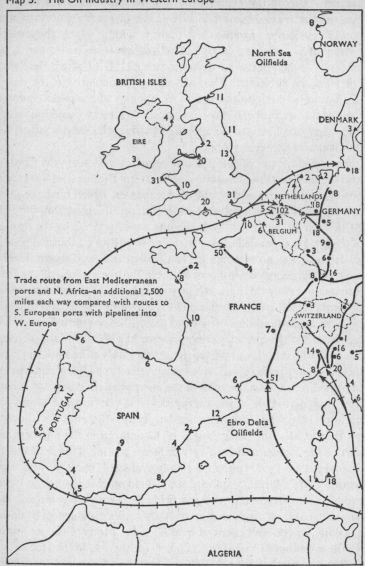

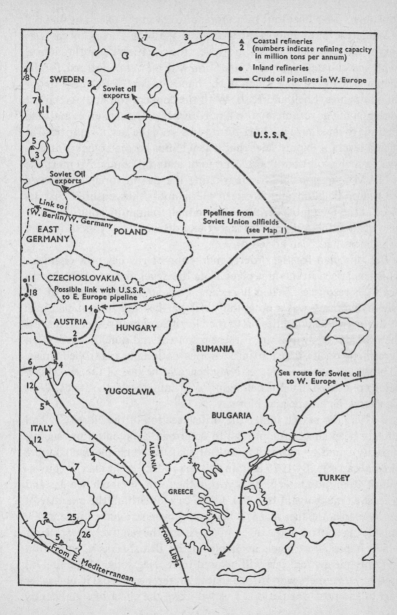

Coastal refineries
(numbers indicate refining capacity
in million tons per annum)
Inland refineries
Crude oil pipelines in W. Europe

7   3

SWEDEN   3

Soviet oil
exports

8

7   11

U.S.S.R.

5

3

Soviet Oil
exports

Link to
W. Berlin/W. Germany

EAST
GERMANY

POLAND

Pipelines from
Soviet Union oilfields
(see Map 1)

11

18

CZECHOSLOVAKIA

Possible link with U.S.S.R.
to E. Europe pipeline

14

AUSTRIA

2

HUNGARY

RUMANIA

6   4

12

Sea route for Soviet oil
to W. Europe

5

YUGOSLAVIA

ITALY

12

BULGARIA

7   4

ALBANIA

TURKEY

3

GREECE

2   25

5

5   26

From Libya

From E. Mediterranean

consumers who turn to it in preference to even the cheapest fuel oil.

While the most important source of Western European gas was confined to the Netherlands, however, the situation never threatened to get out of hand so far as competition with oil was concerned, for the Dutch fields were very much in the hands of two of Europe's major oil companies, Shell and Esso. With the cooperation and agreement of the Dutch government, also a part-owner of the resources and also anxious to maximize its short-term gains from the gas, it was priced at such a level for export sales that it would not become quickly attractive to major oil consumers. The joint state/oil company enterprise – NAM – responsible for marketing the gas in foreign countries – France, Belgium and Western Germany – thus ensured that its price at the Dutch border was high enough to limit its ability to compete against fuel oil once transport and distribution costs to foreign consumers had been added on.

But this plan for the orderly marketing of gas has now changed. This has arisen in the first place from the development of the North Sea's gas resources. When it became evident that the whole of the North Sea basin was a potentially rich gas-bearing zone, the nations of Europe with shorelines on to the North Sea got together to discuss the problem of ownership of these resources and quickly reached an agreement on its division into various nationally controlled areas. Exploration of the resources lying beneath the bed of the sea is now being conducted in areas belonging to Britain, the Netherlands, West Germany, Denmark and Norway.

By 1969 the search under the British section of the North Sea had already been successful enough to determine a potential productive capacity equal to more than half of that of which the Dutch were already capable. By 1975 Britain will be producing the energy equivalent of 40 million tons of oil a year in the form of North Sea gas and at least as much again by 1980. In the case of Britain the quantity of gas available, the fact that it is being sold by a national entity entirely outside the control of the oil companies, and the relatively low price at which it has been made available to the British Gas Corporation certainly means that gas will be used to replace some of the fuel oil used by consumers who turned to it in preference to coal in an earlier part of the post-war period. This will have the effect of significantly slowing down the growth of the oil industry in Britain over the next ten to fifteen years, as gas moves up to take a position of providing as much as one-quarter of the total primary energy requirement. Repetition of the Dutch, British, and, most recently, Norwegian successes in the search for natural gas in other continental shelf areas could well produce enough gas in north-western Europe to provide over one-quarter of the total energy demand within the whole of this densely peopled and industrialized part of the continent.

For more easterly and southerly parts of Western Europe there are yet other sources from which this third primary energy can be made available. This involves importing international gas on a very large scale from the known gas fields of Northern Africa – via a pipeline or liquefied natural gas tankers from the massive fields of Algeria and Libya across to southern Italy and possibly southern Spain; as liquefied natural gas from Nigeria and other more distant producing areas; and also via large-diameter pipelines running into Austria, Switzerland, West Germany and Italy, from the virtually limitless gas fields of the U.S.S.R. and, via the U.S.S.R. or Turkey, from the gas fields of Iran (see Map 6, pp. 114–15). The development of pipeline technology makes this very long-distance transmission of gas into the markets of Western Europe economically feasible. Gas will thereby become available in the consuming countries at prices which will enable it to compete with oil products in a wide variety of end-uses, especially in the light of the rapid and continuing increases in oil prices which Western Europe has had to face since 1973. (See Chapter 3 for a discussion of Russian gas in Western Europe.)

Thus, Europe's energy economy will soon become based on three fuels, in much the same way as have the fuel economies of the U.S.A. and the U.S.S.R. This must be partly, at least, at the expense of the existing markets for oil – those markets in fact which oil has secured from Europe's other indigenous resource, coal, in the post-war period so far. Such a development will be welcome in every country of Western Europe, for many governments have expressed increasingly great concern over their countries' undue reliance on imported energy from politically unstable parts of the world – even though they didn't necessarily pursue appropriate policies to limit the degree of dependence. However, while oil remained as the only alternative to

Map 6. Natural Gas in Western Europe

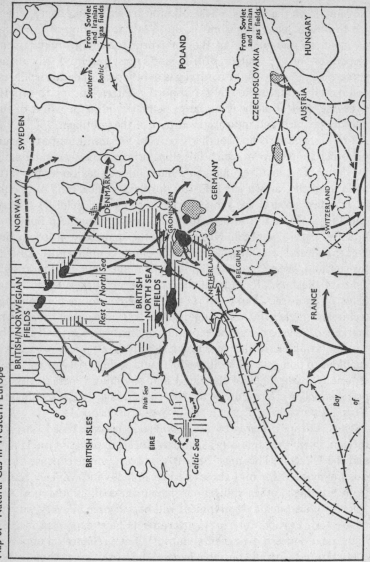

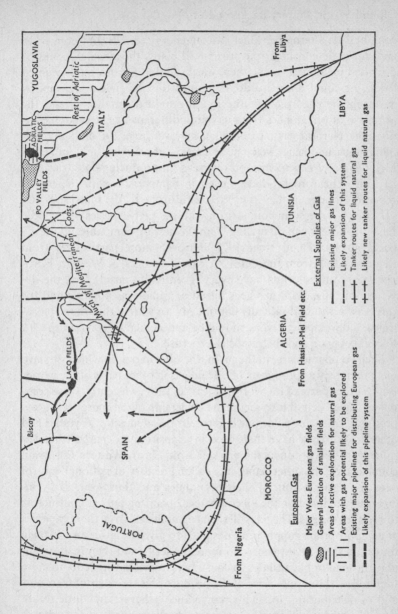

European Gas

◖ Major West European gas fields

◍ General location of smaller fields

||||| Areas of active exploration for natural gas

┃ Areas with gas potential likely to be explored

━━ Existing major pipelines for distributing European gas

╍╍ Likely expansion of this pipeline system

External Supplies of Gas

━━ Existing major gas lines

┼┼┼ Likely expansion of this system

╫╫╫ Tanker routes for liquid natural gas

┿┿┿ Likely new tanker routes for liquid natural gas

From Hassi-R-Mel Field etc.

YUGOSLAVIA

Rest of Adriatic

ADRIATIC FIELDS

PO VALLEY FIELDS

ITALY

From Libya

LIBYA

TUNISIA

ALGERIA

Coast

North of Mediterranean

LACQ FIELDS

Biscay

SPAIN

MOROCCO

PORTUGAL

From Nigeria

coal, and an alternative which offered energy to industry, commerce and domestic consumers at prices well below those which could be provided by domestic coal, there was little that Europe really wanted to do, or could afford to do, to reduce this dependence, except by ensuring the expansion of the refining industry at home, and the purchase of oil supplies from as many different overseas sources as possible. Natural gas introduced a new variable, for not only is it indigenous, and hence welcome as a means of reducing the continent's high degree of dependence on overseas oil-producing countries, but it is also cheap to produce – even in comparison with the much-reduced oil prices achieved in Western Europe by the mid-1960s and very much more so in comparison with the higher prices for Middle Eastern and African oil arising from the new oil companies/O.P.E.C. countries agreements since 1971 and even more particularly from those resulting from the O.P.E.C. cartel since 1973. Western European governments thus have every incentive to ensure that the development of natural gas goes ahead as rapidly as possible and for this reason will undoubtedly continue to be willing that the exploration and development work should be undertaken by companies with long experience and the requisite expertise.

Such companies are, in the main, the oil companies which we have met previously as producers of oil and gas in other parts of the world. But in other parts of the world, at least until very recently, these companies have been able to secure the ownership of the energy resources produced by their operations in return for a payment of royalties and other taxes. They have then been in a position to charge whatever prices for their products the markets would bear. Western European countries, on the other hand, have a long history of national control over the basic sectors of their economies and thus seem likely increasingly to insist on the oil companies operating only as contractors to produce the gas. The gas will then be purchased from the companies at an appropriate supply price designed to give the latter an adequate return on their investment – no more, no less – and then made available through public utilities to consumers at prices which do no more than reflect the supply price of the product plus the costs of transport and of distribution. In such circumstances, there seems little doubt that natural gas will greatly enlarge its markets, partly at the expense of imported oil, and provide an important new element in the 1970s and the 1980s within Europe's energy economy.

When the potentialities of natural gas are coupled with the increasingly likely large-scale development of nuclear power stations, a phase already under way in Britain, Western Germany and France, in each of which at least one large – 1,200 MW or more – atomic power station will be commissioned each year in the 1970s (in part, at least, in place of new oil-fired thermal power stations), Western Europe can be seen to be on the threshold of containing the increase of oil's contribution to its energy economy. And it seems not impossible that the markets in absolute terms for some products will decline. This is particularly so in the case of fuel oil – against which coal will still be protected especially for electricity generation in Britain and Western Germany. Fuel oil will also lose potential outlets to nuclear-power developments and will be substituted by natural gas in many areas and end-uses. This process had already started in the Netherlands by 1968 as natural gas became the preferred fuel in most end-uses, and since then the use of fuel oil has declined by about 30 per cent. However, the total oil requirement is likely to continue to rise slowly overall because of its use in sectors – particularly motor transport – where there are as yet no satisfactory alternatives to oil-fired internal-combustion and diesel engines. This likelihood of a changing pattern of product demand will necessitate changes in refining programmes in order to reduce the fuel-oil output, which has hitherto been at a maximum. Refining may thus become even more closely tied in with petrochemicals (whose feed-stocks and fuel requirements can absorb the refinery output for which other markets do not exist) and move the refineries for preference back to the coastal areas, where petrochemical developments are usually more appropriate.

These changes will have serious repercussions for the oil industry itself, but for Western Europe its post-war oil crises – arising out of political difficulties in the Middle East – should by 1980 be but a spectre of the past. In the meantime, however, Europe has to face the most serious crisis of all in terms of its dependence on imported oil: the post-1972 crisis arising out of the control over oil supply which has come to be exercised by the oil-producing countries – a development not initially unwelcome to the major oil companies which saw the constrained supply system as a means of achieving increased profitability through monopoly pricing. Given the dominant role of oil in Europe's energy economy, this crisis may yet involve rationing and other constraints on the use of oil products for a period of several years. In fact, one can argue the need for 'preventive rationing' to eliminate the producers' certainty of gain from inevitable rises in demand, so serving to alter the balance of power between the parties concerned.

Beyond this period of difficulty, however, there is the promise of a greatly reduced dependence on imported oil opened up by the large and exciting new discoveries of oil resources under the North Sea where, by mid-1973, enough oil had already been discovered to justify the possibility of an annual production of up to 300 million tons from Norwegian, British and Dutch waters by the early 1980s (see Map 7). This is certainly only the beginning of the development of Western Europe's off-shore oil resources which could, by the middle 1980s, be supplying most of Western Europe's total oil requirements – especially if between 1974 and the end of the decade there is a serious restraint on the demand for oil either as a result of the very much higher prices which will have to be paid for O.P.E.C. oil (see Figure 1) or as a result of the introduction of rationing systems.

In addition to this important development there are the recently improved prospects of diversifying supply sources by importing Australian, Alaskan and northern Canadian as well as African oil. Thus after three decades of great concern over oil by European planners and governments, the continent should, by the early 1980s, be able to afford to adopt a somewhat more relaxed attitude. And coupled with the lessening of fears about the security of supplies, there could then be some relaxation of the need for the European-wide surveillance of oil price levels, the development of which became essential during the period of rapidly escalating prices after 1973. Given the pressure of competition both between oil supply sources and between oil products and other energy sources, oil prices by then seem likely to be able once again to take adequate care of themselves – that is, as seen from the long-term point of view of European governments concerned with oil import costs, and of European

Map 7.   North Sea Oil Developments — March 1974

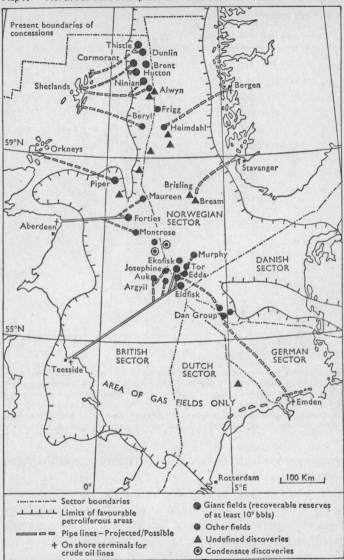

Present boundaries of concessions

Thistle Dunlin
Cormorant Brent
Hutton
Shetlands Ninian Alwyn
Bergen
Frigg
Beryl
Heimdahl

59°N Orkneys
Stavanger

Piper Brisling
Maureen Bream

NORWEGIAN
SECTOR
Aberdeen Forties
Montrose
Murphy
Ekofisk Tor
Josephine Edda
Auk
Argyil Eldfisk

DANISH
SECTOR

Dan Group

55°N

BRITISH
SECTOR GERMAN
SECTOR
Teesside DUTCH
SECTOR

AREA OF GAS FIELDS ONLY
Emden

Rotterdam 100 Km
0° 5°E

Sector boundaries
Limits of favourable
petroliferous areas
Pipe lines — Projected/Possible
On shore terminals for
crude oil lines

● Giant fields (recoverable reserves
of at least 10^9 bbls)
● Other fields
▲ Undefined discoveries
◉ Condensate discoveries

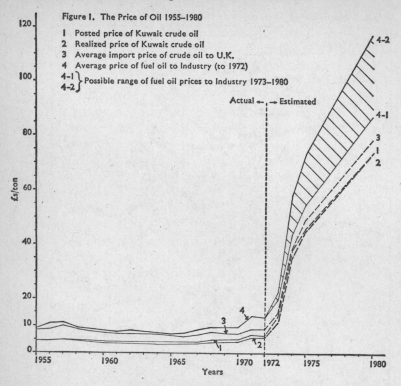

Figure 1. The Price of Oil 1955–1980

1   Posted price of Kuwait crude oil
2   Realized price of Kuwait crude oil
3   Average import price of crude oil to U.K.
4   Average price of fuel oil to Industry (to 1972)
4–1
4–2 } Possible range of fuel oil prices to Industry 1973–1980

Actual ← , → Estimated

The diagram clearly shows how steady the prices of oil remained for a period of 15 years. In real terms (after allowing for inflation and the falling value of the £) oil became cheaper. The increases up to 1974 have already occurred – beyond 1974 we simply extrapolate a further 10 per cent per annum increase in crude oil costs (4 – 1) and in crude oil costs and profit margins (4 – 2). There could, of course, be events which will undermine this price development but there is no sign by March 1974 that the consuming nations are willing to constrain their demands for oil sufficiently to cause the system to break.

consumers concerned with the cost of oil at factory gate or delivered to a domestic storage tank.

Europe's 'battle for oil' is now all over bar the shouting, except for the very difficult period up to 1980 or thereabouts when the alternatives to imported oil will not be available in large enough quantities. This gives a period of time during which O.P.E.C. countries and the international oil companies between them will be able to squeeze much more money out of European consumers for their oil requirements. Thereafter and within the framework of constraints which will be introduced into the system by overall energy policies (national and European Community), the companies concerned in the trade seem likely to have to be content with limited profit margins on the highest possible volume sales they can achieve.

With such low margins – which, moreover, are likely to be subject eventually to pressures arising from increasing competition from other energy sources – the companies concerned will have to devote increasing attention to the problems of alternative continental-scale supply and distribution patterns. A wrong choice in this respect could easily eliminate the profit element entirely. The changes in the technology and the economics of refining and transportation and the changing geographical and product requirement patterns of oil demand further complicate the situation, so much so, in fact, that there seem to be striking differences of opinion between companies, which usually, in making use of the same information, arrive at roughly the same conclusions about what best to do in any given situation. Thus, for example, one company chose to serve its European refineries indirectly through a massive terminal in Southern Ireland at which oil is received in 300,000-ton tankers and dispatched to various European countries in 50,000–100,000-tonners. Another company sees the trans-European (south to north) pipeline system, with refineries strung out along it in consuming centres, as the primary pattern of distribution at which to aim. Others see the south North Sea coast of West Germany, Britain, the Netherlands and Belgium as remaining the major growth area in the development of refining facilities. As a result of such contrasting plans, the geography of the European oil industry seems likely to become even more complex in the period that lies ahead – particularly in the light of contrasting company (and country) interests in the development of the North Sea resources.

Finally, the structure of the industry poses another set of problems. In particular, its low degree of 'Europeanization' in face of the still-increasing private U.S. companies' dominance of the European oil scene creates a situation which may not be acceptable to a large part of European political opinion in a gradually strengthening economic framework. In the 1970s this could lead to some efforts to 'Europeanize' the industry in a way not dissimilar to the 'nationalization' of the older-established energy industries in an earlier period of Europe's political history and/or to the floating of many new European oil companies using locally raised finance particularly for the development of the North Sea resources – the Norsk Oljeselskap, floated on the Oslo stock market early in 1971 with an enthusiastic response from many tens of thousands of small investors in Norway, was the first example of this kind of development and since then there have been several other examples.

Other routes towards ensuring a greater strength for local companies in the oil scene include both that adopted in France – where a powerful state oil entity (E.R.A.P.) has been established – and that in West Germany where the government has forced a set of small companies to merge to produce a viable oil company able to operate at an international level. However, it seems that much of this could have been more efficiently and effectively done at a European level rather than within individual countries. Such a European approach to the challenges and opportunities of the oil industry in the 1970s may yet become a part of the overall moves towards more economic and political integration in the continent over the next decade.

6: Japan: The World's Biggest Oil Importer

Apart from the few major oil-producing countries which at the present time appear to have little else of potential economic value – and whose economies are therefore based on the continuing production and export of crude oil – Japan stands as the country most susceptible to economic distress in the event of a major upset in the international oil industry. This has been clearly demonstrated in the oil crisis situation which developed in 1973. The Japanese economy and the country's international economic standing have both suffered unexpected shocks. Its position and its problems resemble in kind those of Western Europe (see Chapter 5), but in degree they are significantly accentuated by the interplay of a series of factors which will be examined later in this chapter.

Japan's position in this respect is a relatively recent one. Its pre-war economic development and wartime exertions, like those of Western Europe, were essentially coal-based. This coal was domestically produced and was supplemented by two other energy sources: firstly, by a great deal of 'non-commercial' energy, which may be defined as any combustible materials which could be collected or gathered (for example wood or straw) to provide peasants with their limited requirements of heat and light; and secondly, by hydro-electricity, particularly in the 1930s when a great deal of the country's hydro-electricity potential was developed. The country's needs for oil up and into the war period were, therefore, limited mainly to a small amount for motor transport and for the armed forces. During the war the country's small indigenous oil resources, plus installations which were captured in the Dutch East Indies and Burma and repaired sufficiently to yield some oil, met the needs of the fighting forces. Japan suffered less than Germany in this respect.

In the immediate post-war period the initial rehabilitation and growth of the country's industry and transport had to be based mainly on the energy that was indigenously available – coal and hydro-electricity. The latter was quickly brought back into full production – and even expanded – with the help of the U.S.A. The former depended partly upon mines that were approaching the end of their useful life and on an ageing mining force which was relatively unproductive – the description of the Japanese coal industry's problems savours of the language familiar to those with knowledge of the coal industries in post-war Britain and Germany. In addition the mines were remote from the main industrial areas (see Map 8). Still, in spite of all the difficulties, the coal had to be secured and government help was given to the privately owned mines. Production increased, but by no means fast enough to satisfy the demands of an economy which by the end of the 1940s and the beginning of the 1950s was beginning to show a great potential, partly as a result of the enforced changes in the structure of Japanese society during the American occupation. Somewhat reluctantly, therefore, but in the face of necessity – and with the encouragement of the U.S. military administration – the Japanese started to encourage the expansion of the oil industry. As far as encouraging consumption was concerned, assistance was given to power stations and other large industrial users to convert to oil. In order to make the required products available at as low a cost in foreign exchange as possible, the government turned to the rehabilitation and massive extension of the old-fashioned, small and inefficient oil refineries. For crude oil, as in Western Europe, could be imported at a lower foreign exchange cost than oil products, and in the face of a crippling shortage of foreign exchange – and, temporarily, of the means of earning it – crude-oil importation certainly had to be encouraged. But even the expansion of the refineries caused economic problems in view of the amount of capital needed and the fact that much of this capital had to be spent on equipment and expertise available at that time only from the U.S.A. Thus, capital and foreign exchange scarcity seemed likely to be a stumbling block to this solution to the energy 'crisis'.

In 1950, therefore, the government took a decision which it has since lived to regret but which was probably unavoidable at that time. In conflict with the traditional Japanese attitude towards foreign

Map 8. Oil in Japan

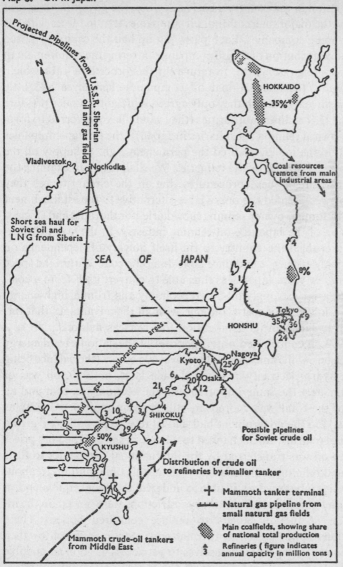

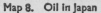

Projected pipelines from U.S.S.R. Siberian oil and gas fields

N

HOKKAIDO

←35%→

6

2

Coal resources remote from main industrial areas

Vladivostok

Nachodka

Short sea haul for Soviet oil and LNG from Siberia

SEA OF JAPAN

2

4

5

8%

1

3

Tokyo

HONSHU

35 36 9

24

3

exploration areas

gas and

Kyoto

Nagoya

25

3

6

20

Osaka

21 5

12

2

8

2

3 10

3

4

SHIKOKU

9

Possible pipelines for Soviet crude oil

50%

KYUSHU

Distribution of crude oil to refineries by smaller tanker

✚ Mammoth tanker terminal

⊢⊢⊢ Natural gas pipeline from small natural gas fields

◈ Main coalfields, showing share of national total production

▲ 3 Refineries (figure indicates annual capacity in million tons)

Mammoth crude-oil tankers from Middle East

participation in the country's basic activities, the government agreed to allow the major international oil companies to join forces with the local refining companies. Each party put up half the capital required with the contribution of the oil companies covering the requirement in terms of foreign exchange. In return for this procedure – for which, incidentally, the international oil companies themselves had little enthusiasm and to which they only agreed reluctantly, under pressure from the U.S. military authorities (they would have preferred to form wholly-owned refining subsidiaries in Japan) – the foreign companies putting up the money secured the permanent right to supply all the crude oil ever needed by the refineries. We shall return to examine the later criticism of these procedures, but in the circumstances they probably represented the only viable alternative to the establishment of wholly foreign-owned refining subsidiaries for the rapid and efficient expansion of the Japanese oil-refining industry. In the event this expansion enabled the country to rid itself quickly of dependence on increasingly expensive and unreliable domestic coal. Within the space of a very few years Japan was thus able to convert itself from a coal-based to a very strongly oil-based economy and from a high-energy cost to a low-energy cost economy, with all the advantages that this brought to Japan in its competition for overseas markets.

In 1950 oil contributed only 7 per cent of the nation's total energy requirement, while coal contributed over 60 per cent (the balance being mainly hydro-electricity). Only a decade later, in 1960, oil was of approximately the same importance in the economy as coal and its share of the total was, moreover, still growing rapidly. Already as early as 1955 the government had had to reverse its policy of giving assistance to firms which changed to oil, for, in spite of the high prices at which oil was transferred by the international companies to their associated refining companies in Japan at this time (and up to about 1957), oil products were still able to undercut their coal equivalents in the market place. In 1955 statutory restrictions were placed on the installation of fuel-oil boilers to replace coal-fired boilers. These restrictions applied even to thermal power stations, which by then were almost falling over themselves to get access as soon as possible to the lower-cost oil fuel. However, the trend to oil could not be reversed by such steps, for the price differential in its favour over coal started to widen. On the one hand coal prices continued to rise under the stimulus of rapidly increasing wages paid to miners (the important cost element in mining in most parts of the world and even more so in Japan, where labour productivity in coal mining was particularly low) and because of increasingly difficult physical conditions of coal mining. On the other hand, oil prices started to fall as a result of competition between the growing number of importing and refining companies seeking markets, and the availability after 1957 of crude oil on the world market at prices below those formally posted by the international 'majors'.

In the late 1950s even the high annual increase in oil consumption of the earlier part of the decade (averaging 15 per cent per annum) seemed small as consumption more than doubled in the three years from 1957. Then right through until 1964 it averaged almost 25 per cent per year. In 1958 Japan was the world's seventh largest oil consumer: it has gradually climbed the league table and now lies third, with a consumption of over 200 million tons in 1973. In 1957 consumption had been less than 15 million tons. But the growth of oil demand and the growth of its relative importance in the total energy requirement of the country does not appear to be at an end. The continued rapid growth of the economy, and the continued ability of oil to compete with the coal that is still produced and with the remaining and less attractive opportunities for the development of hydro-electric potential, are still producing annual rates of increase in oil demand of more than 10 per cent. Rates of growth have been so consistently high that all forecasts of the future demand for oil made in the last twenty years have been proved too conservative. A 1962 estimate for 1967 indicated an oil consumption of a little under 100 million tons, but the actual figure was about 8 per cent higher and growth rates until 1973 continued to be higher than those written into the estimates of the earlier part of the decade. It is thus possible that present forecasts, such as the one produced in 1967 by the Energy Commission, could still err on the low side. Even so, total demand for energy is expected to grow from its present annual level of about 300 million tons of oil equivalent to over 800 million tons by 1985. Oil currently accounts for nearly 60 per cent of the total, but by 1985 it is estimated that its share will be over 75 per cent, giving a requirement for that year of

127

over 600 million tons – approximately three times the 1973 level of consumption. This estimate assumes that nuclear power will grow quickly enough to meet almost two-fifths of the remaining energy need, and this is probably an optimistic assumption in the light of the considerable difficulties that still exist in building successful nuclear power stations – particularly in a country as earthquake-prone as Japan.

As this brief survey shows, the Japanese economy has quickly become, and will remain for the foreseeable future, one whose well-being is inextricably tied to the oil industry. One should note, however, that since 1970 Japan has started to worry a great deal about the environmental impact, in respect of both atmospheric and water pollution, of such an intensive use of oil. Between then and 1973 measures were taken to limit these adverse effects – particularly as far as requirements for pollution control were concerned – and there were already indications that these were beginning to slow down the rate of increase in oil use. More recently, however, this motivation to restrict the use of oil has been further strengthened by the oil-supply crisis arising out of restraints on production in countries of the Middle East (on which Japan mainly depends for its imports), and then again by the rapid rise of oil prices since October 1973. The impact of these will certainly be to heighten the degree of concern for efficiency in the use of oil, and to encourage the use of substitutes.

Nevertheless, for Japan it remains highly unlikely that there can be an increasing contribution to the country's energy economy by a still significant coal industry, as in the case of the U.K. or Germany. The Japanese planners hope that coal production can be stabilized at a little over 50 million tons per year, but at least until the 1973 oil crisis there were serious doubts whether even 20 million tons could really hope to compete. The British coal industry reduced to the same proportionate share of the energy market would be no more than a quarter of its present size, and even the most pessimistic estimates of its chances never saw it being reduced to less than 50 per cent of its 1971 production level of 150 million tons. Japan does not have the immediate promise of the very large resources of natural gas that Europe can already count on (as a result of the development of natural gas, the European oil industry has lost much of its growth prospects for the 1970s). Nor have large oil resources yet been found in Japanese off-shore waters. And, finally, Japan has no existing nuclear power industry with many years of experience in producing nuclear electricity and with the domestic technology and know-how that make nuclear power virtually an indigenous fuel, as north-west Europe has. Japan will no doubt ultimately achieve this, but in the meantime nuclear development promises to be costly in terms of foreign exchange. Even in 1974, therefore, in spite of the fundamental changes in the international oil supply and price position, Japan's continued reliance on increasing quantities of imported oil seems certain – and justifies the argument advanced at the beginning of this chapter that no country, outside some of the major oil-producing nations, has more to be concerned about as far as international oil is concerned.

It is not surprising, therefore, that successive Japanese governments have worried about oil to an increasing degree, and their degree of concern has been gradually reflected in an increasing willingness and intention to do something about it. In the early post-war period official concern lay principally with the foreign exchange cost of oil imports and thus the industry merited the special kind of treatment that it received – official blessing for joint ventures whereby foreign capital part-financed the expansion in refining. Apart from this special treatment, oil also occupied an important place in the general control exercised by the government over all imports. Because of the acute shortage of foreign exchange a complex government system of allocating funds for imports was gradually developed, and, as part of this system, the oil industry had to argue its case for foreign funds twice a year and have its arguments weighed against the claims of other sectors. Because oil was essential to the country's recovery and because its foreign exchange cost was not a dominant element in the total foreign exchange requirement, the industry was given high priority and met only temporary difficulties in the occasional periods of financial stringency through which Japan passed in the fifteen years after the end of the war. Nevertheless, from accounting for only about 8 per cent of the value of imports in 1950, oil's share of the total rose gradually through the decade until it reached 16 per cent in 1960, in spite of the falling crude-oil prices that Japan enjoyed over the last three years of the period. Thus, the government did use its allocative powers to ensure that preference was given to refinery proposals which incorporated plans for or possibilities of petrochemical developments, as the encouragement of this industry was another means of improving the country's balance of payments, both by import substitution and by the development of an industry with export potential. From very small beginnings in the mid-1950s, petrochemicals in Japan were thus encouraged to expand so quickly that by 1966 the Japanese petrochemical industry was second only in size to that of the U.S.A. in production and in exports. From four small complexes in 1958 the industry expanded to eleven major ones – all associated with the oil-refining industry of the country. Thus, oil imports were made to pay for themselves as far as foreign exchange costs were concerned by providing the raw material on which much value could be added in the manufacturing in Japan of large quantities of petrochemicals with their readily available export markets.

The method by which foreign exchange for oil refiners was allocated sought to encourage the companies to search the world's producing areas for the cheapest supplies of crude oil and, similarly, the methods of apportioning exchange allocated for the import of refined oil products (principally fuel oil, which the Japanese refineries did not produce in sufficient quantities to meet the heavy peak demands) also sought to stimulate the purchase of low-cost supplies. The ending of import controls in 1962, when, by international agreement, Japan agreed to liberalize its trading régime, foreshadowed an end to this system of close government control, not only over the oil industry's imports in particular but also over its activities in general. This was viewed with official consternation in the light of the increasing significance of oil in the Japanese economy and the knowledge that these essential supplies of energy were really out of the control of the Japanese themselves and in the hands of a small group of international – mainly American – oil companies and an even smaller group of oil-producing nations in a politically unstable part of the world. About 80 per cent of Japanese oil imports were tied – by long-term contracts – to those few international oil companies whose financial assistance in promoting refinery expansion the government had been obliged or persuaded to accept, first in 1950 but also through much of the period since then. Apart from the initial need to accept financial and technical help from the United States to get its oil-refining industry off the ground, the continued rapid expansion of refining in Japan throughout the 1950s and into the 1960s put such a severe strain on the local capital market that all Japanese refining companies were more or less continually obliged to accept loans from the international companies to finance development or expansion. In return the international companies concerned sought and obtained guaranteed crude-oil outlets. To make the degree and dangers of dependence even worse, over 80 per cent of Japanese oil imports originated in the Middle East and so Japan found itself dependent upon the goodwill of the governments of Kuwait, Iraq, Saudi Arabia and Iran for the security of its oil supply.

In view of the obvious economic, political and strategic implications being generated by the rising tide of oil imports, the Japanese government decided that it could not afford to 'liberalize' oil. It resolved, therefore, to replace the control it had had through the import system with a direct control of the industry exercised through new oil legislation. In 1962, concurrently with the Japanese liberalization of its trading régime, a new law was passed concerning the oil industry. Though this was essentially 'enabling' legislation, it did give the government the possibilities of very wide powers by means of which it could control the oil industry in almost all its activities. The implementation of these powers would depend on the outcome from time to time of the more or less continuing discussions between the government and its agencies on the one hand and the different sectors of the oil industry on the other.

The new law not only provided for the continuation of the measures of control over prices and refinery expansion that had previously existed, but also enabled the government to insist on outlets being found for all home-produced and any Japanese-produced oil. Its intention was to limit the growth in the foreign exchange cost of the commodity and to curb the power exercised by the foreign companies and governments over Japan's energy. But this was not all, for the law, as passed by the Diet which sought to strengthen it beyond the intentions of the government, added further scope for building up Japan's position in the oil world. Thus, the law created the possibilities of financial aid and tax exemption for the exploration and development of Japan's own oil and gas reserves; it promised assistance to Japanese refiners to give them more freedom in making their crude-oil purchases; and it allowed the establishment of a national corporation to market indigenous and Japanese-produced overseas crude oil – termed 'classified crude' – developed by national companies. Powers were also given to this corporation to direct such classified supplies to other refiners.

The readiness, willingness, ability or need of the government to implement in its entirety such a far-reaching piece of oil legislation did not, however, materialize immediately. In fact, reporting in 1966, the Petroleum Committee of the Energy Council was able to note that little had been achieved in fulfilling government policy, which in theory sought to promote low-cost secure supplies provided, at least in part, by fully integrated Japanese companies. In the years 1962–5, the new legislation made little difference. Thus, crude-oil import prices, which had fallen year by year from 1957 to 1962, thereafter remained almost constant, in spite of a growing availability of crude oil in the world. 'Tied' crude still accounted for 80 per cent of total supplies and was permitted in even at an average cost per barrel 10 cents higher than 'free' crude oil. There had been little development of overseas ventures apart from the gradual development of the field discovered by a Japanese Consortium in the Neutral Zone in the Persian Gulf in 1959. Initial development of this field – the Khafji field – had been rapid by world standards, but then output was restricted by the unwillingness of refineries in Japan controlled by foreign companies to take more than a very limited amount of its crude oil. The company – Arabian Oil – almost in desperation because of its need to achieve a higher cash flow from its investments, tried to sell an interest in the field to American companies in return for their right to take up to 20 per cent of the crude oil available. Thus, oil production, developed initially to feed the Japanese markets with Japanese-produced oil, was being forced into other markets because no room could be found for it in Japan – even with Japanese demand expanding at a world record rate of about 20 per cent per annum! By 1966, Khafji crude still provided under 10 per cent of Japan's total crude-oil supply. Finally, attempts to use Soviet oil as an alternative to the predominant Middle East international oil companies' supplies had been little more than half-hearted and in 1966 it provided under 5 per cent of the total.

All this the Petroleum Committee of the Energy Council found depressing, expensive for Japan, and not in the country's best political and strategic interests; and it recommended several lines of action involving much greater government intervention in the oil industry. It called for a 10 per cent reduction in the 1966 level of crude-oil import prices by 1970. It recommended a reduction in the proportion of 'tied' oil imported by Japanese refineries to 50 per cent or less of their requirements, justifying this figure by reference to the maximum equity interest of 50 per cent that the supplying companies had in these refineries. It also suggested that the state should be responsible for overseas oil exploration and development ventures and for promoting indigenous sources of supply so as to bring their contributions up to 30 per cent of the total oil requirement by 1985. Finally it advocated larger imports of Soviet oil, which would ultimately be achieved through a pipeline from the Siberian fields to the Pacific coast of the U.S.S.R., with the U.S.S.R. supplying the oil in return for the supply of Japanese steel and other equipment for the line (see Map 8).

Since then, the government has moved in these recommended directions, risking eventual conflict with the international companies. Japan now felt strong enough to face such a risk and had also seen how many European countries had gained what they wanted from the same oil companies through a policy of toughness rather than of appeasement. Refining companies have gradually been 'persuaded' to accept more Khafji crude. Negotiations on the import price levels of other crudes became more or less continuous and prices were gradually brought down, at least until the beginning of the period of constrained supply in the early 1970s. Negotiations with the Soviet Union over supplies from Siberia via pipeline to the Pacific coast were re-opened and, having been given even more point by the disruption of Soviet supplies from the Black Sea to Japan caused by the closing of the Suez Canal after the Middle East war of June 1967, have since been successfully concluded with an agreement in principle to go ahead with the project. The effect of this agreement, when it is fully operational in the early 1980s, will be to increase Soviet oil supplies to about 15 per cent of Japan's total imports. In the meantime, the short-term problem of transporting Soviet oil to Japan arising from the closure of the Suez Canal was resolved in a way which clearly illustrates the 'internationality' of the oil industry, for Iraq and B.P. joined Japan and the U.S.S.R. in solving it. Soviet oil to Japan was replaced by B.P. oil from Iraq, and B.P. in turn took an equivalent amount of Soviet crude oil out of the Black Sea ports for use in its markets in Western Europe, whose normal supply from East of Suez had also been disrupted by the Canal closure!

However, of greater importance in revising Japanese oil policy since 1966 has been the series of decisions taken to try to increase the supplies of oil under Japanese control and hence available at a lower foreign exchange cost. In October 1967 a Petroleum Development Public Corporation was formally inaugurated to coordinate and promote development and production by Japanese companies, to give direct financial aid and to guarantee loans from other sources, to lease exploration equipment and to give whatever technical assistance and guidance might be required. The cost of the programme, designed to lift the Japanese-owned share of oil provision to 30 per cent of a steadily increasing total, was evaluated at £1,500 million by 1985 and this, together with a medium-term plan for exploration and development overseas costing over £400 million by 1975, was to be financed under arrangements made by the Ministry of Industry and Trade, which hoped to combine private funds with government loans and other assistance. There is little doubt that the Japanese government really meant business in this direction and the steps announced had by 1970 already produced significant results. Khafji crude has been entirely earmarked for Japan and attempts by the company to sell it elsewhere have not been approved. An interest has been bought in a Canadian company for a joint exploration programme in Canada; a link has been formed with an American company to investigate the Canadian Athabasca tar sands; an Alaskan Oil Resources Development company has been formed and has joined forces with Gulf Oil to exploit acreage in Alaska; the Indonesian Petroleum Development company has been expanded and both government and private funds are financing the development of promising off-shore discoveries in North Sumatra and Kalimantan;

an interest has been bought in an Australian company for w
both in New Guinea and Australia itself; and various exploratoi̟,
negotiations were started in several Latin American companies.

Japan's foreign oil ventures by 1973 under the auspices of the gov-
ernment-financed Japan Petroleum Development Corporation totalled
more than fifty and thus meant very much more than the isolated
production efforts of the post-war period up to 1966, when activities
were still limited to the Persian Gulf Neutral Zone and to an agreement with Pertamina, the Indonesian State oil entity. The Japanese
have, in fact, committed themselves to large exploration expenditures in many parts of the world – though most notably perhaps in
Abu Dhabi in respect of two separate projects. The first involved
successful competitive bids for onshore and offshore acreage in the
very promising oil-bearing zone of Abu Dhabi in the Middle East.
These concessions were won by consortia of Japanese companies
in the face of international competition from established oil producers
of the U.S.A. and Western Europe and involve total minimum exploration expenditures of almost $50 million by 1975 even if no oil
is discovered at all. Given the nature of the concession areas this seems
highly unlikely, however, for they abut on to existing producing
areas of high potential. If the Japanese companies strike oil quickly
and move ahead as quickly as their fellow countrymen did in developing the Khafji fields in the early 1960s then oil from Abu Dhabi produced by the Japanese consortium will make a significant contribution
to the needs of Japan's refineries by the middle of the 1970s. This
expected flow from Abu Dhabi to Japan will be further increased as a
result of the second project there. This project involved the purchase
for a total of almost $600 million of a 50 per cent share in B.P.'s proven
oil-rich concession there. The price paid appears to have been related
to the existence of agreed reserves amounting to 80 milliard barrels of
oil. The development of these will be of importance even in relation
to Japan's astronomical requirements for crude-oil imports, and the
profits from them will enable further exploration and development
work to be self-financing. The next decade, in other words, could
well be marked by as rapid a growth in Japanese financed and controlled oil production as the last one has seen in Japanese oil consumption. The likelihood of this is made stronger when one recalls the

anticipated by the mid-1980s, which could be as
ons per year even after allowing for constraint
for both price and conservation reasons, and
the very strong reaction in Japan against the
companies when they collectively decided to raise their
following their agreements with O.P.E.C. in 1971 and 1972.
The only major development that could seriously affect this evaluation of the rapidly rising demand for imported oil (other than a world
depression) is the successful discovery of natural gas in the Sea of
Japan, which is now being explored by Shell in a joint venture with a
Japanese company – the first time that a non-Japanese company has
been permitted to participate in mining and oil exploration in Japan
itself (see Map 8, p. 125). Other companies are also to join in the
exploration of Japan's continental shelf, but so far there is no indication of potential supplies of gas of the order of those in north-west
Europe.

Fortunately, the growth rate of the Japanese market makes the
possibility of a serious clash with the international majors over the
new oil policy somewhat remote. There will probably be room for
everyone in such a massive operation, and profits for all that are
efficient. But the potentially serious and inevitable conflict of interest
between state and international companies is clearly there, in much
the same way as we have already seen it at work in Western Europe
as well as in the producing countries. The pathway that the companies
have to tread between these conflicting interests is a narrow and
dangerous one, and one false step in Japan – as in many other
countries – could see them effectively squeezed between opposing
nationalisms. And in the case of Japan this would be particularly
disastrous, for here is the world's largest and most secure market for
international oil for as far ahead as it is possible to judge, in spite of
the shock administered to the Japanese economy by the traumatic
events in the international oil world since 1973. These events caused
Japan not only to modify its policy towards Israel (see Chapter 8)
but also to look to a much more direct involvement with the Middle
Eastern oil-producing countries – a development which has still
more serious implications for the future role of the international oil
companies in Japan.

7: Dependence on Oil in the Developing World

This chapter is concerned with the last grouping of countries: those which have interests in common arising from their underdevelopment and low living standards and which participate in the economic system of the non-communist world. Often their participation is only marginal, through the export of some primary commodity or another to the industrialized countries in return for which foreign manufactured goods are imported for use by the minority of the population interested in such things. At the same time many – or even most – of the people of such countries pursue their own subsistence or largely subsistence ways of life and are virtually unaffected by such external trading relationships in the light of their very rudimentary wants. There are a very large number of such countries – over 100 in Africa, Latin America and South East Asia – and their general economic and social problems have been investigated in much post-war literature. Our concern with them is as consumers of oil and here one has to note that almost all of them make use of oil as their most important source of energy – other than that collected or gathered within the framework of a subsistence way of life (see Map 9). Their position in this respect differs from that of the industrialized nations, where, as we have seen in earlier chapters, coal has in most cases been the main source of energy until a significant switch to oil occurred in quite recent years. It also makes their economic positions more precarious than those of any group of countries in the world as a result of the four- to five-fold increase in oil prices in 1973–4.

Since almost all developing countries are aiming at rapid economic development, they face the need to increase their oil supplies very quickly. Many of them give a great deal of attention to their relationships with the world of oil – not only with the international oil companies and the governments of the countries from which they work (the

137

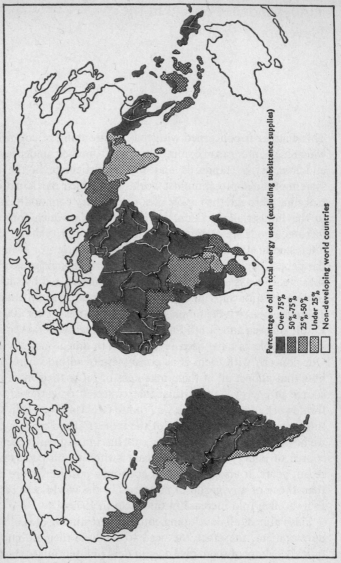

Map 9. Dependence on Oil in the Developing World

Percentage of oil in total energy used (excluding subsistence supplies)

Over 75%
50%-75%
25%-50%
Under 25%
Non-developing world countries

U.S., Britain and the Netherlands) but also with other large countries like Italy, France and Germany which can offer some lessons and help in dealing with oil companies and with the oil-producing nations. Incidentally, the oil-producing nations are also developing countries and, as we have already seen in Chapter 4, they have had problems specially related to their function as producers of a single primary commodity. They have at least, however, unlimited quantities of oil and gas available for their own use; favourable balance of trade positions as a result of their oil exports; and significant government revenues arising from the payment of oil royalties and taxes by the oil-producing companies. And, as we have previously seen, their ability to charge much higher prices for oil since 1973 has finally eliminated any problems that they might earlier have been said to share to some degree with those countries of the Third World which do not export oil. The developing countries we are concerned with in this chapter lack the considerable advantages of the oil producers and, as will be shown later, increasingly consider themselves the means, in part at least, whereby the oil-producing countries secure their wealth! To the governments of many underdeveloped oil-consuming nations, it long appeared that oil prices were so arranged as to transfer income from themselves to the wealthier oil-producing countries; they have been more than confirmed in this view by the 1973–4 attitudes of the oil-producing countries to the adverse effects of the higher oil prices on their economies. They would like to change this situation in the light of the increasing gap in incomes *per capita* that has opened up between the developing oil-producing nations on the one hand and the developing oil-consuming nations on the other – but, given their apparent inability to bring about any change in the present arrangements, the discrepancies seem likely to get worse.

The developing oil-consuming nations thus share some interests in common with the consuming nations of Western Europe and Japan (see Chapters 5 and 6). But these latter nations are powerful both from the point of view of their political status and also from their position as considerable consumers of energy and were thus gradually able until 1971 to secure their increasing demands for oil at prices which moved downwards in response to their political and economic pressures. In contrast, the world's developing countries lack both political and economic power. Politically, many of them are only recently independent and are feeling their way with difficulty in a complex world in which the organization of the oil industry is but one of many problems with which their limited number of experienced diplomats and technical experts have to deal. Economically, they are such small users of oil products that their markets are not necessarily attractive to competing suppliers, particularly when compared with the markets of Europe. Thus, their concern over oil and oil prices has been fraught with difficulties throughout the post-war period and their position with respect to the oil sector can in large part still be interpreted as a neo-colonialist one. This will be explained later in the chapter.

Before going on to that, however, we must examine in a little more detail the position of these countries as energy consumers, noting that underdevelopment and a low use of energy go hand in hand. This correlation has been established in numerous studies over the last thirty years or so, and one finds that the *per capita* use of energy in countries like India, Brazil, Ghana and many others may be calculated in terms of hundreds of pounds of coal (or coal-equivalent) per year, while more developed nations consume thousands of pounds per head. At the two extremes lie the U.S.A., with an annual *per capita* consumption of over 20,000 lb. of coal equivalent, and at the other, Nepal, with only about 20 lb. per head per year. Though one cannot talk of low energy use as causing economic underdevelopment there is nevertheless some element of 'circular causation', with bottlenecks in energy supply making economic advance difficult.

A case study of such difficulties was made by the author in the Cauca Valley of Colombia in South America. There, under the stimulus of favourable conditions for both agricultural and industrial growth in the post-war period, the demand for energy far outstripped the ability of the local, small-scale coal industry and the public electricity authority to provide it. As a result industrialists in particular had to resort to costly expedients to ensure that they could continue to operate. The cement company, for example, had to integrate back into coal mining to ensure its required supply of fuel, using some of its scarce managerial abilities and capital in an activity divorced from its main interests. Other manufacturing plants, unable to rely on the public electricity supply (which became overloaded at peak periods and thus had to cut off supplies to some customers) but requiring a guaranteed availability of electricity, were forced into the expensive expedient of providing their own small diesel-generated units whose fuel costs *alone* were higher than the price which the manufacturers had expected to pay for public electricity. With such bottlenecks – and the kinds of efforts and costs incurred by consumers to overcome them – it is only to be expected that potential development is limited by the unwillingness of new firms to put themselves in the same position or for existing firms to expand as quickly as they might otherwise have done. Thus the pace of economic development is slowed down.

Such energy bottlenecks occur particularly when developing countries make a start along the pathway towards economic development, for this inevitably leads to a period of rapidly rising rate of energy consumption. As societies emerge from a largely immobile, subsistence-type economy into one in which transport, both of goods and people, becomes more significant, in which urbanization becomes of greater importance and in which industries are established to make use of the country's resources, so the demand for energy starts to rise rapidly, because transport – particularly motor transport, which is nearly always the preferred mode these days – is very energy-intensive. Moreover, urbanization involves taking men and their families from a rural peasantry or labour force. Families which previously collected or produced their own very limited energy requirements for simple heating and lighting purposes now crowd together in the slums of the emerging urban centres and have little access to wood, other vegetable matter or animal dung for their energy needs. Instead they come to rely on kerosene or, at a somewhat later stage, when they are officially connected to, or can unofficially tap, the electricity distribution network, on electricity for heating, lighting and cooking. Then, as their mode of living changes from subsistence or semi-subsistence rural to fully urban their demand for energy as a family rises far above the level to which they have been accustomed. Finally, the emergence of industries creates, of course, a completely new demand for fuel and

141

power. This is particularly apparent in industries as energy-intensive as iron and steel and cement, which are just the kinds of industries that many of these countries establish as soon as possible, either to take advantage of the availability of local resources or to reduce the cost of their imports of these products – or both.

For all these reasons one finds in the post-war period – when numerous nations have embarked on such policies of development – that the most rapid rates of increase of energy consumption are in Latin America, South East Asia and, more recently, Africa. In both Malaysia and Brazil, for example, the average annual rate of growth of energy consumption over the last twenty years has been of the order of 12 per cent. These rates are not untypical of those countries of Latin America and South East Asia where economic development plans, centred around industrialization, have been followed now for the whole of the post-war period (or since independence if later than 1945). In the case of most African nations, industrialization and development planning is a more recent phenomenon and the high energy growth rates date back only to the mid- to late-1950s. These rates reflect not only the growth of the economies concerned in terms of total output of goods and services, but also the increasingly energy-intensive character of their development, with a consequent co-efficient of energy use approaching 2·0 (that is, each percentage point rise in economic activities brings about a 2 per cent rise in energy use). This coefficient may be compared with figures of only 0·7 and 0·85 for the U.S.A. and Western Europe respectively during the same period, where the much lower coefficients reflect the lesser significance of additional inputs of energy in the development processes of more developed nations. These relationships are shown in Figure 2. One should, however, be aware that the high percentage rates of growth in energy consumption for developing nations also reflect the low level of energy used at the beginning of the period – in the economies before they started to develop. Even after fifteen to twenty years of

---

The diagram opposite demonstrates how rates of increase in energy use remain higher than the growth rates in the industrialized world and as developing countries depend mainly on oil for their energy this means that their importance as participants in the international oil industry will steadily increase.

Figure 2. The Relationship between Energy Use and Economic Development Over Time

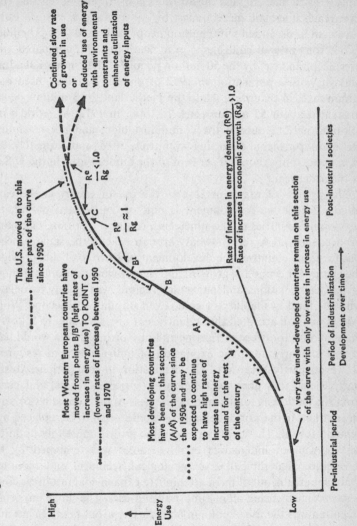

High

Energy Use

Low

The U.S. moved on to this flatter part of the curve since 1950

Continued slow rate of growth in use
or
Reduced use of energy with environmental constraints and enhanced utilization of energy inputs

Most Western European countries have moved from points B/B' (high rates of increase in energy use) TO POINT C (lower rates of increase) between 1950 and 1970

$\frac{R^e}{R_g} < 1.0$

$\frac{R^e}{R_g} \approx 1$

C

B¹

B

A¹

A

Most developing countries have been on this sector (A/A¹) of the curve since the 1950s and may be expected to continue to have high rates of increase in energy demand for the rest of the century

A very few under-developed countries remain on this section of the curve with only low rates in increase in energy use

Rate of increase in energy demand (R^e) > 1.0
Rate of increase in economic growth (R_g)

Pre-industrial period

Period of industrialization
Development over time →

Post-industrial societies

rapid growth in energy use the absolute consumption levels that they have reached are still quite modest by American and Western European standards. Brazil's 100 million people still used only 50 million metric tons of coal equivalent (m.m.t.c.e.) in 1972, compared with over 325 m.m.t.c.e. by the 50 million people of the United Kingdom. Malaya, with a population in 1972 of under 11 million, used only 6 m.m.t.c.e. in that year, while the Netherlands' 13 million people consumed about 55 million tons. In total, in 1972 the world's developing nations outside the communist bloc, and also excluding the main petroleum-exporting countries, used approximately 900 m.m.t.c.e. – only about 40 per cent of the amount used in the U.S.A. in the same year.

The process of rapid increase in the use of energy at the early stage of economic development is not, of course, a new one; the developing countries of the nineteenth century – Britain, Germany, France, the U.S.A., etc. – went through exactly the same process. But for these countries the development of their coalfields provided the energy for economic growth, and the growing economic strength of particular nations and particular regions was closely associated with the local availability of coal. Even up until the Second World War it was still accepted that countries or areas wishing to follow in the economic footsteps of Europe and of North America would have to rely similarly upon the expansion of indigenous coal resources. However, partly because of the dislocation in coal supplies during wartime and the subsequent significant price increases, and partly from the increasing ability and willingness of oil companies to serve any markets in the world, demand for coal started to be replaced by a demand for oil. The idea that economic growth must rely upon the development of indigenous coal resources was tempered by the recognition that difficulties of geological, technical and economic character arising out of most attempts to expand coal resources could be overcome by using oil in almost all end-uses. The single important exception was the use of coke in blast furnaces, but research has now shown that part of the coke charge can be replaced by other fuels, while steel-making processes have been evolved which eliminate the traditional blast furnace entirely. It is not perhaps surprising that most of the progress made along these lines has been in Mexico – one of the fastest-growing of the developing countries but one with very poor coal resources.

This increasingly widespread use of oil in the post-war developing world was assisted both by the inherent physical characteristics of oil and by the organization of the industry. Oil is easy and generally safe to handle even with only limited technical resources and expertise, and could be relatively cheaply shipped around the world in small, as well as in large, quantities and thus could be made available wherever energy was required. In this respect it had, and in fact still has, significant advantages over coal, particularly as far as the ease of handling any quantity is concerned. At the same time, the relatively unsophisticated and divisible nature of oil transport and use ensures that it has a continued advantage over more recent competitors – notably natural gas, whose distribution and use requires an infrastructure economically acceptable only in large-scale use, and atomic power, whose technological requirements are beyond the capabilities of most developing countries.

In addition, because the oil industry is organized internationally, all the facilities were available to supply oil to developing countries. The ready availability of capital within the framework of the international groups, no matter where the opportunity for investment arose, meant that local financing difficulties did not have to stand in the way of the provision of facilities, and the groups, moreover, were orientated not only to acquire universal knowledge of investment opportunities but also act on them. In the case study to which reference has been made – that of the Cauca Valley of Colombia – the vacuum left in the supply of energy by the failure of the local coal industry to expand was quickly filled by the provision of oil by some of the international companies – Mobil, Shell and Esso – or their local subsidiaries, in spite of the complicated supply arrangements which this necessitated. Oil products, in relatively small quantities, had to be lifted out of Colombian refineries on the Caribbean coast (with their crude supply originating in the Middle Magdalena Valley little more than 200 miles – as the crow flies – from the Upper Cauca Valley), shipped by coastal tanker via the Panama Canal to the Pacific port of Buenaventura, and then by rail – and later pipeline – over the Pacific Cordillera Range to depots in the Cauca Valley, from where the products could be locally distributed by truck to industrial and other consumers. Thus, in the Cauca Valley of Colombia, as in every other part of the world where they are permitted to operate, the international oil companies, with personnel used to and willing to work anywhere to further their company's business (and, of course, their own careers), have sought and created opportunities for selling oil by establishing the terminals, depots, etc. needed for their operations. It would be very difficult anywhere in the developing world to find a case where (politics permitting) the international oil companies have failed to respond to an energy 'gap' or failed to produce a profit out of their activities.

Thus, the developing world has gradually become heavily dependent on supplies of oil for its economic advance. In Latin America as a whole, for example, between 1939 and 1972, the total demand for energy increased by approximately four and a half times, from less than 70 million tons of coal equivalent to over 320 million tons. Over this period the consumption of coal rose only from just under 10 to a little over 13 million tons, with its share thus falling from some 15 per cent of the total to under 4 per cent. The bulk of the increase in the overall demand for energy was provided by the expansion of oil consumption. The continent as a whole is now dependent on oil for some 70 per cent of the total energy required (and on natural gas for another 20 per cent). In Africa coal provided about 75 per cent of energy needs in 1955; it is now down to less than 60 per cent and continues to fall steadily. Meanwhile, oil consumption more than tripled between 1956 and 1972 and, moreover, still continues to rise at over 10 per cent per annum. Out of more than 130 countries and territories in the developing world only five – Taiwan, India, South Korea, Zambia and Mozambique – now consume more coal than oil.

As has already been hinted, there are many political and economic problems, often difficult to disentangle, connected with the developing world's need for oil. Politically, there is the conflict between the intense nationalism of the developing nations and the foreign control exercised over the oil sector in their economies. In the main it is the oil companies that have been responsible for the establishment of the complex international infrastructure that gets the oil from the points where it is produced, through the refining processes, and then, in the right quantities – generally small – and appropriate qualities to the markets in the developing countries. There is no doubt that they operate efficiently and reliably, and in many developing countries the local affiliates of the major international oil companies present an enclave of efficiency in a generally less than efficient public and private administration. Their employees are usually smartly turned out; their service stations never seem to run out of the required product; their transport is clean and well maintained; they often produce the only readily available maps of the country; and they sometimes finance or sponsor facilities ranging from technical training centres to young peoples' soccer and baseball competitions. This essentially Western image which they present is, however, sometimes a contributory cause of their difficulties, for to be so wealthy and to be able to afford to be so efficient and such good citizens must mean, according to some of the more vocal parts of many local populations, that they are 'exploiting' the local economy and that the poverty of the many is a function of the wealth of the oil companies.

Oil companies operating in such circumstances become the 'whipping boys' for the 'colonial' powers, which may no longer direct political control but which certainly exercise significant influence through their control over the purse strings. These charges cannot be completely disproved, though they are probably increasingly exaggerated as time goes by. But certainly in the recent past to a large degree, and today to a smaller degree, the oil companies have something of a stranglehold over many of the countries in which they have operated. The companies' pricing policies have been indefensible – though one should note that other nations have also suffered at the hands of the companies' 'posted price and assessed freight rate' pricing system. We saw the impact of this in Western Europe in the immediate postwar period and noted how its disadvantageous effects were overcome not just by the increasing political strength of European governments as they recovered from the war, but also by the intervention of the U.S. government, which found itself paying what it thought to be too high prices for oil to be delivered to Western Europe under the terms of the Marshall Plan.

The system, however, lasted longer and worked even more effectively in the interests of the companies in the case of the developing nations. For example, until the middle 1960s any pretence at competition was eliminated in a joint scheme devised by the major companies for supplying the small markets of West Africa. In this scheme each of the companies involved took its turn at providing a cargo of oil products, with its ship moving from port to port along the coast, discharging into the tanks of all the companies involved their oil products' requirements. Each company charged – and in turn was charged by others – for the oil it supplied on the basis of the posted price of the products involved at the Caribbean port of loading, plus the ocean freight rate published for the voyage undertaken – irrespective of what the costs of oil purchase or transportation had been, and irrespective of the price at which the oil could have been obtained from and delivered by a third party. This West African Supply Agreement persisted until some of the West African countries started to refine their own oil, and up until then constituted very profitable business for the companies involved and led to high prices for oil products in the countries concerned.

For India there were similar penalties to be paid by the nation and its consumers for the import of both crude oil and products through the international companies. Until the war Indian oil imports were priced as though the oil had been brought out of the United States and shipped from the Gulf of Mexico. In fact, the oil mainly came from the much lower-cost fields of the Persian Gulf, only one-tenth the distance from India, or, at worst, from the Dutch East Indies, less than one-fifth the distance of the Gulf of Mexico. During the war freight rates were adjusted under pressure from the British and U.S. military authorities to take into account the Persian Gulf origin of the oil, and after the war the free-on-board prices of imports were adjusted to the new Middle East posted prices, which soon diverged from Gulf of Mexico ones. No later adjustments were made, however, to reflect the steadily falling costs of shipping oil as tankers increased in size and scale economies were achieved. Neither was adjustment made by the international companies serving the Indian market as Middle Eastern oil began to be traded at prices well below those officially posted in the Gulf.

The Indian government was increasingly unhappy about the position during the late 1950s but it was powerless to take any effective action – other than by persuasion – until it had an alternative source available. Persuasion produced no results, but in 1960 the Indian government was offered oil from the Soviet Union at prices which were over 20 per cent less than the delivered price of similar Middle Eastern oils. Armed with this offer, and having formed a national oil company able to handle imports independently of the international oil companies if necessary, the government told the companies concerned to reduce their price. After arguments, threats and counter-threats the companies eventually did so – though not by the full 22 per cent demanded. Since then on several occasions up to 1971 they had to adjust prices still further to allow for changing conditions – and particularly to take note of the prices at which the Soviet Union was prepared to offer suitable crude oil and oil products. It is thus only quite recently, and only in the case of important and relatively powerful developing nations like India, that the nations themselves have had any effective voice in the pricing of commodities which enter into all sectors of their economic life. The developing nations' lack of participation in making decisions affecting their own welfare – and the reservation of those decisions to outside parties – justifies the description of their relationship with the international oil companies as a neo-colonial one. Such relationships have, however, increasingly produced similar reactions to the one just described in the case of India.

The developing nations' main economic problem over oil has arisen from the impact that rapidly increasing imports of the commodity have on their balance of payments positions. Most of these countries – almost by definition – depend upon the exports of one or more primary commodities, and have had export earnings which have either stagnated or, at best, fluctuated to give good and bad years as a result of the rapidly changing supply/demand position for the products concerned. Thus, they have available in most cases only a limited and often a variable amount of foreign exchange with which to make their energy purchases overseas. But as we have already seen, their demands for energy have not stagnated or fluctuated in the same way, but have rather tended to slope strongly upwards. Therefore, in almost all developing countries the foreign exchange costs of oil have risen more or less continuously until in some cases, for example,

Brazil and Argentina, oil came to account for some 25 per cent of the total availability of foreign exchange. It thus became an important factor making for rigidity in the import structure and, through this, created tendencies towards chronic and permanent balance of payments problems and, often, associated inflationary tendencies in the economies concerned. In the light of this the developing countries one by one had to take steps to try to minimize the cost of oil imports.

One way to reduce the scale of the problem was to initiate a change similar to that which we examined for immediate post-war Europe – that is, the substitution of imported oil products by imported cruder oil supplies, the refining being carried out as a domestic industry. This had the effect of reducing the foreign exchange component in the importation of any given quantity of oil, as crude oil could be bought abroad more cheaply than oil products. But the exact similarities with the European situation end there, for the developing nations did not, in general, create the same enthusiasm for the local construction of refining capacity by the international companies as did Europe, where the wishes of the nations usually coincided with the best commercial interests of the companies concerned. Refining had a minimum scale-of-operations requirement given by a through-put of the order of 2 million tons per annum; and few companies had markets of this size in any of the developing countries in the mid-1950s, when the pressure for such developments really began to mount. There were, of course, exceptions to this generalization – one or two of the largest countries, Brazil and India for example, had large enough markets to justify this size of refinery. Even in these cases, however, the market was often spread over vast distances: shared, for example, in India between the main coastal conurbations of Bombay, Madras and Calcutta so that a refinery in one location could not necessarily serve all of the demand areas at an overall cost lower than the alternative of importing products from a large refinery in a producing country.

This problem was sometimes solvable by all the companies concerned agreeing to share refining facilities in different localities. They could arrange exchange deals with each other, and refineries of the minimum necessary size could then be constructed. In this way the refineries in such countries were sometimes financed by the international companies involved in the markets. In other cases, however, other finance had to be sought, either because the companies would not do the job or because the nation concerned did not want them to. The state might perhaps persuade a third party to come in, or agree to it coming in – a party such as E.N.I., the Italian state oil concern, or an oil organization from one of the communist countries with refinery expertise (the U.S.S.R., Czechoslovakia or Rumania). Or the government of the country could attempt to borrow the money itself and construct its own refining facilities.

It might be thought that international borrowing to this end would have been enthusiastically supported by the important lending agencies established in the post-war period to help the developing countries with their capital problems during industrialization. Such agencies have, after all, made a particular point of arranging loans for the construction of hydro-electric plants, roads and other energy and transport facilities which go to make up the economic infrastructure essential for the successful implementation of development plans. Since oil has become such a dominant source of energy for most of these countries, it would appear to be almost self-evident that the financing of refineries would be viewed equally favourably by the international agencies. In fact, until the late 1960s – that is, until after fifteen years of aid and development programmes – no capital for refinery construction was made available for such purposes either from the international organizations such as the World Bank or within the framework of bilateral aid from Western nations such as the credit extended through the U.S. Aid programme. The reasoning behind this attitude was that as private funds were available for building oil refineries, there was no problem of a capital bottleneck in this sector. It was far better, so the argument ran, to make use of the limited amounts of public funds available on projects that could not otherwise be financed at all. Such an argument is valid, of course, providing one accepts that the countries concerned are in a position to negotiate satisfactory financing arrangements with the private companies – and that the countries accept unequivocally the philosophy of the private financing and ownership of an essential part of their economic infrastructure – a 'commanding height' of their economies, in fact. Now the governments of many developing countries did not accept such a philosophy and, in line with an important branch of political thought in Western Europe, where many of the leaders of the developing nations have had their education and have also been politically orientated, they considered that oil refining ought to be directly under their own control. And they suspected that the decisions of the World Bank and other institutions not to give loans for developments of this sort were the results of pressure from the international oil companies anxious to maintain their positions in developing countries. They thus saw the denial to them of official loan-funds for refinery construction as one of the strategies employed by the oil companies in their role as neo-colonialists.

However, for countries as large as India, Brazil, Egypt, Argentina and Pakistan the absence of international loans only slightly delayed the build-up of their refining industries, as they employed various devices for securing the capital and expertise required. Sometimes they played off some international company against another, or offered marketing advantages to the company that agreed to build a refinery. Or they invited refinery bids from other parties. Or they built up the oil-refining industry in the public sector of their economy and secured loans to cover the foreign cost component from whatever sources were available. One by one they have all managed to become more or less self-sufficient in refined products, except for difficulties arising out of their particular patterns of product demand which sometimes necessitate additional imports of certain products and sometimes the international disposal of locally surplus products because it is not economical to have their refineries adjust to such situations. For example, India has to import extra kerosene, which is used extensively for cooking, and to export gasoline, which emerges as a surplus product from its refineries owing to the relatively small number of cars in the country. Incidentally, the existence of such refinery shortages and surpluses within the framework of a single national market is a factor which strengthens the hand of the international oil companies' proposals when refinery developments in a developing country are under consideration. Such companies can – and do – offer, as part of their proposals, to cope with 'shortages and surpluses' within the framework of their international operations. They thus eliminate the practical problems and high costs which can be involved in an international search for limited quantities of a particular product and/or in trying to sell a product of unknown quality on a world market which may already be overloaded with it, but which if it is not sold will not only make the refinery unprofitable but also cause it to work at less than full capacity so as to avoid the over-production of the unwanted product.

Although, by one means or another, the large developing countries achieved fairly easily their objective of building up a domestic refining industry sufficient to meet national needs, the same cannot be said of the much larger number of smaller countries anxious to achieve the same objective, both for balance of payments and industrialization motives. Their difficulties have been both political and economic. Politically they have been less well able to build up a state-owned oil industry which can develop refining as one of its activities; and even when they have been willing and able to do this, or to take other state action to achieve the same objective, they have been in a less strong position than their larger neighbours. Such smaller countries would not be so likely to receive refinery offers from the communist countries, and if they did get them, and then take action on them, they could find themselves at the receiving end of counter-action by the U.S.A. This happened, for example, in 1964–5 in the case of Ceylon, which formed a state oil-importing and distribution agency, accepted Soviet help and oil supplies to get this working, and was then cut off from all U.S. assistance – as the U.S.A. intervened to retaliate in favour of its oil companies, which considered themselves unjustly treated by the Ceylon government.

From the economic side, most of these countries have a total demand for oil products of less than 2 million tons per year, and until recently this was considered the smallest demand which would justify the construction of a refinery. For the companies it remained more profitable to continue supplying such markets out of the large 'export' refineries in the Caribbean, Western Europe and the Middle East, which were built with such markets in view, than to invest capital and managerial expertise in the construction and operation of a series of small refining units. In the case of one Central American country, for example, it was estimated that the net extra cost involved in manu-facturing the products locally in the intended half a million tons per year refinery amounted to 60 cents per barrel more – an increase of approximately 25 per cent – than that of supplying the market from the 15 million tons a year refinery which was processing Venezuelan crude oil near the point of production.

Knowing that they would have difficulties in ever persuading a government to permit product prices to rise by this amount, so as to cover the additional costs involved, and thus appreciating that such local refining would seriously squeeze their profits, the international companies showed little enthusiasm for such developments and used every possible device to stop the development going ahead. But all to little avail. As a result of pressure from the governments concerned, and, much more important, pressure from companies prepared to do such deals as a means of getting access to markets in which they hitherto had no interests, refineries have been built and by now few countries remain without a refinery.

In Central America for example, the first refinery was opened in 1963 on the Caribbean coast of Guatemala. Since then one refinery has been built in each of the other Central American countries and Guatemala now has a second one on its Pacific shore. The total oil-product demand in the five countries is still under 4 million tons per annum – little more than the throughput of what was hitherto considered a minimum-sized economic refinery; yet the seven refineries, with an average capacity of only a million tons per year, offer a total of over $7\frac{1}{2}$ million tons per year. Thus, not only are they high-cost plants by virtue of their small size but their unit costs of production also suffer from the partially unused facilities. As it has been calculated that there is a 1 per cent rise in the unit costs of production for every 1 per cent of under-used capacity, the economic significance of the existence of surplus facilities should not be underestimated. Thus, for the companies this new pattern of providing Central America with its oil requirements appears anything but a lowest-cost method. For the Central American countries, while the refineries led to some foreign exchange savings and created a relatively small number of new jobs in the industry, they also put upward pressure on prices. Though there was, without doubt, some fat to be squeezed out of the profits that the companies were previously making in selling oil products to these countries, much of this disappeared with the development of the refineries and the consequent upward movement of prices was, of course, to the ultimate disadvantage of local consumers. This was particularly dangerous for the largest oil consumers (generally concerned with the basic export sectors such as banana production), who could previously buy their oil requirements cheaply in an open international market (by tender) but who then became obliged at government insistence to buy from the local refinery, and at prices higher than those to which they were accustomed. A continuation of this kind of requirement could well make their operations uncompetitive on the world markets and thus lead to a decline in their activities, to the obvious detriment of the countries' economies.

In such cases it is getting difficult to argue that the establishment of refineries is necessarily justified. Perhaps the countries concerned could have saved just as much foreign exchange, and have enabled prices to consumers to be reduced as well, by insisting that the companies concerned reduced the import prices of their products from the levels of 'posted prices' to the price levels of an open market. The example of Western Europe and of the largest developing countries in encouraging, and even insisting on, domestic refineries is not necessarily one which should have been followed by the smaller developing countries, such as those in Central America, until such a time as their demand for petroleum products justified a large enough refinery. In the meantime, the disadvantages may well have outweighed the advantages.

For many developing nations, however, not even the political and economic benefits flowing (or considered to flow) from the establishment of a domestic refining industry are sufficient to meet their aspirations. They see the prospects of additional foreign exchange savings and other economic benefits, plus more effective political independence, emerging out of the development of indigenous crude oil resources whereby oil imports can be substituted entirely.

The less risky – but often less politically satisfying – way of doing this has been to persuade one or more of the international or other foreign companies to conduct a survey and, if favourable, to undertake exploration and development work. Evidence for the companies' recognition of the powerful potential of such nationalistic feeling can be seen in their willingness to do this on so many occasions

155

over the last decade – particularly when one notes that this coincides with a period in which most companies have had control of or access to more than enough crude oil from the main producing areas to make further exploitation not only unnecessary but also an apparent misuse of their capital resources. One explanation for this apparently irrational behaviour could be their altruism, but this is unlikely, given the hard battle that the companies have on occasion had to maintain their overall levels of profit at an acceptable level. There are two other explanations. One is that individual companies agree to do such work in order to keep other companies and institutions out and thus to minimize the danger that oil will be discovered by others that might consequently set themselves up as rivals in the market. Until quite recently in most countries, the right to prospect and explore for oil could be bought very cheaply and some companies have from time to time undoubtedly secured acreage only to eliminate the possibility of its exploration by other potentially interested parties. For example, some of the international companies with oil concession rights in India and in Pakistan were alleged to be undertaking their searches with less than sufficient enthusiasm and urgency, because they preferred to continue to supply these countries out of their vast, low-cost reserves in the Middle East. Such charges cannot be proved, but from the companies' point of view what they were alleged to have done made sense, even though they denied the allegations. In any case more and more countries are now demanding guarantees of minimum exploration and development programmes from any concessions that are given, and so the opportunities for sitting on possible sources of oil merely to keep out competition or to ensure the continuation of a market for an existing investment in oil-producing capacity in another country are diminishing quickly.

The second explanation for the willingness of companies to undertake searches in new areas arises from the clear indication given to them by the governments concerned that any oil discovered at home will be given absolute priority over imported oil. In these circumstances, foreign companies with investments in marketing and perhaps refining facilities in such a country will have a very positive incentive to find domestic oil – before anyone else does so. Without its own local supplies the company would be obliged to refine and market someone else's domestically produced crude oil. And to make the situation even worse this would probably be within the framework of a system of price controls which all but eliminates the profits from refining and marketing operations, but which still leaves profits to be made out of production.

An excellent example of this occurred in the late 1950s in Argentina, when foreign companies were invited to explore for and/or develop oil resources with the firm promise that any oil found would be guaranteed a market; that it would be paid for at a price at least as high as the delivered price of crude oil from overseas; and that it would immediately replace imported supplies as far as possible. In such a situation Shell and Esso could not afford *not* to participate in the search. They had built up important interests in marketing and refining oil in Argentina, as a result of which their parent international companies were making considerable profits out of selling them crude oil from Venezuela and the Middle East at delivered prices equivalent to posted prices in the Caribbean or the Persian Gulf plus the full freight rates allowed by the quoted assessments (and which were generally much above actual costs). If they found oil from their searches in Argentina then, given the Argentine government's willingness to pay import parity prices for the oil, there seemed every possibility that they would make just as good profits out of this arrangement as out of the pre-existing one. If, on the other hand, they chose not to search but to argue their preference for continuing to bring in supplies from overseas (an argument unlikely to be acceptable to the Argentine government) and another company found oil, then they would be obliged to take it in their refineries instead of oil from their overseas affiliates, and all their profits on crude oil supplies would be lost. Such policies of economic nationalism in many of the world's developing countries have played the most important role in persuading the international oil companies to extend and diversify their areas of search. Today, there are few countries of the world (outside the communist countries) which have not managed to get some kind of an oil survey and development programme going, even where the geological and other physical prospects may not appear too good.

But not all developing countries have been prepared to accept the economic and/or political wisdom of having foreign companies come and look for oil in order to achieve this result. Such countries have chosen instead to establish a domestic oil industry with exploration and production responsibilities. In many ways this represents an extension of the 'commanding height' philosophy – the need for the national ownership of industries which are of fundamental importance to all or most sectors of the economy. In Latin America, most of which has been politically independent for more than a century, such views have been commonplace for many years, and state participation in Argentina, Chile and Bolivia dates back as far as the 1920s. In 1938 Mexico's reaction against the oil companies went much further by the expropriation of all the assets of the petroleum companies operating there and by the establishment of PEMEX – Petróleos Mexicanos – with a complete monopoly over all oil-industry activities from exploration to marketing. The more recent continuation of this attitude is seen in Peru's nationalization late in 1968 of the producing and other operations of the International Petroleum Company – a subsidiary of Esso – and Bolivia's expropriation of Gulf Oil's producing and export operations in 1969.

These well-formulated attitudes emerge from the fact that the companies involved have been concerned with Latin American oil from the earliest days of the industry – and over this long period have locally achieved a widespread reputation of being 'agents of economic imperialism'. This reputation has made the companies susceptible to attack from a wide spectrum of political groups within the Latin American countries, for they thus became involved in the major political issue of nationalism and its associated anti-Americanism of more recent years. In such a situation one can see that there will have been a great propensity on the part of Latin American nations to keep the development of their oil resources in their own hands.

In Chile the state monopoly of oil exploration and production, established first in 1927, has been absolutely maintained ever since, and ENAP – the state company – has gradually expanded its producing operations in the extreme south of the country (in Tierra del Fuego) with the aim of making Chile self-sufficient in oil. The best it has achieved so far is a little less than two-thirds of the country's total requirement and it is now having difficulty in maintaining this share in view of a steadily expanding demand for oil by the industrializing economy and the relative poverty of Chile's oil resources. So far exploration in the northern parts of the country has been unsuccessful and the southern fields appear to be capable of only modest expansion. In Brazil, too, oil exploration and production is a state monopoly, and has been since the formation of Petróbras in 1950. As a result of extensive and expensive searches Petróbras has discovered oilfields in Bahia, which have been producing oil in gradually increasing quantity since 1954, and there are some possibilities of additional output elsewhere from parts of the Amazon basin and from off-shore searches. But Brazil's oil potential, like Chile's, appears to be limited and, so far, Petróbras's level of production has not risen above one-third of the country's requirement.

ENAP and Petróbras argue that without their efforts their countries would have been producing no oil at all, because the international companies would not have found the local efforts worthwhile and would have opted instead to supply Chile and Brazil out of their major supply sources in Venezuela and/or the Middle East. The companies argue a different case, saying that had they been given opportunities to search for oil they would have done so and, moreover, with their greater expertise and resources would have been likely to do rather better than the state entities, whose small oil production has been achieved only at the cost of capital investment which could have found more worthwhile and less risky outlets in other sectors of the capital-short economies of the countries concerned.

To back up their arguments they cite the case of nearby Argentina, whose state oil company's monopoly over production was ended in 1958. This was because of the growing burden of oil-import costs, the state company's long-term inability to raise oil production to more than a third of the country's total needs, and the unlikelihood that it would be able to do much better than this, in spite of the known existence of potentially quite attractive oil areas, owing to the inability of the Argentine exchequer to provide it with the capital required to do the job. Foreign companies were thus invited to participate in the search for oil. With their capital availability and their managerial and technical expertise they were able, within three years of accepting the invitation, to increase production threefold and thus make the country self-sufficient. But technical success appears to have

159

been bought at the cost of a considerable loss of foreign exchange, as the successful companies concerned with the oil exploration and production programme repatriated their profits out of the country. This repatriation, moreover, was at such a high level, a later government claimed, that it more than offset the foreign exchange savings which were achieved by the replacement of foreign crude by domestic supplies. These views were challenged, but so far the validity of the claims and counter-claims on the economic front has never been proved. But what is beyond doubt is the fact that this relinquishing of the state oil monopoly by President Frondizi in 1958 emerged as the major cause of his overthrow a couple of years later. The government which replaced him soon reintroduced the state monopoly, through Y.P.F. (which incidentally soon allowed production to fall below consumption), but even more recently the situation has again been reversed, as a military government in the country decided that the foreign companies were necessary to produce the oil the country required.

Looking at Chile, Brazil and Argentina it seems that the argument in Latin America between those favouring state development, on the one hand, and those favouring foreign oil company development, on the other, has been 'won on points' by the latter. But this conclusion ignores the success of Mexico in producing a state oil entity – PEMEX – which has achieved the basic objective of providing the country with the amount of oil it has needed in the process of development through industrialization. Though one may argue over the wisdom of certain aspects of PEMEX's activities, and though one recognizes that it had a flying start as a result of the availability of oilfields as going concerns at the time of the expropriation, it is still true that PEMEX demonstrates that foreign companies are not essential to ensure that domestically produced oil becomes available to a developing nation anxious to eliminate an import bill for foreign oil of growing dimensions. Thus, in spite of the warnings against spending scarce domestic capital on oil exploration and development – given by the U.S.A. and international lending agencies such as the World Bank, as well as by the international companies – more and more developing countries set up national entities run by the state to pursue the search for oil within their national territories. So far, however, except in the Latin American countries mentioned above, such entities have made very little contribution to their nations' oil supplies.

The reasons for this are not difficult to find. Oil is an elusive commodity and the major requirement for finding it is capital – and moreover capital for investment in an enterprise which may not produce any returns. And very few of the developing countries have sufficiently large amounts of capital to spare for such risky ventures on a large enough scale. Thus, an alternative strategy has been evolved by a few developing countries in order to overcome not only the foreign exchange problems arising from the need to continue to import oil, but also their political dislike for their oil suppliers. They argue that the international companies really act as little more than middle-men in getting oil from producing to consuming areas and, in doing so, 'exploit' both producers and consumers. Why then should producers and consumers not get together in a joint venture to their mutual advantage? This argument has led India to seek to obtain supplies directly from producing nations in the Middle East and in 1967 the first agreement along these lines was signed with Iran. One field has already been brought into production but in spite of the eagerness of India to secure these supplies, negotiated at a lower foreign exchange cost than that involved under the pre-existing arrangements for importing oil, little oil, in fact, moved to India as it proved to be unsuitable for the existing refineries. On the other side of the world in Latin America some attention was given to the integration of Venezuela's ability to produce crude oil and the rest of South America's need for it. Again government-to-government discussions – this time within the framework of the negotiations on economic integration in Latin America – were based on the idea that oil should flow from one developing country to another without the intervention of the international oil companies which have hitherto run such arrangements.

The emergence of political awareness and realism in the countries of the developing world and the creation of instruments of economic policy whereby they can help each other could, in the longer term, help to eliminate the role of the international oil companies in serving them. This will take time; in the meantime, the oil-consuming developing world is going to have to rely on American and European companies to a high degree – with the inevitable accompaniment of suspicion and hard feelings between them as a fact of international life, particularly in the period since 1971 when the companies passed on to the poor importing countries the higher oil prices which followed the agreements between the oil-producing countries and the oil companies. The fact that the companies made these agreements collectively and then raised prices by more than the additional tax burden justified was seen as evidence that their exploitation of the poor oil-consuming countries was increasing. As a result Brazil, for example, immediately announced its intention to make direct government-to-government arrangements for its oil supplies, as well as its intention to redouble its efforts to produce more oil at home: a reaction which seemed likely to become very common in the early 1970s amongst the countries in the developing world which depend upon imported oil for their economic advance.

Their faith in the wisdom of such government-to-government deals has, however, quickly been rudely shattered by the traumatic events in the oil world which followed the establishment of oil-producing countries' control over the supply and price of oil. The poor oil-importing countries quickly found that the 'lucky few' major oil-producing countries in the Third World appeared to have even less concern for their economies and their prospects for economic development than did the 'wicked' oil companies and their owning nations (the United States, Britain and the Netherlands). The latter may have helped to secure a continuation of the oil companies' abilities to refine, distribute and market oil profitably in the developing oil-importing nations; the profits sought and earned were, however, modest (of the order of $1 to $2 per barrel at most) as compared with the extortionate profits which the oil-exporting countries started to earn out of sales not only to the Western world, but also to the developing world in 1973. A profit for the oil-producing countries of $7 per barrel or more (on a commodity costing 10–30 cents to produce) became the expected norm, in spite of the fact that the landed price for each barrel of oil multiplied by the number of barrels needed by the developing countries gave a total foreign exchange cost for the commodity which, as shown in Figure 3, many of them can pay

Figure 3. Developing World Oil-Importing Countries: Impact of Increased Crude-Oil Costs, 1974

Country	Foreign Trade 1973		Balance of Trade	Additional Cost of Oil in 1974 (Estimated)*	Foreign Exchange Reserves (end 1973)
	Exports	Imports			
Ethiopia	285	180	+105	45	114
India	2934	2771	+163	1050	629
Pakistan	983	928	+ 55	220	254
Philippines	1494	1243	+251	550	606
Sierra Leone	145	125	+ 20	22	36
Sudan	401	376	+ 25	105	28
Tanzania	399	363	+ 36	45	na
Thailand	1382	1662	−280	525	1107

*On the basis of likely prices for crude oil in 1974 and assuming there will be no relief from these prices for the developing countries. Note also that most developing countries' balance of trade positions are likely to deteriorate from their generally favourable position in 1973 as the changes in the international oil system cause the demand for other primary products to fall away as a result of recession in industrialized economies.

neither from their annual export earnings, nor from their foreign exchange reserves.

Thus, to buy the oil the developing countries thought they needed will bankrupt their economies (in the absence of compensatory flows of financial resources), whilst not to buy it implies a near cessation of economic growth – given the degree to which they are dependent on oil for their energy needs. Initial pleas by the poor oil-importing countries for help from the oil-exporting countries were, at the beginning of 1974, ignored or rejected – except in special cases (such as Iranian help for Pakistan), and by means of low-cost loans from oil-exporting to oil-importing countries to make cash available for buying the oil imports. Though this offers help in the very short term, it does nothing to assist the longer-term problem of the poor oil-importing countries and it seems inconceivable that some adjustment of the grossly unbalanced position will not emerge over the later months of 1974: perhaps through the creation of a differential pricing system whereby the oil producers charge higher prices to the industrialized world. This would certainly help to sustain the otherwise quickly disappearing support amongst Third World countries for the O.P.E.C. countries, and especially for the Arab members of that

163

organization; it would thus be a politically astute move for the oil producers to make as a means of enhancing their position in the world of oil power. However, even poor oil-importing countries are unlikely to get their oil at anything like the low price they did in the 1960s. They may therefore come to think that, in respect of oil at least, they have more in common with the rich importing countries than with countries they hitherto accepted without question as also being exploited by the international oil companies and their owning nations. And as in the United States, Western Europe and Japan, those countries in the developing world which do not export oil will be giving much more attention and devoting more resources over the next decade to the development of their indigenous sources of energy – such as coal in India, oil shale in Thailand, hydro-electricity in Brazil – and to the establishment of autarkic energy policies.

8: Oil in International Relations and World Economic Development

The preceding chapters of this book have attempted to describe and evaluate the role and significance of oil in several different nations or groups of nations. The contrasting – and in some ways conflicting – interests of the U.S.A., the main producing nations, the principal consuming countries of Western Europe and Japan, the developing nations with their rapidly increasing demand for oil, and the U.S.S.R. and its allies have, it is hoped, been made clear. At the same time, we have had to take into account the growing complexity of the oil industry's organization, for the companies and other institutions concerned with oil have legal, economic and political relationships with the world's nations and inevitably form part of the system which we have had to examine.

Little more than a decade ago there were fewer than a dozen of these entities which really mattered at an international level, and to a large degree they did what seemed best from their own point of view. They took note mainly of each other and they worked together where possible (as in the joint producing companies in the Middle East). Where this was impossible, perhaps because of U.S. anti-trust legislation, they rarely moved in such a way as to upset the others and thus displayed an 'understanding' which to the outside observer might appear to indicate the continued existence of the cartel arrangement of the 1930s. Today, quite apart from national, and in some cases, regional governments, there are at least 150 entities which form part of the oil system. Such large numbers inhibit formal agreements and render complete understanding between them well-nigh impossible even when use is made of mathematical and sociological models and techniques to enable 'predictions' to be made of others' responses to a particular course of action.

But the world oil industry is more than the interrelationship of

165

supply sources and markets, of companies with governments, of companies with companies. The system works within the framework of the larger and even more complex system of the world's political and economic relationships, and this book would be sadly incomplete if there were no attempt even to outline the main points at which the 'oil system' impinges on, affects and is affected by the larger 'international system'. This chapter cannot be exhaustive or even comprehensive and thus we shall instead choose a few cases with which to illustrate some of the general points involved.

At a purely political level, the interrelationships of oil and the Middle East cauldron of instability and change have made the headlines on more than a few occasions since the war. The political stresses and tensions in the area have certainly made their impact on the oil industry, but in return the development of the latter has certainly produced a different Middle East from what would otherwise have been the case.

The tensions in the Middle East arising from the Arab–Israeli conflict have time and time again produced their effects on the oil industry. The initial formation of the state of Israel was immediately followed by the cutting of the pipelines which had previously taken oil from Iraq to Haifa for refining or onward transhipment to Western Europe (see Map 4, pp. 78–9). To this day these pipelines remain broken and unused and the Iraq Petroleum Company was obliged to replace the sections in Israel and Jordan with lines through Syria and the Lebanon, where new refining and export terminals have been built at Tripoli. Israeli territory also had to be avoided when Aramco, a few years later, decided to build the Trans-Arabian Pipeline (Tapline) from its fields in the Gulf coast of Saudi Arabia to the Mediterranean coast. Supply to a terminal in Israel would have been the cheapest way of providing this transportation, but political conditions made this impossible and so an extra thirty miles or so of line had to be laid around Israel's northern boundary. Following the Arab–Israeli war of June 1967 a few miles even of this relocated line now lie in Israeli-occupied parts of Syria, but so far Israel has not interfered with its operations, though, inexplicably, Arab commandos have – thus temporarily closing the line at one stage and interrupting the transit revenues earned by Lebanon, Syria and Jordan.

Right from the start of the conflict in 1947 Israel has been denied Arab oil and so for many years the Haifa refinery, designed to run on Iraq's crude, stood idle. Supplies, first of oil products, and then of crude oil once the refinery had been reconstructed to take oil of other specifications, have had to be brought in from other parts of the world, such as Venezuela. Even then it could be received only in tankers which avoided the use of the Suez Canal, which until its closure in 1967 was forbidden to ships carrying goods to Israel. The international companies marketing oil in Israel were also forced by the Arab states to choose between continuing to do this and continuing to pursue their interests in Arab countries. As the importance of the latter invariably exceeded the importance of the former, Israel had to organize its own refining, distribution and marketing facilities and thus achieved the virtually unique position in the non-communist world of being unable to 'Go Well with Shell' or to share the advantages of having 'tigers in the tanks' of its motoring public!

But Israel's oil problems arising from the continued state of war with the Arab countries have at least been predictable and thus amenable to solution – albeit at a cost of higher transport charges. Less predictable, however, have been the indirect effects on the oil industry of Israel–Arab tensions. In times of the absence of active and large-scale hostilities the oil business could continue working, provided the Arabs' ground rules forbidding contact with Israel were observed; but when the continuous tension has deteriorated into actual warfare the significance of the Arab–Israel dispute for the oil industry has become virtually universal. In both the Suez War of 1956 and the Six Day War of 1967 not only was the Suez Canal closed, with a consequent traumatic effect on the international movement of oil, but the Arab states also tried to use their control over a large part of the world's oil production as a weapon to assist them in their struggle. In 1956–7, the situation arising from the closure of the Suez Canal, the sabotage of some of the pipelines from producing countries to the Mediterranean and the ban on shipping Arab oil to Britain, France and certain other countries produced several serious consequences. It led to the short-term rationing of oil products in Western Europe. It immediately gave rise to increased prices to enable the companies to cover increased costs arising from their need to buy more oil from more expensive areas (notably the U.S.A.) and from the longer tanker journeys required for Middle Eastern oil round the Cape of Good Hope. And it produced intense diplomatic pressure on the part of the U.S.A. and other Western nations to get Egypt and other Arab countries to abandon their use of oil as a political weapon. This just succeeded and the Western European economies escaped major close-downs by a hair's breadth.

Ten years later, in 1967, Middle Eastern oil was even more important to most of the world's industrial economies, for in the meantime low oil prices had encouraged its replacement of coal to such an extent that oil had become the dominant industrial fuel in most countries (see Chapters 5, 6 and 7). Moreover, motor transport had grown rapidly in importance in these countries, too, since the mid-1950s and the transport sector of the economies concerned had become largely dependent on oil products. This time, therefore, it seemed that a repeat of the Arab nations' 1956 actions must cause a major breakdown. At first, the pattern of 1956–7 appeared to be repeating itself as the Canal was once again closed and reports of bans on oil movements to certain countries were announced by governments and oil workers of producing nations. But this time there was no sabotage to the Mediterranean pipelines; the bans on shipping oil were, in general, lifted after a few days and the world's unused tanker capacity (which existed partly because of the over-ordering of tankers following the Suez crisis) was quickly chartered to move the oil round the Cape of Good Hope – a route which was, in fact, already being taken by the largest tankers as they were too large to go fully laden through the Canal anyway. Moreover, in the decade since the last crisis new oil-producing capacity had been developed in other parts of the world – notably Libya and Algeria – while other areas of relatively low-cost production – for instance Venezuela – were working at less than their full capacity. On this occasion, therefore, Western Europe was not denied the oil it required and the only penalty it had to pay for trouble in the Middle East was a small and temporary price increase to cover the additional transport charges.

The continued closure of the Suez Canal between 1967 and 1974 certainly altered the relative abilities of different countries' oil (and companies for that matter) to 'compete' in the world markets and in particular worked to the advantage of Venezuela, Libya and Nigeria, whose oil does not have to go through the Canal to reach Europe. But the Middle East producers have continued to grow and it is somewhat ironic that the single most important interruption in oil supply arising from the Canal's closure was the U.S.S.R.'s inability to send oil from the Black Sea to Japan. Fortunately for the U.S.S.R., whose oil trade with Japan constitutes an important source of foreign exchange earning, it was possible to arrange a 'swop deal' with B.P. – also badly affected as a company by the Canal closure because of the dominance of Middle Eastern supplies in its total oil availability. Under the terms of this agreement oil was taken out of Iraq by B.P. for shipment to Japan and was traded on a ton-for-ton basis with Soviet oil delivered from Black Sea and Baltic Sea export terminals to B.P. outlets in Western Europe. It is possible that such an arrangement could continue even with the re-opening of the Canal, for all parties would benefit from the overall reduction in transport costs incurred.

But whether or not the Canal was ever again opened for oil tankers became almost a matter of indifference to the oil companies concerned. Minor adjustments to their production patterns, coupled with their major decisions to achieve, as quickly as possible, the ability to move oil in tankers whose size and speed made it less costly for them to reach Europe or the U.S.A. via the Cape, marked an important turning point in the history of the Canal as a primary route for the international movement of oil. And if this development in tanker technology was not sufficient to seal the demise of the Suez Canal as a growing thoroughfare for oil, then the new multi-million-ton pipelines designed to carry oil from the Red Sea to the Mediterranean will certainly do so (see Map 4, pp. 78–9). One of these is an Israeli pipeline which has been built from Eilat on the southern shore of the country to the Mediterranean coast, following Israel's securing control of the Gulf of Aqaba with its occupation of the Sinai peninsula. Given an Arab world which accepted Israel and Israel's right to benefit from transhipping Middle East oil to Europe, then the pipeline would make very good sense indeed. But since it does not accept these ideas, then the continuing economic viability of the pipeline is seriously undermined, for none of the Arab countries will agree to their oil passing through the line. Thus the only oil in large quantities that can make use of it is oil from Iran. Even this possibility is limited whilst most oil in Iran continues to be produced and shipped by companies that also have large interests in the Arab states and which would thus not dare to get overtly involved in the Israeli project, for the reason given earlier in the chapter (see p. 167). The only other large-scale possibilities for its use, other than for moving oil to Israel itself, are, in fact, quite remote. One *might* be the north-to-south movement of Soviet oil bound for India, Japan and other Far Eastern markets, but this demands such a fundamental switch in Soviet political strategy in the Middle East away from its support for Egypt and the other Arab states as to make it appear a very remote possibility indeed. The second could be the south-to-north movement of Australian oil by companies new to the international oil business and thus without interests in the Arab countries to consider. This development depends on both a large-scale build-up in Australian supplies and the securing of markets for these supplies in European countries where the large international oil companies are well established. Neither of these will happen overnight, and they cannot be relied upon to provide the economic justification for a really large – and hence low-cost – trans-Israel pipeline. Therefore the likelihood of a major expansion in its capacity is small indeed until there is a peace treaty between Israel and the Arab nations. The only exception to this conclusion would be if Iran, which has now decided to take over complete control of its oil industry and thus retain the ownership of much more oil in transit to centres of consumption than has hitherto been the case, felt strong enough to ignore entirely Arab feelings over the question and so take full advantage of possible economies to be gained in moving its oil via this pipeline to Western and Eastern Europe. One should note, moreover, that Iran does have a transport alternative to this politically somewhat dangerous use of Israel's line. This is the proposal for a very large-diameter crude-oil pipeline to take Iran's production directly from the fields to the Mediterranean coast in Turkey. As can be seen from Map 4 this would not only have the effect of reducing by about 75 per cent the distance over which the oil has to travel to reach the Mediterranean (compared with the use of the Israeli line) but it also avoids crossing any country other than Iran and Turkey. This development would eliminate the main opportunity which Israel has for becoming an important crude-oil transit country.

The second project, however, is free from the political problems that affect the likely use of the Israeli pipeline. This is an Egyptian development for twin 42-inch diameter lines from Suez to Alexandria capable of transporting 80 million tons of oil a year (increasing to 125 million with the addition of more pumping stations) and with facilities for loading and unloading the largest tankers now anticipated at both Red Sea and Mediterranean ends of the line. It can be interpreted partly as Egypt's answer to the threat of the Cape journeys of the large tankers, but it might have come even without this development as an alternative to widening and deepening the Canal itself to provide the extra capacity which would be required mainly for additional oil traffic. Though the Suez pipeline will be subject to the same dangers as the Suez Canal in times of hostilities, the fact that the line will be fed by tankers of such a size that the alternative of a Cape routing for them is also possible in the event of trouble has led the companies to decide to use its facilities – as it gives an opportunity for big enough cost-savings to offset the relatively limited amount of capital they must invest in terminal and storage facilities. However, given the continued tension between Israel and the Arab world it seems highly unlikely that any major company will willingly put all its eggs into this particular basket. The Suez pipeline can therefore promise to do little more for Egypt than retain some part of the trade which, in the absence of super tankers and political hostilities in the Middle East, it could reasonably have expected to secure in moving oil from the Middle East to Western Europe and North America.

Egypt's keenness to press ahead with this pipeline project, to be completed in 1975, adds one further piece of evidence to support the contention that the Arab states after 1967 began seriously to re-evaluate the use of their control over the industrialized world's oil requirements as a weapon in their geo-political struggle against Israel and its alleged Western allies. In 1956–7 unilateral decisions on the part of Arab governments, and/or particular elements in their countries, to close down oil production and oil transport facilities affected the consuming countries and international companies

171

more seriously than it affected their own interests. But thereafter the producing countries moved into a position in which their own benefits from oil increased very rapidly and in which their immediate and longer-term economic and political viability came to depend increasingly on keeping their oil flowing.

By contrast, some consumers of Middle East oil sought to decrease their dependence on this particular flow of oil because they were not content merely to await the next unilateral decision by the Arab states to turn off their essential energy requirements. As previously shown, the U.S. decision in 1959 to introduce mandatory quotas on crude-oil imports was taken partly because of concern for security of supplies from the Middle East. Japan – with a greater dependence on Middle Eastern oil than any other major industrial nation – has, as shown in Chapter 6, been encouraging national companies to develop oil resources elsewhere and persuading other companies supplying oil to the Japanese market to diversify their sources of supply. The countries of Western Europe, which collectively take the bulk of Middle East oil and which at the time of the Suez War depended on it for 75 per cent of total oil supplies, reacted to some degree to the dangers and risks of too rapid a change to imported oil as the basis of their energy economics. Without the fear of interruptions to those supplies, most West European countries would have had even fewer inhibitions about pursuing cheap-energy policies based on imported Middle East oil than was the case between 1958 and 1970. Instead, indigenous coal was given some degree of protection, while alternative supplies of imported energy, including coal from the U.S.A. and oil from the U.S.S.R., were welcomed as a means of reducing the risks. Still more recently, the risks attendant upon a continuing high degree of dependence on Middle Eastern oil have also helped to accelerate interest in Europe's own natural gas and oil potential. In fact, the already discovered potential of North Sea and Dutch gas, plus good prospects in the Adriatic and Baltic Seas, plus the development of the newly discovered indigenous oil resources, seemed by 1970 likely to be able to eliminate much of the annual rate of growth in the market for imported oil in West Europe by the end of the decade. (Up until then there was felt to be little real danger of a reduction in Middle Eastern supplies of oil, given the agreements in 1971/72 between the oil-producing countries and the international oil companies over the supply and price of oil up to 1981.)

These attitudes and developments have not gone unnoticed in the Middle East, even though in public opinion media they receive little publicity compared with references to the industrialized world's dependence on Middle East oil. This could account for the relatively limited support, in terms of oil sanctions and other interruptions to oil supplies, given to the Arab cause in the 1967 war. It was surely not co-incidental that only two new producers – Libya and Algeria, less sophisticated in the oil business than the longer-term producers of the Middle East proper – persisted in boycotting certain markets for more than a few days. In Saudi Arabia, Kuwait and Iraq, as well as in the smaller and newer producers of the sheikdoms of the lower Persian Gulf, nothing was permitted to occur which would have meant a long-term interruption of supplies. The 'boycott' was restricted to certain destinations and certain ships (depending on nationality); and no really serious steps appear to have been taken to ensure that the com-panies did not get away merely with observing the letter, but not the spirit, of the boycott decisions. The companies reorganized their supply arrangements so that all bans on particular oils to particular destinations by particular ships could be observed, but they switched tankers and cargoes so that no nation went short of oil (and, in doing so, incidentally helped to demonstrate the validity of their claim that they can act as neutral intermediaries in moving oil between hostile governments). In other words, the Middle East oil-producing nations appeared to have made up their minds that, in both the short and the longer term, they themselves were likely to suffer the most from simply 'holding the West to ransom' over oil.

Thus, since the 1967 war, at a series of Arab conferences held to determine future policy, a new philosophy towards the use of oil as a means of achieving desired ends began to emerge. In brief, the new policy was to make deliberate use of revenues from exported oil to provide the financial base for the achievement of political ends. The scope for this new policy – emerging not only from the growth in total exports, but also from the growth in revenue per barrel, which rose from about 30 cents in 1946 to about $1 by 1970 – is clear. In 1972 the Middle East (including Libya and Algeria but excluding

Iran) exported over 5,000 million barrels of oil and secured some $5,000 million in revenues. The small monthly payments of approximately $5 million being made by two of the major Arab oil-producing nations (Kuwait and Saudi Arabia) to Egypt while the Suez Canal is closed, and to Jordan for an indefinite period, to help with the costs of the Palestine refugees and the loss of its West-bank region to Israel, was a first small indication of the possibilities which exist for using oil revenues for political ends.

There now appeared to be a chance that oil revenues alone would be used to achieve the geo-political aims of the Arab group of states, with two main results. Firstly, there would be a flow of oil from the area unaffected by political crises, as the producing countries increasingly attached more importance to ensuring the continuation of revenues from oil than to using oil as a political weapon. (Though this did not, as has been clearly demonstrated since 1973, exclude the use of oil as an economic weapon against the rest of the world: this, however, was a general reaction of oil-producing countries, rather than one related specifically to Arab producers in a Middle East context, and is discussed fully in Chapter 9.) Secondly, as a result of the economic and political advantages that oil revenues can buy, there would be an Arab Middle East with greater internal cohesion and a more significant geo-political potential among the blocs of the world in the latter part of the twentieth century. With the achievement of the latter in 1973, it was to become somewhat ironic to find the commodity which originally helped to divide the region into spheres of influence of competing outside powers, and which later emphasized national rivalries within the region (creating 'have' and 'have not' nations in the Arab world), emerging to provide the means whereby greater regional cohesion and strength between the Arab nations became a reality in 1974 – albeit through the 'use' of an unfriendly but commercially necessary outside world.

But the interpretation so far of the relationships between oil and geo-politics in the Middle East has been restricted to a consideration of the impact of the Arab–Israeli conflict; and important though this is, it is not the only geo-political consideration involved in an area which has been a centre of world interest and conflict for many centuries. Our limited concern here is merely to evaluate the significance of oil in interesting outside powers in the region and in influencing their policies. The earliest outside interest in the region's oil came from Britain and Germany, with the latter more active through its influence in the pre-First World War Turkish empire. Its activities were not, however, very successful in comparison with exploration in Persia, which provided more than enough oil for Britain, whose political control over the rest of the Persian Gulf area was largely used therefore to inhibit possible oil developments by others. Germany's interests were, of course, eliminated by its defeat in 1918, when the division of the former Turkish empire into British and French spheres of control led to a general understanding between the two countries to divide the spoils as far as oil was concerned. Thus, the newly formed state of Iraq, where the prospects of oil appeared good, lay on the frontier of British and French influence, which necessitated the participation of both British and French capital in a consortium created to initiate oil exploration. To the west the former Turkish empire lay wholly within the French sphere, but Syria and Lebanon – given the technology of the period – turned out to have little by way of oil prospects until, at a later period, they offered routes and export points which could be utilized by the pipelines to the Mediterranean from the producing areas further east. French oil interests were thus quite limited. Britain, on the other hand, gradually extended its oil interests to other parts of the Persian Gulf, where its earlier informal political authority was formally confirmed in 1919.

In the inter-war period British firms discovered oil resources along the coast, particularly in Kuwait. But the opportunities for marketing Middle Eastern oil at that time were not great enough to give an incentive to develop these facilities, for existing fields in Iran and Iraq were quite capable of producing whatever oil could be sold out of the Middle East. The oil-selling potential of the Middle East was effectively inhibited by the world oil-pricing system, dominated by the U.S.A., and the existence, unofficially before 1933 and officially after that, of an international oil cartel. These attributes of the international oil industry – controlled essentially from the U.S.A. – enabled the U.S.A., Mexico and, to a lesser degree, Venezuela and the Dutch East Indies to maintain their dominant role in world oil markets and thus restrain the expansion of known Middle East resources. But as the prolific nature of the Middle East oilfields and the low cost of extracting oil from them gradually became known, the U.S.A. showed increasing interest, and the political efforts of Washington were linked with the commercial and technical efforts of the American oil companies in an attempt to gain access to the oil wealth of the region. This meant a diplomatic struggle with Britain and France, as well as rivalry between oil companies of the different nations involved, and eventually, as a result of both political and commercial pressure, the U.S.A. secured an entry to Middle East producing areas. The British government managed to keep American interests out of its most important producing and refining facilities in Persia but it was forced to allow them into Iraq and the Persian Gulf states. In Iraq, the consortium, in which British and French companies retained an interest, came to be dominated by a group of U.S. companies, while in Kuwait the concessionary company became 50/50 British and American. Thus, by the outbreak of the Second World War in 1939 the U.S.A. had already won for itself a position of virtual parity with Britain and a stronger one than France, in spite of the latter's longer-standing oil interests in the region.

During the war the British military presence throughout the area secured what were considered to be vital British interests, but once the U.S.A. entered the war its great reserves of personnel and equipment quickly gave it a military influence of little less significance. The defeat of France in 1940 more or less eliminated French influence in the Middle East, with Syria and Lebanon, the former French dependencies, quickly achieving independence. By the end of the war Britain and the U.S.A. had 'tied up' the region in political terms and thus paved the way for their oil companies to rush in to take advantage of the concession areas which they had secured within the framework of this colonial situation. Internally, as we have already seen, Britain and America now faced the impossible task of keeping the area under political control. As oil became more important, ran the British and American argument, so greater control became more necessary. But political control could not be maintained within the framework of the traditional colonial relationship, and the two outside powers were gradually obliged to acquiesce in the demands for independence. Associated demands from the oil-producing countries led to the previously described re-negotiations of the oil agreements to give the countries concerned much increased financial returns from, and even some control over, the activities of the oil companies. It was this combination of political and economic moves towards independence for the Middle Eastern countries which gave rise to concern, not only in Britain and the U.S.A., but also in all the other countries which depended on the region's oil, about the security of supplies. There has thus been a period of over twenty years of such uncertainty, dating from the Iranian nationalization of its oil industry in 1951 and marked by what usually proved to be temporary and partial disruptions of the oil flow as a result of the difficulties stemming from the Arab–Israeli conflict. Similarly, disruptions have also occurred from time to time related to the breakdown of negotiations over prices and other issues between the producing countries and the companies holding the concessions. This set of issues, however, culminated in the traumatic events of 1973 and 1974 whereby the relative power of oil companies and oil governments was fundamentally altered – a development which is the subject of the next chapter.

Anglo-American efforts first to secure and then to maintain direct or indirect control over Middle East countries were only partly motivated by their desire to ensure the 'rights' of their companies to explore for and develop Middle East oil and to guarantee its transhipment to world markets. In part, they were dictated by the postwar fear that the Middle East might become increasingly susceptible to political intervention by the U.S.S.R., which, it was suspected, had not only a political interest in the Middle Eastern countries but also an economic interest in securing control over the region's oil. Some students noted the rapidly increasing demand for energy within the Soviet Union and assumed that this demand could not be met by production within the country's boundaries. They also recalled the very early post-war efforts by the U.S.S.R. (up to 1948) to secure concessions for oil exploration and development in the northern parts of Iran, which they had militarily controlled, by agreement with Britain, from 1941. It was therefore predicted that the U.S.S.R. would seek access to Middle East oil and would do this not on commercial terms through purchases from the producing companies (or even countries) but within the framework of a political effort to secure the support of the growing Arab nationalist movement. In the face of this threat, the U.S. and the U.K. governments forgot their earlier differences on the sharing of the Middle East's oil wealth and, emphasizing the need to present a united front in the region against the common enemy, attempted to sell to the Middle East countries the idea of the peripheral anti-Soviet alliance as developed in Western Europe through NATO. It was from these efforts that CENTO emerged, in which one of the most important oil-producing countries of the Middle East – Iran – decided to participate. Behind this 'screen' provided by Turkey, Iran and Pakistan, Anglo-American interests in the Middle East were felt to be more secure and both diplomats and oil investors breathed a little more easily once the Treaty had been signed in 1955 (see Chapter 2).

With hindsight, one can see that this concern about Soviet oil intentions in the Middle East was exaggerated, for the U.S.S.R. proved to have more than enough oil and gas within its own borders to meet its growing requirements. In fact, the rapid development of the Soviet oil industry enabled the country not only to change from a coal-based to an oil- and gas-based economy but also, by the late 1950s, to become a potential rival to the Middle East in terms of oil exports (see Chapter 3). Middle Eastern producing countries and companies now faced the challenge of a new competitor and one, moreover, which was prepared to cut prices of its exports of oil and gas in order to break into the markets controlled by companies with large-scale production in the Middle East. It would, indeed, appear to be the very success of the U.S.S.R. in this respect that has recently encouraged and enabled it to conclude some commercial arrangements with Middle Eastern countries over oil and gas.

It has, for example, agreed to purchase large quantities of Iranian natural gas (to be exported by a pipeline link between the two countries), mainly because this gas is nearer to Soviet consuming areas than some of its own unutilized resources of Siberia, and hence available at lower cost. It will also enable the U.S.S.R. to use this Iranian gas to replace both domestic oil and natural gas, which will then be available for export, earning more foreign exchange than the Iranian gas will cost. The Soviet Union has also agreed to help with the marketing of oil produced from those parts of Iraq that are to be exploited by the latter's new state oil company, which will also depend on the Soviet Union for financial and technical help. This offer could well form the basis for the kind of exchange arrangements described earlier, whereby the costs of supplying U.S.S.R. export markets in the Far East are reduced by taking these requirements from the Middle East and using Soviet supplies themselves in the closer and more accessible European markets. In view of the continued rise in Soviet oil and gas production, linked with the repeated discoveries of new fields in the vast areas of potentially petroliferous sedimentary basis of the U.S.S.R., there seems little chance that the Soviet Union itself will have to rely other than marginally on the Middle East for its energy supplies. Though it may well try to exploit political opportunities in the Middle East for extending its influence there, the motivation for this in the short to medium term will certainly not be to secure access to energy supplies which it must have for its economic development, in the same way that Western Europe, Japan and even the United States, to some degree, have come to depend on such supplies.

The one remaining motive for Soviet intervention lies in a deliberate attempt by the U.S.S.R. to gain control over Middle East oil supplies in order to deny them to those countries that depend on them, but such a deliberate policy would be regarded as tantamount to an act of war by the West and hence likely to bring the confrontation which neither the U.S.S.R. nor the U.S.A. seeks or desires. Such a dangerous policy by the Soviet Union would appear to be out of keeping with the realities of great-power relations in the 1970s and, in any case, hardly worth the risks involved. There is no guarantee that the denial of one, two or even three national sources of Middle Eastern oil would cause much more than temporary supply problems to a Western world where the fundamental problem over energy still appears to be one of long-term surplus rather than shortage, in spite of appearances to the contrary in 1974 when time is still needed to switch from institutionally scarce O.P.E.C. oil to other sources of energy supply. Such a policy would, of course, not necessarily be favoured by the Arab nations, given their continued need for revenues from oil sold to the West to provide the foundation of their political and economic strength. They would be very unhappy with a Soviet attempt to eliminate their exports.

It is thus in the Middle East that the interrelationship of oil and international politics are at their most significant and their most complex. Elsewhere their interrelationship is usually of a bilateral character, affecting the national interests of a particular country and the U.S.A., through its ownership of the majority of the companies that operate in other parts of the world. These bilateral manifestations of the difficulties arising over the importance of oil and the form of its organization internationally have, however, tended to escalate to multilateral proportions in the case of Latin America, where an almost continent-wide consensus exists over attitudes to oil and the largely American companies concerned in its production and distribution.

Individually over the last thirty years, or more in many cases, the countries of Latin America have viewed the oil industry as a particularly effective manifestation of U.S. imperialism. Over this time, one Latin American country after another has fought its own national battle with the international oil companies. These battles have ended either in complete expropriation and an entirely nationally owned industry, as in Mexico in 1938 and Cuba in 1961, or in the establishment of national companies such as E N A P in Chile or Petróbras in Brazil. These entities are given a dominant role in the national oil scene, and the international companies are relegated to providing crude oil, services and know-how but without control over the way in which the industry is run. So strong have national feelings been over this issue that governments have sometimes been brought down because they have seemed likely to make too great concessions to the outside countries. Perón was overthrown in Argentina in 1955 – after ten years of popularity in office – when a deal with an American oil company appeared likely to thwart popular feeling on the subject. Frondizi, another President who followed shortly after Perón, and who when elected to office pledged to maintain the *status quo* over oil, fell even more quickly after he implemented steps to bring in foreign companies to help Argentina to find oil. More recently, President Belaunde Terry of Peru was overthrown because of the agreement he made with Esso over the working of the latter's long-discovered reserves in the country (see also Chapter 7).

But now such individual bilateral conflicts are being 'multi-lateralized' through the cooperation of the state oil companies within Latin America, and the evolution of a petroleum policy within the framework of the formation of free trade areas and/or common markets within the continent. To date the state entities and the civil servants involved have done little more than talk and draw up statements of intent, or sign proposals for cooperation which could not possibly be implemented. But sooner or later and especially since 1973, given the motivation to do something very positive about oil as a result of the massive price rises for the commodity, the organization that has been formed with headquarters in Peru, Asistencia Recíproca Petrolera Estatatal Latinoamericana (ARPEL), will take positive steps towards assuming control and direction over intra-Latin American trade in crude oil and petroleum products, and over the determination of patterns of production and refining in the region, with all that this implies for intervention in investment decisions which the international companies so jealously guard as their own.

Already, some advance in this direction is seen in the case of the European Common Market. This is slowly moving towards a multi-national agreement on energy policy which will involve a common policy towards the international oil companies. They will be constrained to work within the new regional framework laid down by the political authority and will have to justify their attitudes and actions not only to the governments of the individual countries which make up the Community, but also to the Common Market authorities as well. Again, moves in this direction have been greatly stimulated by the new difficulties and dangers of the international oil scene.

Finally, one must note that oil is involved even in the world's growing concern with racial problems – at least in so far as these are reflected in the rest of the world's relationship with South Africa and Rhodesia, the two countries which are deliberately pursuing policies of racial segregation and built-in inequalities in their multi-racial communities. Whether or not their policies are a domestic matter of national interest only is not our concern here – if they are, then of course they are outside the competence of the world's comity of nations to judge, except in moral terms. We only have to observe that the international community has chosen to intervene in their racial policies and that oil has been picked out as an instrument of such intervention. In the case of the dispute between Britain and Rhodesia over the illegal declaration of independence by the latter, the first economic sanction applied by the former was to prohibit the supply of oil to the rebel régime. Support for the sanction was sought specifically amongst the world's oil producing and transporting nations (as well as generally through the United Nations) and British naval units were stationed off the Portuguese East Africa port of Beira (through which oil for Rhodesia was received for onward transportation by pipeline to the refinery at Umtala) to prevent tankers from completing their journey. With all the neighbouring states committed to the policy of denying oil to Rhodesia, Britain's action would eventually have been successful in crippling the country's economy. It would also have made life unpleasant – if not impossible – for Rhodesia's white inhabitants. This could have been achieved in spite of the fact that Rhodesia is less dependent on oil than almost any other country in the world (except for those with still largely subsistence economies) as a result of the local availability of high-quality low-cost coal, which still provides the basic fuel for industry and the railways and, together with hydro-electricity from the massive new station at Kariba on the Zambezi, for the production of electricity. Rhodesia, however, had neighbouring states ready and able to support it over oil sanctions, and both South Africa and Portugal made oil products available across their national frontiers. They thus limited the impact of oil sanctions to little more than nuisance value; the nuisance being the somewhat higher prices which had to be paid by consumers in order to meet the higher transport costs of getting the oil by road or rail from the neighbouring countries, instead of through the recently constructed crude-oil pipeline from Beira, and the temporary rationing of petrol for use in private cars. Even this, however, proved to be unnecessary between May 1971 and January 1974, when Rhodesian supplies through South Africa were affected by the oil boycott on the latter country by the most important Arab oil producers in the aftermath of the October war with Israel.

The effectiveness of oil sanctions against Rhodesia failed between 1966 and 1973 because they did not extend to the other two countries of Southern Africa. Such a possibility has long been given serious consideration by the Union of South Africa in its economic–strategic planning – not unwisely in the light of repeated calls for such action against it from many parts of the world. But again South Africa has cheap coal in abundance (cheap, incidentally, largely because of the availability of low-cost African labour), which is given additional protection against possible competition from oil by its location on the inland plateau. Most of the country's energy consumption is located here, and coal has to stand only limited transport costs in being moved to consumers – in marked contrast with the transport charges which have to be met to get oil from the port of import to the main demand centres. Moreover, these costs have been kept higher than they would otherwise have been by the government's insistence, until very recently, that this oil traffic had to be moved by the state-owned railways. After much pressure from the oil companies a pipeline from Durban to Johannesburg was authorized, but only when the companies agreed to accept the participation of the railways in the project – a device by the government which not only aimed at maintaining railway revenues and profits, but also one which could have the effect of increasing the charges above the minimum possible, thus maintaining some protection for coal.

Nevertheless, oil consumption has been increasing rapidly, particularly in those end-uses where oil products have no rivals, and the vulnerability of the economy to international sanctions over oil is thus increasing. Government recognition of this has been accompanied by action designed to minimize and contain its effects. Of most immediate significance has been government sponsorship of the oil from coal plants at Sasolburg. So far, nowhere else in the world has the large-scale production of oil from coal been economically possible in peacetime conditions. Even in South Africa, with its low-cost coal and relatively high delivered prices of oil products, the development of such facilities has only been carried forward because of the government's willingness to provide the limited subsidy required, in return for the guarantee that this provides a minimum availability of oil products for military and other strategically necessary uses. The seriousness with which the government saw the risks to the country's oil supply is demonstrated by its decision in 1968 that the oil from coal plants should be more than doubled in capacity with a view to the eventual production of about 30 per cent of South Africa's petrol and diesel oil needs in 1974. The South African government has also required the gradual build-up of stocks of crude oil and oil products in an effort to improve its short-term bargaining power in any crisis. It has in part been prepared to finance these itself (particularly stocks of products required for possible military use) but has also required an undertaking on the part of the oil companies concerned that they will hold large stocks at their own expense. This requirement was, indeed, made one condition of the franchise given to oil companies to build or expand refineries.

For the longer term the government has followed two lines of action to meet the threat. Firstly, it has encouraged and sponsored petroleum exploration in the far from favourable geological conditions of the Union, most of which is composed of geological provinces in which oil is thought not to occur. In the limited areas of oil potential however – such as the Karroos immediately behind Cape Town and in South West Africa – exploration has been pushed ahead, though with very little success so far. Very significantly, encouragement has recently been given by the government to persuade the companies to look at the country's rather difficult and narrow continental shelf. As a result, exploration in several off-shore areas is now under way, with somewhat more promising results. Oil production on any scale in South Africa, however, is still a matter for conjecture – and, on the part of the South Africans – of hope. They do, however, take some encouragement from the recent expansion of oil production prospects in Angola, where significant off-shore oilfields have been found. Here the now almost certain production by 1975–6 of relatively large amounts of oil surplus to the requirements of Portugal and Portuguese African territories could find its way by coastal or even overland connections to South African refineries without fear of intervention by the outside, anti-South African world. These discoveries in Portuguese territories, coupled with the oil sanctions against Rhodesia and the intense South African interest in the subject, constitute the principal arguments in favour of the formation of a Southern African bloc in which mutual assistance over oil would be a main area for negotiation. This would help to minimize the future degree of economic control that the outside world can exercise over these countries and territories by using oil as a weapon.

South Africa does not, however, see the outside world as unanimous in its attitude towards it over oil and this leads on to the second line of action which it is actively pursuing. This is a diplomatic 'offensive' designed to secure agreement on the part of other nations to continue to supply it with oil in the face of 'world opinion'. Much of this activity was, of necessity, conducted in secret, but what eventually emerged to public view was an agreement with Iran. Iran is to supply the crude which will go to a partly Iranian-owned refinery in South Africa. This means, of course, that Iran would have a significant national interest in continuing to allow oil to be loaded for South African destinations, even in the event of international action to impose sanctions. The government has tried to secure similar guarantees from the foreign companies working in South Africa. It is highly likely that all have given an assurance that they will do what they can should the occasion arise, but French companies in particular appear to have satisfied the South African government in this respect to a greater degree than have the American or British ones – perhaps reflecting contrasting government attitudes to South Africa.

Finally, South Africa has decided that the minimization of the oil risk also provides an economic case for pursuing 'southern hemisphere' solidarity. Since the late 1960s South African diplomats, particularly those concerned with oil, have been active in South America, and there are signs that they believe that the contacts they have made could lead to an oil flow should it turn out to be required. Whatever they are thinking of Venezuela or Argentina as possible supply points is not clear, but the existence of a government less unfavourably inclined towards South Africa in the latter country as compared with the former points in the direction of a future possible involvement of South African interests in Argentinian oil potential. Looking around the southern world the other way, South Africa must also be very encouraged by the significant finds of oil and gas made in Australia in recent years, for South African markets could be among the most attractive of any in the world for any oil or gas which Australia has surplus to its own requirements. In the light of these significant preparations which South Africa is making against all eventualities it seems unlikely that the use of oil as a means of taking diplomatic action against it (in respect of its racial policies) will be any more successful than were the wartime efforts of the allied nations between 1941 and 1945 against Germany, when even that country's military machine managed to secure the fuel that it required.

Alternatives and other stratagems are always available to a nation to secure essential oil. There are, for example, usually high profits to be made out of sanction- or blockade-breaking by those individuals or individual companies prepared to take the risks involved. And, in any case, it is very unlikely that unanimity of action on such an issue by all interested parties can ever be achieved. Thus, one must summarize the potential use of oil in international disputes as having little more than nuisance value. Short-term rigidities in oil supply arrangements, indicating a possible means of exercising control and authority over unfriendly nations, quickly dissolve into relative insignificance with the alternative arrangements which can and will be made by the unfriendly nation. In the medium term, they disappear altogether with the development of alternative strategies for obtaining requirements. Such 'oil crises' are therefore perhaps overplayed in the day-to-day reporting of events, while, at the same time, the diplomatists and others actually concerned in the ordering of events perhaps already evaluate such problems as the reciprocal of the column inches they receive in the world's press!

It is significant that – with the exception of Western concern over the U.S.S.R.'s oil diplomacy in the Middle East – the post-war East–West struggle has not had overmuch concern with oil as such. The Soviet Union has pursued a policy of self-sufficiency in oil but has shown itself sufficiently flexible to attempt to arrange 'swop' and other deals with private enterprise companies in the West. On the other hand, NATO has laid down ground rules about trading in oil with the Soviet Union, but when these were ignored by Italy it did not appear to give rise to much real concern. It also attempted to restrict sales of certain oil-industry equipment and pipelines to the U.S.S.R. and its allies, but the attractions of the Soviet markets for these commodities made any such collective policy unworkable, as first one ally then another made offers to the Soviet Union as a means of keeping surplu. producing capacity in their steel and other industries fully occupied.

In other words, strategic concern over oil has tended to evaporate quickly because of the substantial economic gains that could be made by all parties concerned by keeping the oil flowing. These included the use to be made of oil revenues by the major producing countries; the economic effect of substituting high-cost coal with low-cost oil in countries like Japan and West Germany; and the importance of the availability of oil products in almost all corners of the earth in order to break the energy bottleneck in the initial industrialization of an underdeveloped country. This well-nigh universal importance of oil in the process of economic development has provided its most funda-mental influence on the relationships between the world's nations up to 1973 – and gave rise to the whole complex set of issues that have been briefly examined in this book. As already indicated in previous chapters, however, the world oil system did take a quite remarkable shift in its organization and power structure in 1973 when the produc-ing and exporting nations took control over the supply and price of oil by means of their collective action. In so doing they threw the rest of the world into confusion over oil in particular and over attitudes to energy in general, and thus caused a need for a re-evalua-tion of the world of oil power. This issue is dealt with in the final chapter.

: The World of Oil Power in 1974

It is almost five years since the first edition of this book was written. This period has certainly confirmed the general rule, stated in the Introduction, that a day rarely passes without oil being in the news. The text of the original eight chapters has thus been much changed to take note of developments in the years since 1969. The world of oil has continued to expand so that the companies in the industry have continued to do the same, whilst the producing countries have enjoyed rising government revenues from their increasing sales of oil abroad, as well as from their abilities to increase their revenues per barrel of oil sold. Everywhere in the world, oil has continued to increase its share of the total market for energy.

The single most important reflection of this trend was the success of oil in ousting coal from its position as the principal energy source even in the United Kingdom, where the economy had previously been built up on the strength of the indigenous coal resources and where, thanks to continuing investment in the industry in the 1950s and to a relatively low-paid mining force and governmental help, the coal industry had managed better than in other parts of Western Europe to fight off competition from oil. Even so, in September 1971, oil in Britain finally took over as the most important source of energy in the economy, and its use has since continued to expand, whilst the use of coal has continued to decline. In 1973, oil provided about 47 per cent of total energy use and coal under 40 per cent. In the meantime, on the other side of the globe, Japan leapt further ahead as the world's most important oil-importing nation and, in 1972, its imports exceeded 200 million tons for the first time, making Japanese concern for its overdependence on oil produced abroad (and almost entirely by non-Japanese companies) even more pronounced than was suggested in Chapter 6. This increasing concern has been reflected in Japan's widening and intensifying oil and gas operations, which are now proceeding apace not only on its own continental shelf, but also, through the efforts of state-helped and state-encouraged Japanese oil companies, in many countries in every continent of the world except – up to early 1974 – Western Europe. Even here, however, increasing Japanese interest has been shown in the investment opportunities offered by the major oil and gas developments on the North Sea and on other parts of Europe's continental shelf, and by the time this book is published it seems likely that there will be Japanese involvement in this one remaining area.

Elsewhere, the developing nations, under the impact of deliberately fostered industrialization policies and a general inability to produce sufficient energy at home quickly enough to sustain their economic growth, imported steadily increasing quantities of oil from the main oil-exporting areas; and, though many of them tended towards the use of state trading and the construction of nationally owned refineries etc., they still largely depend on the international oil companies for their increasingly important flows of oil. At the same time, the United States, as a result of domestic policies which constrained the rate of development of its indigenous oil and gas resources, started to become a rapidly developing importer of oil from 1968 onwards and, as shown in Chapter 2, was thus obliged to review and eventually, in 1972, abandon its oil import quota system, leading to an expectation for a continuing rise in the quantities of Middle Eastern oil which would have to move to the United States. This expectation gave rise to numerous projects for the construction of crude-oil terminals and/or refineries on Caribbean and Bahaman islands, where the mammoth tankers, required to ship the crude oil from the Middle East, could discharge their cargoes. (On the mainland of the U.S.A. itself no east-coast port could accept tankers bigger than 100,000 tons.)

More important, however, than the effect that this increasing demand for oil had upon physical developments such as shipping, infrastructure developments and so on, was its effect upon the attitudes and policies of the different elements in the world oil-power system. In order to appreciate the significance of this it seems most useful to recapitulate the main elements of the system as it emerged, in order to put the fundamentally changed situation of the present period clearly into perspective.[1]

The oil world became an unstable system shortly after the end of the Second World War. Until then a few international oil companies – organized within the framework of a cartel which had first emerged to protect the industry's profits in the difficult economic circumstances of the 1930s – had largely controlled the supply and price of oil. There was little interference either from the countries in which production happened to be concentrated or from consuming countries, most of which used oil simply as a fuel to supplement the indigenous coal or hydro-electricity on which most of them then depended. The international companies, moreover, effectively organized their activities around the world behind the guarantee of security offered by the political and/or military presences of the United States and the United Kingdom, which between them provided the home base for six and a half of the seven international oil corporations (with the remaining half – the Royal Dutch part of Shell – domiciled in the Netherlands).

Instability in this apparently stable system, however, first appeared, paradoxically, when the United States took action to ensure that its tough domestic line against cartels and monopolies, through the medium of its anti-trust legislation, also affected the foreign operations of American companies. This action, moreover, more or less coincided with another which further undermined the traditional organization of the oil industry by the oil companies. This was the insistence by the administrators of the Marshall Plan that the oil companies should cease to charge for the oil they sold to Europe (which was to be paid for out of Marshall Plan Funds) as though it came out of expensive fields in the United States and as though it were transported from the Gulf of Mexico. Thus, a posted price system orientated towards non-U.S. points of oil production and freight rates related to actual, rather than to hypothetical, movements of oil around the world was introduced.

At the same time there were other blows to the stability of the oil

1. The next few paragraphs essentially paraphrase developments which have been described at length in other parts of the book.

system which turned out to be even more significant. The most notable was the rise of nationalism in the oil-producing countries, which, with their knowledge of the rapidly increasing demand for oil in an industrializing world, quickly came to appreciate that the exploitation of their oil reserves in a physical sense was also exploitation in economic and political senses as well. They successively took steps to improve the returns they received from the oil companies' operations. Thus, in 1951 there was the important agreement on a 50:50 sharing of the profits between producing country and producing company. After this, agreements between the two parties brought other changes in the concession-style arrangements, further tax-rate changes and an early form of 'participation' by the producing countries in production activities, such as those negotiated in Indonesia and Iran. Overall, the companies had to learn to live with increasingly expert opponents and within the framework of a world political and economic environment which viewed them as 'aggressors' against the interests of the oil-rich countries.

At the consuming end of the system, the industrial nations of Western Europe (and Japan) pursued policies which aimed at securing increasingly essential oil supplies (oil in most cases having quickly become the most important energy source) at as low cost as possible. Some countries, like Japan and France, controlled the companies' activities very severely; others, like Italy, sought to launch their own rival organizations to look after national oil supplies; and still others, like Sweden and West Germany, encouraged the development of imports from elsewhere, notably from the Soviet Union – which made a post-war reappearance on the oil market in the late 1950s – in order to bring downward pressure on prices. But, paradoxically, it was again the United States itself which gave the biggest help in breaking the price levels of oil to importing nations when it determined in 1959 to pursue a 'fortress America' oil policy and to limit its imports to about 12 per cent of the expected demand in any one year. Over the previous few years a large number of American domestic oil companies (as contrasted with the American-based international companies) had established operations abroad for the first time in order to find lower-cost oil to sell back in the U.S.A. Their anticipated sales outlet was now blocked by the newly introduced U.S. oil-quota import system and they had to seek markets in other parts of the world. In these markets the combined impact of additional supplies and of new companies aggressively seeking marketing outlets (in contrast with the international majors, which preferred 'orderly' marketing) brought a cheap oil era to Western Europe, Japan and elsewhere and a steady decline in the profitability of the oil industry.

Thus in a situation of pressure from the oil-producing countries for more tax revenues, on the one hand, and price weakness for most oil products in many of the world's markets, on the other, the oil companies became something less than the profit centres of the earlier post-war period. This situation, coupled with the complicating and adverse effects of political difficulties in the Middle East, out of which area most of the crude oil supplying the world markets originated, made the outlook less than favourable and sent the companies scurrying into diversification exercises and into a search for a solution which would bring some greater element of stability to their fortunes.

This pattern of development had, of course, led to the general ability of the world's oil consumers to secure their needed supplies at a steadily falling real cost (as shown in Figure 1) and had also produced the situation in which other energy sources had found it increasingly difficult to compete with oil – both leading to the very high growth rates in oil demand over the period. But for the oil-producing countries, the oil companies and the U.S.A. the situation had, for different reasons, become unacceptable and we here hypothesize that each party thus had both a motivation and a wish to see the situation changed.

The initial requirement for a changed distribution of power in the oil system was a re-evaluation by the oil-producing countries of their status and strategy; and this, in turn, required much more effective political action than they had hitherto succeeded in taking. Such increasingly effective action has, however, become apparent since the late 1960s, and so initiated the important new developments which have affected oil and world power in the last four years. The overthrow of King Idris of Libya, and the establishment there of the revolutionary government under Colonel Gaddafi, led to the strongest political action ever taken by an individual oil-producing country. Given the strength created for the new government by the accumulated revenues arising from the rapidly rising oil production of the large number of corporate groups which had been granted concessions to operate in Libya since 1960, and given the impact of the previously mentioned external changes in the world oil-supply system on the country's competitive position, the new government could really afford to 'get tough' with the companies concerned – and, using appropriate tactics, the government tackled them one by one.

The threat of a forcible curtailment of levels of production was generally enough to get the companies to agree to raise the price at which they 'posted' their oil for export – and thus increase to an even higher level the revenues per barrel that they paid to the Libyan government. The one or two companies that chose to test the revolutionary government's intentions in this respect quickly found that it meant what it said and so fell into line – or else were nationalized.

Libya's get-tough policy was quickly noted by other producing countries, and similar action elsewhere also produced agreements by the companies to pay increased revenues to the countries concerned. Hitherto in the oil world, unilateral action on the part of individual countries had, as shown in earlier chapters, been constrained by the fear that the companies concerned would cut back their oil production and investment plans in the country and make it up by expanding their output and activities elsewhere in the 'better-behaved' parts of the oil-producing world! It had, of course, been partly in response to this fear that the Organization of Petroleum Exporting Countries (O.P.E.C.) had been formed. Now it, too, given the changed attitudes of its member countries together with the previously described changes in the post-1970 overall international oil supply/demand relationships, was able to take collective action of a kind which had previously been impossible because it would have been rendered ineffective by competitive (rather than cooperative) responses by its member countries.

The subsequent success of O.P.E.C. in achieving a consensus amongst its members for collective action – as agreed at its Caracas meeting in December 1970 – marked the beginning of a significant change in the power balance between the various groups with an interest in oil. O.P.E.C. now became a sort of trade union of the oil-producing countries. But in the changed circumstances of the time it was, moreover, accepted and even welcomed in this role by the same oil companies which at first, ten years previously, had declined even to recognize its existence at all and which later had come to view it as something of a nuisance. This success of the oil-producing countries in forming a politically and economically significant organization has, of course, significance even outside the framework of the oil industry, for its success in this direction was the first amongst producers of primary commodities at an international level and seems likely to provide a model for the producers of other commodities, such as bauxite and copper, which are not only essential to the economies of the world's industrial nations, but which also occur on a large scale in a relatively small number of developing countries.

Returning, however, to oil itself, events between the late 1960s and the early 1970s produced another equally significant change in the international oil industry's organization. This was the move towards the re-establishment of an international oil agreement by the companies responsible for most of the oil that enters world trade. Their motivation was clear: profit protection in a situation in which they expected to have to pay steadily increasing taxes to the producing countries and thus needed to be able to pass these increased costs on to their customers. Hitherto, the main barrier to such collective action on the part of the companies had been the United States' legal restraints on such agreements through the working of effective anti-trust legislation, developed – in part – because of earlier oil-industry propensities to act collectively! The oil companies now, however, in the period immediately after the Libyan and O.P.E.C. action described above, managed to persuade Nixon's administration that there was a real danger of a crisis in world oil and that the solution to the crisis lay in their taking concerted action in their negotiations with the producing governments. Thus, early in 1971, the companies secured the right to work together, without legal interference, and so became able to reach collective agreements with the oil producers. Though the companies created the appearance of fighting O.P.E.C.

tooth and nail over the agreements – as they sought to keep their increased tax obligations to a minimum and to delay participation in (that is, nationalization of) their oilfield and other assets as long as possible – they certainly recognized that their best hopes of future profitability, and even survival, depended on successful cooperation with the major oil-producing countries.

The latter, in turn, initially accepted the idea that they needed to work with the international oil companies in order to keep the oil, and thus their revenues, flowing. Thus O.P.E.C./oil companies collusion became a fact of the oil-power system of the early 1970s – with the positive encouragement of the United States.

The U.S.A. wished, indeed, to see the establishment of a new collective stability in the oil system for two reasons. In the first place, it sought to provide a basis for a renewed effort to find a political solution to the Middle East conflict, arguing that higher revenues and a greater degree of economic certainty for the Arab oil-producing nations would make it easier for them to accept a compromise in their dispute with Israel, and so bring greater political stability to the whole of the Middle East.

Secondly, given the fact that the U S.A. was fed up with a situation in which the rest of the industrialized world had access to cheap energy (and which the U.S.A. itself could not have because of its underlying belief in a policy of autarky in its energy policy), it deliberately initiated a foreign policy which aimed at getting oil-producing nations' revenues moving strongly up by talking incessantly to the producers about their low oil prices and by showing them the favourable impact of much higher prices. It was, of course, assured of the cooperation of the largely American oil companies in having these cost increases, plus further increases designed to ensure higher profit levels for the companies, passed on to the European and Japanese energy consumers, so eliminating their advantage over their competitors in the United States. And, in as far as the U.S.A. itself would be affected by the higher foreign-exchange costs of the increased amount of foreign crude oil that it expected to have to import, even this would be offset entirely, or to a large degree, by the greatly enhanced abilities of the U.S. oil companies to remit their increased profits back to America.

195

Thus, within the framework of a re-evaluation of how their best interests could be served and the consequential establishment of what might be termed a somewhat 'unholy alliance' between the United States, the international oil companies and the O.P.E.C. countries, the stage was set for changing the international oil-power situation as it had evolved over the previous fifteen years.

From the companies' point of view, of course, acceptance of the producing countries' terms on increased taxes and on the idea of participation (another device for increasing the share of the profits going to the countries) implied a major increase in their tax-paid costs. This meant that the weakness in the market places of the oil world had to be eliminated – as permanently as possible – if the companies were to earn what they considered to be adequate profits. The actual timing of the O.P.E.C. success and the companies' acceptance of it can, in fact, be correlated with the occurrence of a hardening of the oil-market situation in 1970 due to the combination of a set of unusual circumstances – a strong demand for most oil products in most markets in a period of general economic advance, a shortage of refinery capacity in Europe and Japan and a temporary scarcity of tankers which was aggravated by the politically occasioned closure of the Trans-Arabian pipeline. The fact that oil prices strengthened as a result of this set of circumstances now gave the oil companies the public-relations opportunities to start to persuade oil consumers that there was an oil supply crisis – not only of short-term but also of long-term dimensions – and that this, coupled with the imposition of the 'swingeing' new taxes in the producing countries, inevitably meant significant and continuing rises of oil prices over the foreseeable future. The U.S. energy crisis – certainly a real one, but nevertheless an essentially short-term crisis arising out of domestic issues – and the impact of the conservationists and the environmentalists, added further strength to the inevitability-of-higher-prices-for-oil arguments. And the public was persuaded of the oil companies' case!

The climate, in other words, was established for an attack on oil consumers' interests – with the elimination of the cheap energy (and essentially low-profit energy) to which Europe, Japan and elsewhere had, by 1971, become very accustomed. Temporarily, the factors mentioned above could be relied on to secure the situation, but their ephemeral nature meant that the safeguarding of the longer-term position required positive action on the part of the companies. Fortunately, their ability and new opportunity to work and negotiate together with the oil-producing countries gave ample opportunities for strategic marketing discussions – and for a decision to tackle the inbuilt propensity for price weakness in Europe. This market was the critical one, for it was to Europe in the past ten years that 'distress' supplies had found their way in their search for outlets. The appropriate device to achieve this end was obviously a moratorium on the expansion of the infrastructure through which oil is moved and marketed in the continent (particularly in refining and pipelining facilities), accompanied by some element of rationalization in the complex company structure involved in the marketing of oil products in Europe. Thus, expansion projects were slowed down and some companies – for example Gulf, Shell and B.P. – decided to pull out of certain national markets and/or products, whilst in the case of some products – for example aviation fuels – there was evidence of an agreement that existing suppliers of particular customers were accorded the right to continue to have the business without the fear of price undercutting by other companies All this, of course, fell far short of the establishment of a formal cartel of oil companies – or even a repetition of the 1933 'As Is' agreement, under which the oil companies formally agreed to leave market shares etc. as they were However, given the understanding between the companies, and the fact that almost all of them were involved in the collective discussions which were required to reach agreement with the oil-producing lands, it promised to be enough to get some high degree of 'sanity' and 'orderly marketing' into the hitherto cut-throat and generally chaotic market situation in Western Europe.

At first, three factors combined to undermine the strategy (though it should, nevertheless, be noted that most oil prices in most countries did go up by more than enough to compensate the companies for the higher taxes they were having to pay in the producing countries and for other increased costs, with, of course, favourable effect on oil-company profit margins). In the first place the weather was against the oil companies, for Europe had a series of warmer than average

197

winters and this, of course, played havoc with the expected demand for heating oils. Likewise, demand for industrial fuels was less strong than expected because of the slow-down in the rate of European economic growth. The companies did, of course, recognize the likely temporary nature of these two factors and were thus prepared to 'sit out' their influence.

The third factor, however, was potentially much more dangerous to the companies' strategy in that it threatened to get worse over time. This was Western Europe's newly found large-scale sources of natural gas, which, as the fuel preferred by most customers in a wide variety of end-uses, threatened to lead to stagnation in the growth of oil markets. However, though the factor threatened to get worse, it was, nevertheless, eminently controllable in that most of the gas production in Europe was undertaken by one or other of the international oil companies, which thus had the option – on the basis of some pretext or another – of ensuring that production was held back. This happened in both the Netherlands and the United Kingdom, where the future development plans for the expansion of the energy source were significantly restrained. It was assumed that the worst effects on the profitability of oil markets arising from the growth of the availability of natural gas would be over by 1974, when with average or worse than average winters plus a resumption of industrial growth in the continent, the increased demand for oil could be expected to lead to traumatic results as regards the prices for most products. And with the European market 'under control', with orderly marketing replacing the competitive situation of the twenty years since the mid-1950s, the oil companies could reasonably further assume that markets elsewhere in the world would take care of themselves. The tax and cost increases in oil production etc. could be more than passed on to consumers – with consequentially highly favourable conditions for higher profits.

In brief, the competitive nature of the oil market between the middle 1950s and 1970 has proved to be an aberration in that we have since seen the scene set for a reversion to the more normal oil industry pattern of producer's control over the supply of oil. Until 1973, however, it was intended and accepted that this would once again be under the leadership and direction of the major international oil companies – even though they, in turn, certainly recognized that the greater part of the enhanced profits to be made out of the restrained supply situation would flow to the producing countries, whose interests, the companies thought, would thus be served to the full satisfaction of the countries concerned. Thus, the Teheran and Tripoli and other negotiations in 1971 and 1972 between the companies and the producing countries could be viewed as an attempt by producers – both companies and governments – to achieve a satisfactory *modus vivendi*, within the framework of which somewhat increased profits and greatly increased revenues, respectively, could be achieved. What the companies essentially had in mind was the establishment of orderly oil marketing in place of the chaotic and limited profitability situation of the previous fifteen years.

The strategy depended not only on the producing countries' willingness and ability to work together – a development which was achieved through the increasing effectiveness of O.P.E.C. – but also on their continuing to accept the idea that the major oil companies had an essential role to play in the international oil industry. And this was not only in respect of their role in transporting, refining and marketing the oil, but also as decision-takers on fundamentally important matters such as levels of production and the development of producing capacity in different countries. In this respect the companies interpreted their responsibility as one in which the supply of oil was expanded more or less *pari passu* with the expectation of an average 8 per cent per annum rate of growth in demand.

This grand strategy for an orderly world of oil, though representing a significant enough change in itself from the situation of the previous fifteen years, has, however, now been undermined by the recognition by the producing countries that they do not need to cooperate with the multinational oil companies, and that they can themselves take absolute control over decisions on price levels and on the levels of production. During 1971 and 1972 there were already straws in the wind which indicated that the oil-producing nations were moving towards the assertion of control over supply. These straws came in various forms – expropriation of company assets (for example Libya, Algeria); unilateral decisions to fix maximum rates of offtake (for example Kuwait); the unwillingness of other producers to accept production expansions scheduled by the companies (for example Saudi Arabia); and close national attention to the horse-trading between companies of their oilfield assets in producing countries (for example Abu Dhabi). By mid-1973 one could already predict the steady development of an oil-supply crisis based on the expectation that producing-country control over production and development decisions would gradually become the norm, with unilateral decision taking by the oil-exporting countries replacing the 1970–71 agreed bilateralism between countries and companies.

The renewed outbreak of war between Israel and the Arab states in October 1973 and the latters' decision to use oil as an economic and political weapon in their struggle provided the motivation for the accentuation and acceleration of this process. It was a situation in which two of the major industrialized regions of the world – Western Europe and Japan – had not only allowed themselves to become almost entirely dependent on O.P.E.C. oil for sustaining their economic systems, but had also failed to take any effective counteraction, even in the light of the deteriorating outlook for the viability of their cheap-energy policies as a result of the changed post-1970 oil situation. Western Europe failed even to take a serious look at the option of an indigenous energy policy opened up by the prospects for North Sea oil and gas production on a very large scale indeed.

Thus, within three months we arrived at a state of imbalance between oil supply and potential oil demand which would, without the war and the Arab's use of the oil weapon, have taken perhaps three years to develop. Had we had the three years, then there *might* have been time enough for adjustments to have been made to the structure of demand – though, as pointed out above, there was no evidence between 1971 and 1973 of any European or Japanese realization that radical action was in fact required. By now the required adjustment is harsher and much more difficult – if not impossible – to make without serious problems of unemployment and a supply-generated depression in the Western world, and it calls for a range of decisions whereby life-styles will be changed to a marked and perhaps a hardly acceptable extent.

In the meantime, however, what appears *still* to be necessary is a general acceptance – in Europe and Japan, as well as in the United States, where the government already seems to be ahead of the generally more optimistic consensus of opinion – that the world of oil has undergone a near-instant revolution and that there will be no return to the unlimited supplies of O.P.E.C. oil once the politics of the Arab–Israeli dispute have been settled. The depth of the changes may be measured by the absolute control which the producing nations have now taken over decisions on the level of posted prices, on the amount of oil to be produced and on the choice of customers with which to trade. Whilst as far as the Arab states are concerned there is no doubt, of course, but that recent decisions involve the use of oil as a political weapon in the struggle with Israel, the more fundamental nature of the change of attitude amongst the oil-producing countries is clearly reflected in decisions on oil supply and price by the five non-Arab members of O.P.E.C. Thus, Iran started the procedure of auctioning royalty oil (rather than selling it to the companies at a price related to the posted price) and having secured up to $17·30 per barrel for it – compared with the posted price at the time of $5 per barrel – then led the December 1973 move for a doubling of the officially posted prices – and even then still talked in terms of yet higher prices in the near future.

Ecuador, the newest O.P.E.C. member and a potentially important alternative source to Middle Eastern oil for the United States, unilaterally increased its already high posted price to a level higher than elsewhere in the world. Meanwhile, Nigeria, a member of the Commonwealth and presumably, therefore, an even closer friend of Britain than the Arab states, declined to increase its oil exports to the U.K. and took full advantage of the constrained supply to maximize its revenues. And finally, the first act of the newly elected President of Venezuela was to announce in January 1974 that his country had no interest in increasing oil production beyond the levels already agreed and he has more recently indicated that a cut-back may be more appropriate in order to ensure the continuation of price increases – the type of attitude which Venezuela had propagated for ten years with its fellow O.P.E.C. members before finally getting them to accept the strategy.

For non-Arab, as well as Arab oil exporters, their motivation and

201

ability to keep the oil supply constrained is thus becoming increasingly strong – given, firstly, the way in which they have eliminated the power of the multinational oil companies and turned them simply into their agents for physically implementing those essential decisions over the supply and price of oil which they have already taken; and secondly, given the degree to which their attempts massively to increase their return on each barrel of the limited supply of oil have been successful over the last few months.

As a result O.P.E.C. oil is now very high-cost energy indeed but, behind this incontrovertible fact, lie strongly contrasting interpretations of the strength and motivation of the oil-producing countries – and hence contrasting ideas about the strategies that the industrialized world should follow in response to the very serious situation.

Under the leadership of the United States, most industrial nations appear to be persuaded that the oil-exporting countries are either unwilling or incapable of maintaining their present policy of supply limitation and increasing prices. Thus, it is argued, strategy should be based on a declared set of both shorter-term and longer-term measures which add up to a package designed to undermine the unity of O.P.E.C., so as to get the oil moving in the volumes which the industrialized world has calculated it requires over the next five to seven years and at prices which the rich importing countries can just about afford. This then requires the further assumption that the oil-producing lands can be persuaded to continue to circulate the enormous oil revenues which they will inevitably receive, and so provide the mechanism both for automatic adjustments of balance-of-trade difficulties and the means whereby demand in Western economies can be kept at a high level, with a consequent diminishing of the chances of high unemployment and recession or depression. Thus, there emerged a set of American proposals which, on the one hand, sought to ensure the flow of enough oil at lower prices than have been set since December 1973 (so as to moderate the adverse monetary and general economic impact of the impossible supply-constrained, high-price situation) and, on the other hand, threatened the medium-term undermining of the O.P.E.C. supply control through the development of alternative resources. The strategy thus combined an appeal to the better nature of the O.P.E.C. countries' leaders with a warning of longer-term consequences for them if they failed to heed the plea! Confrontation or nor, it set out a programme of action designed to get power back to where it was thought properly to belong and where it could be rationally and reasonably used; that is, with the Atlantic Powers plus Japan. The final proposal in the United States' package – that is for a continuing dialogue between rich consuming nations and the oil producers – thus seemed, at worst, to be an afterthought, or, at best, an indication of a willingness to talk about the implementation of an already determined strategy. The very fact of the existence of a package of proposals which pre-established a preferred strategy, and which, by implication, all but eliminated all other possible strategies, hardly seemed an approach likely to be acceptable to the O.P.E.C. countries!

France interpreted the situation differently. And did her attitude really have no other behind-the-scene supporters – given the fact that Britain, Germany, Italy and Japan, amongst others, had been acting in much the same way, by making special supply arrangements with particular O.P.E.C. countries? This suggests that these other countries were, at best, schizophrenic in their views and, at worst, devious, in the light of the inconsistency involved in their also supporting the U.S.A., which certainly objected to such 'barter' deals, seeing that they undermined the basis on which their strategy was based!

For France – and possibly others – the required strategy thus started from an acceptance of the irreversibility of what had happened. Accept the inevitable they argued, and then aim at securing a flow of oil, the quantity of which will be guaranteed (thus making national planning much easier) and the prices of which will reflect what terms could be obtained at the time, rather than the still higher ones which would undoubtedly be sought later. And, in so securing the required flow of oil, also achieve guaranteed outlets for advanced technological hardware (which might otherwise find itself without sufficient purchasers) and, furthermore, develop the necessary *rapprochement* with the relatively unsophisticated O.P.E.C. producing countries and win them over by kindness and help!

It must be remembered, however, that 'special arrangements' in the oil world are by no means new and, in particular, that France previously pursued such a policy in the period following the independence of Algeria, for a combination of political and economic reasons. The background to this French approach over the last ten years, and the results achieved, is thus a valid precedent – not only because of the international implications arising from the search for special relations, but also because of the implications that any oil eventually imported as a result of the establishment of special relations has to be found a market, thus generating a requirement for a government-controlled refining and marketing policy.

The historical reasons for the development of French policy towards oil lie beyond the requirements of this chapter except to point out, as shown already in Chapter 8, that it emerged in part out of the disconcerting effect, in the 1930s and the early post-war years, of French exclusion from an interest in the important oil-producing areas of the Middle East – a region of long-standing concern to France – as a result of the very powerfully backed diplomacy of Britain and the United States. In French eyes, the international oil industry developed into something which was little short of an Anglo-American conspiracy.

France's initial search for independence from this 'conspiracy' lay, naturally, in the state-sponsored and state-financed exploration in overseas parts of the Union, most notably Algeria. Here, however, really significant success in the search for oil pre-dated Algerian independence by only a few years, so frustrating the efforts to achieve independence in oil.[1] The negotiation of Algeria's independence was, of course, partly concerned with agreement over the country's oil resources, and though France's success in eventually negotiating a privileged position with respect to oil exploration and exploitation was interpreted as an indication of her ability to secure a special relationship at the expense of the Anglo-Americans, one can, with hindsight, see that it was really Algeria rather than France which

1. Ironically, the main benefits of France's large expenditures on oil exploration in North Africa probably flowed to the Anglo-American companies, given the incentive provided by Algerian discoveries for them to move quickly into neighbouring Libya to confirm that the North Africa oil province extended out of the area of French influence. Libya soon proved to be a more prolific oil-producing country!

needed such a relationship at that time. Algeria, in its immediate post-independence period, was, in fact, neither politically nor economically attractive to the international oil companies. At that time, the companies had access to more oil than they knew what to do with, as a result of a decade of great exploratory successes in the 1950s, from countries which offered greater stability and security than did Algeria. Thus, any interest they might have had in Algeria would have given that country's oil low priority indeed for development, as compared with possibilities in other parts of the world. Algeria's preferred strategy therefore lay in its ability to maintain its oil as franc-zone oil and so achieve guaranteed entry to the French market, where the system of controls over refining and marketing in general – and the controls over the activities of the international companies in particular – meant that opportunities enough would be created for selling Algerian oil at prices well above the going market rate of the period. Moreover, as the international companies operating in France would have to use a certain percentage of Algerian oil, an incentive would be created for them to invest in Algerian oil resources.

Thus, the special relationship between France and Algeria was achieved at the expense only in part of the international oil companies. As a result of it they certainly lost opportunities they would otherwise have had for moving larger quantities of their own lower-cost crudes from fields in other parts of the world to France – and thus they lost the profits which they could have earned on such oil-supply arrangements. It is, however, conceivable that this loss of profits could have been offset in large part, or even entirely, by the fact that the generous refining and marketing profit margins built into the French-controlled system at that time enabled them to make more profit by handling Algerian crude in France than they could have made in a freer market situation using their own crude oils, given the way in which intensive competition between an increasing number of suppliers elsewhere in Western Europe had, by that time, brought the price levels of most products down to lower levels than the guaranteed prices in France.

In larger part the success of the special relationship between France and Algeria depended on France's and French consumers' willing-

205

ness to pay more for oil supplies than would have been necessary in the absence of the relationship. This willingness derived, apart from the 'anti-conspiracy' consideration, from the search for security of oil supply which the link between France and Algerian oil was supposed to produce. Even this, however, turned out to be somewhat illusory, for, once the economics and politics of the international oil system changed, Algeria proved to have little or no compunction, first, in unilaterally changing the terms of the special agreement – to make the oil even more expensive to France – and then in essentially revoking it by not only demanding a price in excess of that which even France was prepared to pay, but also requiring the withdrawal of the French oil companies through whose activities the physical flow of oil had largely been maintained – not only from Algeria to France but to other parts of the world as well. Thus, in spite of the special relationships, the French oil companies in Algeria managed to survive only a little longer than the non-French companies which had either withdrawn or been expelled in the previous two or three years. French or non-French made little difference in a situation in which Algeria wanted to go it alone and felt that world oil politics and economics had so developed to make this possible.

In the meantime the idea of special relationships as the bases for policies towards oil had been further extended by France. Politically this followed from the *rapprochement* with the Arab world after the Middle East war in 1967. (Alternatively, the oil policy can, of course, be viewed as an inherent part of the general agreement with the Arab nations or, even, as one of the main motivations for seeking the *rapprochement*, given that difficulties with Algeria were already become apparent by 1967.) In practical terms the special-relationship policy required the creation of a strong, entirely state-owned French oil company. Out of this policy emerged E.R.A.P. (based initially on the pre-existing smaller state oil entities), which was to accept the responsibility for promoting French interests in as many oil-producing, or potentially oil-producing, countries as could be persuaded of the validity of a special relationship with France. This persuasion was not unsuccessful, and E.R.A.P. quickly became a concessionaire (or a contractor on behalf of a local oil state company) in Iran, Iraq, Saudi-Arabia, Libya and so on, as the French aim of having French companies produce an amount of oil at least equal to the total consumption of oil in France was vigorously pursued. The special relationship emerged, in part, of course, out of France's arguments that its exploitation of another country's resources was qualitatively different from that of the Anglo-Americans. But it was due in much larger part to E.R.A.P.'s general willingness to pay more than the competition for the right to seek oil and, having found it, to produce it under conditions of agreement with the host country which inevitably made the tax-paid cost of the oil almost inevitably higher than that for alternative supplies of oil – an identical procedure, of course, to that which had previously been adopted in France's relationships with Algeria.

In many cases the exploration and development programmes continue to proceed as planned, with French expenditure on exploration for oil, which amounted to about $300 million in 1965, expected to be at least double this amount by 1975. However, not even the considerable political and economic attractions of the special relationships have been sufficient to achieve the ends which France sought in Iraq, which, preceding even Algeria, was the first Arab country to show that it perhaps did not, or could not, differentiate between the economic exploitation of its resources by France on the one hand and other capitalist nations on the other! The setback to French policy aims arose in 1968, when Iraq did not accept French proposals for the exploitation of the North Rumaila oilfield, which had been expropriated from the Iraq Petroleum Company a couple of years earlier, but preferred instead to go it alone with help from the communist world – a pattern to be repeated fairly soon after, as pointed out above, in the case of Algeria.

There is thus good cause to suggest that the implementation of a special-relationship oil policy, even within the framework of a very deliberate general foreign policy orientated to achieving such an aim, is not particularly easy and straightforward. This is especially so in a situation in which the countries with which the relationship is sought are not necessarily only concerned with getting the best possible economic return from their oil or, and even more frustratingly, with pursuing a policy which is conditioned by the same logic and consistency as that of the seeker of the relationship. This is seen clearly in the case of Iraq, where the rejection of the French proposal to develop North Rumaila was turned down in favour of letting the Iraq National Oil Company do the work itself, in a situation in which there was little doubt that I.N.O.C. had neither the technical nor the financial capabilities at that time of undertaking the field's development. In this case the offer of assistance by the Soviet Union no doubt turned Iraq away from a special relationship with France to an even more special relationship with the U.S.S.R. as part of the new alliance between the Soviet Union and Arab countries in the post-1967 Middle East war period.

We must thus recognize the ability and willingness of the oil-producing countries unilaterally to change the terms of agreed special relationships, when they find themselves in a stronger bargaining position (either as a result of alternative, preferred offers, as in the case of Iraq, or simply because their oil has achieved a higher value, as in the case of Algeria), as a fundamental barrier to the success of such a strategy by oil-consuming countries, in that it eliminates the essential rationale of the policy – that of ensuring a high degree of security of oil supply. French experience to date is not a particularly happy precedent on the basis of which to persuade the rest of Europe that a special-relationship strategy is necessarily going to be of much help in the medium- to longer-term search for greater security over energy supplies. This is especially so as Europe as a whole, or even particular parts of it (such as the E.E.C.), has much less political justification than France for thinking that there are any very good reasons why oil-producing countries should ever consider the idea of a special relationship, except as a short-term expedient on their part to secure a greater share of the profits to be made out of oil production at present prices, or as a means of pushing prices to higher levels so that the opportunity for the producing country to make profits can be significantly improved.

The producing countries' position in the 1974 search by consuming countries for special relationships with them is, in fact, even stronger than this argument suggests, for there is little similarity with the situation in international oil as at the time when French policy was first evolved. When France was seeking its special relationships there was, firstly, a weak international oil market which gave producers an incentive to consider alternative arrangements for marketing their oil; and, secondly, there was not much by way of competition from alternative offers, putting France in a buyer's market for such deals. By the beginning of 1974 – and for the next half-decade or so – the producers have established a controlled supply of crude oil such that there will be competition for buying 'special arrangements', so establishing a seller's market in the commodity and minimizing the chances of achieving security-of-supply arrangements from the policy.

There is also another important consideration relating to special-relationships policies. This is the necessary effect of the results of such relationships on national energy policies. For, as already pointed out, the achievement of a tied source of crude oil in large quantities, with the intention of making it – at least on the part of the buyer – a more or less permanent arrangement, implies a domestic energy policy which assures refining capacity for the crude oil concerned and markets for its products in competition both with other oil and with other energy sources. In France this has meant the continuation, and the strengthening from time to time, of the long-established system for controlling the importing, refining and distribution of oil. The French companies largely responsible for implementing the special relationship in terms of the flow of oil have had to have certain shares of the domestic market reserved for them. Other companies with refining capacity in France have had to accept 'special-relationship' oil as part of their throughput – all necessarily leading to a supervised and ordered marketing system in which 'competition has been sluggish at best and the government has kept prices high' (Adelman).

Now there is, of course, nothing inherently unreasonable or necessarily unacceptable about this situation – providing one accepts the basic underlying economic and political organization philosophy that it implies. One should note, moreover, that in a period of rising oil prices on the world oil market, as a result of the control over supply now exercised by the producing countries and companies, there is no reason why such a system should give consumer prices any higher than those in the non-ordered and non-government-controlled marketing system, and it may well, over a longer period of time, give generally lower prices.[1] At a European level, however, the philosophy of E.E.C. policy (even amongst the 'Six' and now even more so among the 'Nine', with Britain's weight thrown in in favour of competition) remains orientated towards the idea of competition in the market place as far as energy is concerned. One must, however, observe that this stands in danger of becoming even more of a façade than it has so far been (given earlier protection for particular fuels). For the oil companies responsible for producing and selling most of Europe's energy are, in fact, collaborating with each other internationally in order to keep supply sufficiently below potential demand (at a given price level) so as to increase prices and achieve higher rates of profitability on their activities. However, it is at least possible to maintain the façade of competition in the market place if nothing is done to change the fundamentals of Europe's oil-supply position, whereas the establishment of special relationships in the French style necessarily implies the extension of the French system of organization of the domestic oil sector to the rest of Europe – and this could cause as serious disagreements as have had to be faced over the evolution of a European agricultural policy.

Thus, given the realities of the contemporary world oil situation and of European-level philosophy towards the energy sector, the idea and implications of special relationships between oil-consuming countries or regions and oil-producing countries or regions (aiming, in the short term, to supplement and, in the longer term, to replace the organizational framework by which Europe's oil has been provided to date largely by the international oil companies) do not appear to be particularly valuable or relevant to the problems of securing certain access to oil in the medium to longer term at prices which have any relationship whatsoever to the cost at which the oil can be produced plus even generous payments to the governments of the producing countries.

This, as we write at the beginning of March 1974, neither the American-sponsored strategy, based on a hoped-for disintegration

1. Witness the way in which the differentials between traditionally higher oil-product prices in France and the lower prices in competitive markets like Western Germany have gradually been eliminated or have disappeared altogether in the period since 1971.

of the O.P.E.C. cartel, nor the French strategy, requiring successful long-term special relationships with the existing important oil-producing and exporting countries, would appear to be entirely firmly based and/or appropriate. On the one hand, the French view of the inherent strength and stability of the O.P.E.C. cartel seems to stand up to much closer examination than the alternative hopes of the rest of the Western nations for an early break-up of the oil-supply system. Though the differences, in other fields of endeavour and interest, amongst the O.P.E.C. countries are clear to see, it is difficult to find any real motivation why any one exporting country should try to undermine the success of the cartel. Oil producers, both rich and poor in terms of financial resources, and large and small in terms of their physical potential to produce oil, could hardly do better individually than they are doing collectively, for they can all get as much or as little money as they want by modest adjustments to their volumes of production and/or by large adjustments to their prices. Neither pleas nor threats from the Western world (unless backed by the ultimate threat of the use of military forces) can easily alter this situation for one or more of them – unless King Feisal can be persuaded that it is his duty to save the civilization of the Christian world!

Stranger things have perhaps happened in history – but not very often. Or should he be expected to save the Western world's economic system in his own interests? This presupposes that he and his fellow oil producers consider that their interests are generally identifiable with those of the West. But there seems to be no justification for such a view, as the world emerges from a long period of 300 years in which the West has kept its interests very much to itself! And if the West's 'threats' to make itself self-sufficient in energy as soon as possible are successfully carried through, is the result really an adverse one for the O.P.E.C. countries? By then (the early 1980s at the earliest) they will have accumulated enough funds to be able to live off the interest, and so have a minimal interest in selling oil anyway – as, indeed, has been clearly stated time after time by the other main personality involved, the Shah of Iran, who expects his country to have a whole set of non-oil interests by the 1980s. However, success for this American-sponsored strategy will, at least, ensure the Western world of its required flow of energy by the 1980s. This is an important enough aim in itself – if the industrialized world can only survive the next seven years!

But if the French are probably right in their evaluation of the inherent strength of the O.P.E.C. system, then they are undoubtedly wrong in their reaction to it, in that each additional step taken by France (and others) to barter goods for oil strengthens the hand of the cartel without really doing anything to ensure a flow of oil (given the continuing ability and the possible motivation of the producers to reduce production at will and, moreover, their further ability to turn off the need for further technological help at any moment in time). At the same time the French attitude diverts our attention – and our resources – away from the immediate and pressing need to stimulate and accelerate the production of indigenous (or other alternative) energy sources. Both psychologically and in physical terms the French strategy inevitably undermines our efforts in this direction.

An attempt to re-establish a world in which oil power is shared would seem to lie in an appropriate combination of elements from the two conflicting sets of views and a required third element to complete the strategic response of the oil-consuming world. The so-far omitted third element is the increasingly urgent need for the industrialized world to accept the idea of an austerity economy for as far ahead as can be currently seen. During this time it must aim at using as little O.P.E.C. oil as it possibly can and, moreover, probably allow it to be physically secured through the well-tried systems of the international oil companies which, of course, retain their competence and expertise in the transportation and distribution of the oil and which now, moreover, almost have the appearance of being disinterested parties in this battle of strategies! This alternative policy certainly offers no guarantee of security – except that inherent degree of security which emerges out of a sharing of the risks between as many nations as possible – but neither do the American nor the French policies! It also requires a wartime-like system for the allocation of whatever oil becomes available to the essential sectors of our societies and for the production of goods and services which will accelerate the production of our alternative energy sources. An unpleasant prospect certainly, but not an impossible approach. With passing months and years, certainly it is a policy which will bring us steadily closer to a situation in which we can revert to more normal patterns of activity – in part based upon the use of alternative energy resources including the expected greatly increased amounts of indigenous oil and gas.

A controlled oil demand, in other words – through rationing and other non-pricing allocatory procedures as well as through appropriate uses of the pricing mechanism – is a positively desirable energy strategy for Western Europe, rather than simply a tactical response to a crisis (though it may also be the latter in the very short term). Given this view, the recent debate in most European countries on the need for the rationing of petrol and other products becomes inappropriate and even irresponsible. The real question is not whether there are enough products in stock – or the possibility of making enough products from crude-oil supplies expected – to make rationing unnecessary, but, rather, how much the demand for these oil products can be reduced, without serious economic effects, below the pre-1973 level both now and for a period of years ahead, in order to eliminate the pressure of demand on the controlled supply.

Such a strategy obviously means inconvenience – if not real hardship – and it just as obviously means important changes in the life-styles to which affluent Western consumers have become accustomed. The most notable of these perhaps is the elimination of the motor-car as a status symbol, and its relegation to a usually convenient, and sometimes even a socially acceptable, means of transport, as even 'business users' are restricted to a petrol allowance related to the most economical vehicles and to speeds which persuade them to use alternative means of transport for all but the shortest and the most inconvenient journeys. The journey to and from work in the one man/one car traditional way also becomes the allowed exception (for good and sufficient reasons) rather than the general rule. In brief, the ownership of particular types of cars and their use has to be justified by factors other than the ability of an owner – or his employer – to pay for it and for the petrol it uses – even at £1 per gallon!

As with passenger transport, so with freight movement. Freedom of choice to utilize energy-intensive trucks or even aircraft must be restricted in order to ensure the re-allocation of freight transportation to less energy-intensive rail and water modes. And again this implies intervention by means other than the price of fuel (perhaps by regulatory procedures or by differential rates of taxation on the transport modes) and the need to start restructuring the transport sector of our economies.

And similarly in other uses of energy. Households might be given the 'right' to consume a certain quantum of fuel and/or electricity (with the allocation related to family size, location, age of house and other factors) at 'reasonable' prices (say, at prices related closely to those to which we have become used in recent years). Consumption above the allocated level, however, might well be regarded as a 'luxurious' use of energy and be appropriately penally priced, so introducing an effective constraint on demand.

For industry and commerce one must envisage a requirement in which each enterprise is required to post and, if necessary, to justify its 'energy budget' so as to enable the community to judge the degree to which efficiency in energy use is being achieved. And for the electricity authorities, the most significant wasters of primary energy, there must be a requirement for the immediate replanning and restructuring of the supply and distribution system, so that a much larger part of the 70 per cent losses of primary energy input involved in the centralized production of electricity can be recovered for commercial and residential heating and for industrial steam raising.

All this adds up to a very significant – and a quite deliberate – restraint on freedom of consumer choice over energy use in the strategic interests of a continent much too heavily dependent on foreign oil. Such a diminishing of the freedom of choice will be generally offensive in itself; it also involves an extension of bureaucracy and implies significant changes in values which society has created over the last generation in particular. It may thus be triply unacceptable. But the alternative of continued dependence on high cost and still uncertain supplies of oil from overseas – with the possibility of chaos being externally generated in our society at any moment in time – is surely more unacceptable. And perhaps we can bear in mind that we have for long accepted a precedent for such a controlled approach to the use of a scarce commodity, that is, control over the use of the land – something which many Western societies have achieved, or sought to achieve, by means other than the use of the pricing mechanism alone. This aim has also been justified in terms of ensuring that the interests of society as a whole, rather than just parts of it, are taken into consideration.

In this analysis of the fundamentals of the new world oil-power situation we do, of course, implicitly recognize the valid element in the French view – that of the inherent strength of the new structure of the international oil system as it has emerged from the traumatic events of the four years since 1970. By ceasing to worry exclusively about how to come to terms with it and by leaving the international oil companies to do their best to supply enough oil to keep our economies going, albeit at the expense of the Western world's conspicuous consumption, the period of austerity will probably turn out to be much shorter than expected. For the action will, in itself, serve to undermine the strength and unity of O.P.E.C., as the demand for all oil moving outside the traditional supply system is eliminated and as the companies quickly regain some element of choice in deciding which countries' oil to buy.

On the other hand, the strategy explicitly recognizes the validity of the U.S. view on the need to achieve self-sufficiency in energy as soon as possible and by ensuring that we turn all our attention and all our efforts in that direction will mean that we reach our objective sooner rather than later. Over the last fifteen years Europe has come to accept the idea of an open energy economy, in which cheaper, readily available supplies of foreign oil rapidly achieved the dominant role, to the detriment even of known indigenous energy resources. This is especially true of coal, which, though physically plentiful, has remained unused as hundreds of coal mines in Europe have closed down over the period. It is also true of the hydro-electricity potential which has not been developed, and even of small, but nevertheless useful, resources of oil and gas which have been left unexploited. Europe has, in fact, been irresponsible towards its resources and has left its 'talents' unused – and been noticeably led astray in this respect by the persuasion of the international oil companies, with their earlier interests in maximizing sales of foreign-produced oil to Western Europe.

Nations thus became convinced that Western Europe either could not, or should not, pursue an autarkic energy policy – in marked contrast with both the United States and the Soviet Union, where import minimization has generally been a declared objective of national policies. And even when a quite modest exploration effort in northwest Europe's off-shore waters demonstrated an availability of tremendous resources of both oil and gas, Europe still pretended that they would not, or need not, make any essential difference to the situation. But if complacency about the development of the energy economy was understandable – even if inappropriate – whilst the international oil system apparently remained unchanged, there is certainly no longer any excuse for a continuing failure to investigate the option of an autarkic energy policy.

The motivation for a European project 'Energy Independence 1985' (compared with the U.S.A.'s 'Project Energy Independence 1980') lies in the tremendous burden of cost and uncertainty which continued reliance on imported oil places on the European economy. On the other hand, the opportunities for even being able to consider the idea of self-sufficiency in energy emerge, firstly, out of the constrained demand policy – as just suggested – and, secondly, from the potential for oil and gas production from the North Sea basin.

Fortunately, indeed for Western Europe the medium- to longer-term supply position can now be guaranteed out of the potential for oil and gas production which is currently under development within Western Europe itself and the rapid and systematic development of which should now, in fact, be forming the cornerstone of Europe's policy towards the industry. In the chapter on Western Europe (Chapter 5) indications are given of the medium-term potential and a map (Map 7) illustrates the basis of discoveries etc. on which oil and gas production can be rapidly developed.

On the basis of the more than twenty or more giant oil and gas fields and at least sixty other significant finds of oil and gas already made, plus very modest extrapolation of continuing success in finding new fields, as a result of what is now becoming the world's most intensive ever exploration effort, the 1980 and 1985 production levels for oil and gas in Western Europe, as shown in the 'alternative estimates' columns in Figure 4, can even now be confidently predicted as being achievable from the resource base and technical standpoints. Neither is there any doubt but that the quite limited amount of investment capital required for the resources' exploitation will be forthcoming. (It is limited in relation to what Western Europe has been used to investing each year in its energy sector and also limited in relation to what we shall have to spend on importing O.P.E.C. oil at an average delivered price which now seems likely to be nearer $20 per barrel than even $15.)

Figure 4. Conventional[1] and Alternative[2] Views on Europe's Energy Supply to 1985

	1973 Approximate Actual Use		1980 Estimates Conventional		Alternative		1985 Estimates Conventional		Alternative	
	mmtce[3]	%[4]	mmtce	%	mmtce	%	mmtce	%	mmtce	%
Total energy	1,550	100	2,250	100	1,900	100	2,850	100	2.350	100
Oil-Total	970	63	1,500	66	835	43	1,825	64	840	36
(i) Indigenous	30	2	50	2	500	26	195	7	640	27
(ii) Imported	940	61	1,450	64	335	17	1,630	57	200	9
Gas-Total	135	9	265	12	575	30	385	14	790	34
(i) Indigenous	125	8	215	10	500	26	300	11	640	27
(II) Imported	10	1	50	2	75	4	85	3	150	6
Coal-Total	400	26	280	12	310	16	310	11	350	15
(i) Indigenous	360	23	205	9	230	12	220	8	250	11
(ii) Imported	40	3	75	3	80	4	90	3	100	4
Primary Electricity	45	3	210	10	180	9	330	12	370	15
Total Indigenous	560	36	680	31	1,410	74	1,045	37	1,900	81
Total Imported	990	64	1,570	69	490	26	1,805	63	450	19

1. Based on O.E.C.D., E.E.C. and various national estimates of future energy supply and demand as published in 1972.
2. The author's own alternative estimates assuming a restrained rate of growth of energy demand and increased indigenous production of oil and gas.
3. Millions of metric tons of coal equivalent.
4. Percentages do not always add to 100 because of 'rounding off'.

The only real doubt over the development of the potential lies in the seeming continuing indifference by the nations of Western Europe to work for the achievement of the political agreements essential for ensuring maximum levels of production as quickly as possible. This applies even within the framework of the E.E.C., particularly as regards Dutch gas and British oil, and even more so in the continuing apparent lack of urgency over the need to mend the political fences between the Community and Norway which, by 1985, could have enough oil production surplus to its own requirements to provide the total needs of Denmark, Sweden, Germany and much of the Benelux countries as well!

However, in spite of the present lack of political will in Western Europe for an active and collective indigenous energy policy, one perhaps still remains optimistic that a further worsening of the international oil-supply situation will eventually produce a European-wide motivation for agreement on the rapid exploitation of indigenous oil and gas reserves. How great the reward could be for such a policy is shown in the 'alternative estimates' columns of the table – for which estimates there is also an assumption that the austerity-type economy described above will also be brought in, leading to a 15 per cent reduction in the expected rate of energy use in 1980 (1,900 instead of 2,250 mmtce) and a 17·5 per cent reduction by 1985 (2,350 instead of 2,850 mmtce). Essentially one contrasts the 37 to 63 per cent relationship between indigenous and imported shares of the energy market in 1973, and the 'conventional' expectation that even this adverse position will worsen still further, with the alternative possibility which shows a rapidly declining degree of dependence on imported energy to give over 80 per cent self-sufficiency in 1985. What this implies in terms of oil imports is the difference between their conventionally expected 65 per cent increase from 1973 to 1985 and the alternative estimate of their 80 per cent decrease over the same period. By 1985 Western Europe's total need for oil imports would be a mere 135 million tons (=200 mmtce) instead of the conventionally expected more than 1,000 million tons – or even the 625 million tons or so per annum in the period before the oil crisis!

Beyond 1985 it is more difficult to be certain about the options, but it can be said even now that there are very good chances indeed that Western Europe's ability to produce indigenous oil and gas will continue to increase ahead of the rate of increase of the demand for energy for *at least* the rest of this century. A computer-based simulation of the future development of the North Sea oil and gas

Map 10. Western Europe – Potential Offshore Areas for Oil and Gas Production

NORTH SEA	Offshore areas where extensive oil and/or gas deposits have been located and which are under active development.
Irish Sea	Offshore areas where preliminary exploratory work has been undertaken and where drilling will soon start with high expectations of success.
N.W. Spain	Other interesting offshore areas with relatively shallow water where there are geological expectations of oil and gas structures and where exploration will begin before 1980.

province[1] shows, even on the basis of a limited twenty-year period of continuing discoveries, that oil and gas production will continue to build up into the middle 1990s, with the range of possible peak production lying between 650 and 850 million tons of oil per annum – or at least as much oil as the continent is likely to need! Even this, however, does not exhaust the potential availability of European oil and gas, given that there are very much larger regions of the continent's off-shore shelf which still remain to be explored. The number and extent of the potential areas for oil and gas production are shown on Map 10. Over the coming decade these regions will be successively opened up by new exploration efforts, and there is a very low probability indeed that none of them will contain large quantities of oil and gas. Europe will thus be able to sustain, over a very long period indeed, its now certain medium-term ability to achieve self-sufficiency or near self-sufficiency in its oil requirements. It is within the context of this highly favourable outlook, once the very difficult period up to about 1980 is past, that appropriate political and economic decisions are required for achieving not only a continental-wide integrated oil system, but also a pricing system for energy in Europe related to the cost of producing indigenous energy rather than to the monopolistically determined price of internationally traded oil. This would ensure that Western Europe is not too seriously disadvantaged compared with the United States, where the domestic economy has already been protected from the international escalation of oil prices and where there remains little doubt that the country will now see self-sufficiency in energy as one of the cornerstones of its economic policy for the foreseeable future.

But these very important Western European oil discoveries are not the only ones which could be exploited and so help to undermine the present dominant role of the O.P.E.C. countries. Every major oil-importing country is taking a new look at the possibility of indigenous oil and natural-gas occurrences, particularly those

1. This model has been developed in the Economic Geography Institute of Erasmus University, Rotterdam, from where anyone interested may obtain a full description of it and a copy of a paper setting out the implications of the development.

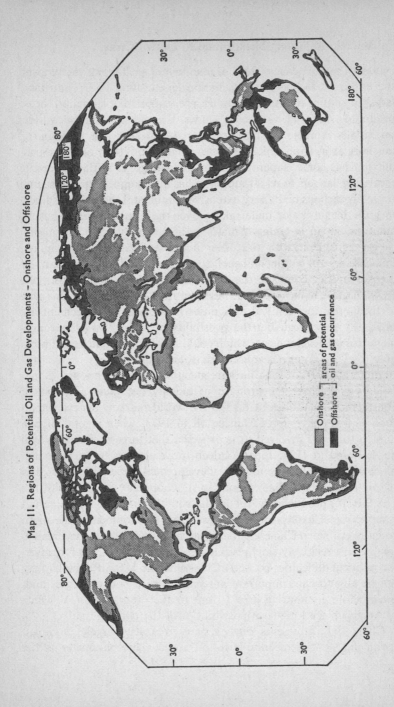

Map II. Regions of Potential Oil and Gas Developments – Onshore and Offshore

Onshore ⎤ areas of potential
Offshore ⎦ oil and gas occurrence

countries with extensive areas of continental shelf from which, given the improved technology of off-shore exploration and production, large quantities of hydrocarbons are expected eventually to be produced. As Map 11 clearly shows, the non-communist world's potentially valuable off-shore areas are several times larger than the on-shore areas from which, to date, almost all of the world's oil production has come. Japan falls into this category. With the rapidly escalating dangers to its oil supply, it has now stepped up the search for hydrocarbons on its very extensive continental shelf. This is likely to grow into a major undertaking over the next five years, but, in addition, Japan is taking a major political initiative in attempting to get agreement with the other countries which border on the immense area of continental shelf to the south and west of Japan. As these countries comprise the two Koreas (North and South), the Republic of China, Formosa and even the Soviet Union some way to the north, the political difficulties in the way of agreement are obviously very great, but the possibility of at least *ad hoc* arrangements for oil development, which could be of great economic importance to all the countries concerned, is far from remote.

Quite apart from such an agreement with its neighbours, China holds out considerable promise of quickly becoming a source of considerable quantities of oil for the world market. In fact, Japan took its first deliveries of Chinese oil in 1973, when a total of one million tons was involved. It is expected that three million tons will be delivered in 1974. Japan, indeed, now appears to be attaching more importance to the ultimate development of very large supplies of oil from China than it does to its cooperative efforts with the U.S.S.R. for producing oil for Japan from the known Soviet Siberian reserves (see Chapter 6 for details of this development). The more recently evaluated Chinese possibilities may, in fact, provide a reason for Japan's relatively slow response to the Soviet project for, given the political difficulties between China and the U.S.S.R., Japan may not be able to have important agreements with both countries and, thus, before committing itself to one or the other, obviously wants to weigh up the long-term possibilities of the two alternatives.

China thus represents one element in a still largely unknown parameter on the medium-term oil scene. This parameter is the degree to which oil production for export can be achieved from countries which are unlikely to want to join the O.P.E.C. cartel and whose attitudes to the pricing and development of their oil and gas resources will be very different from those of the member countries of the producers' club. Other countries involved are Australia and Canada, where, as in China, vast potentially oil-rich areas have hardly yet been tested. Already, however, major recent discoveries in Australia suggest that it could become a net oil exporter by 1975 (as well as a certain exporter of natural gas in a liquefied form) and some reports from Eastern and North Canada suggest that not only do the solutions to the United States' future needs for imported oil lie with its northern neighbour, but that Canada will also have resources available sufficient to sustain an important export trade to Western Europe and/or Japan in the 1980s and the 1990s.

In brief, the medium- to longer-term outlook for the build-up of significant oil-production potential, not only in areas which are large oil users but also in areas which could become important new oil exporters, is probably brighter now than they have been at any time in the whole post-1945 period of dependence of the energy-using world on the oil reserves of the Middle Eastern and one or two other countries. These potentials are important in two respects. Firstly, they undermine the validity of the spectre of a physical shortage of oil in relation to the world's increased needs in the last fifteen years or so of the present century. This spectre has recently become an important talking point for 'futurologists' and has even been gaining some influence in governments' attitudes towards energy policies (as, for example, in the Dutch attitude towards the rate of depletion of the Groningen gas field, from which production has been limited so as to ensure gas supplies for domestic consumers in the late 1990s). However, forecasts based on oil and gas reserves already known and those which can be confidently extrapolated from the known reserves plus the high degree of confidence one can have in finding new reserves from areas, such as those mentioned above, which remain to be explored, show that there need be no physical shortage of oil in the foreseeable future, especially if we take a little more care in our patterns of oil use. This implies, as previously indicated, the introduction of transportation policies which pay more attention to the efficiency with which energy is used, the initiation of energy budgeting for all major development projects so that contrasts in the energy requirements of alternative methods of achieving a given aim can be clearly revealed and taken into consideration in the final decision and, finally, a serious investigation into ways and means of eliminating the current wastage of some 70 per cent of the energy input that is involved in the production of electricity in conventional power stations. Thus will it be possible for a conventional energy economy, based largely on oil and natural gas, to see the world's development through at least until the second quarter of the twenty-first century. By then we can remain confident that technological developments will have made clean solar and fusion energy commercially possible as substitutes for conventional energy – without having to bother in the meantime with the massive development of what appears to be relatively unsafe and potentially radioactively dirty nuclear power.

Secondly, the potential development of alternative oil supplies diminish the medium-term effectiveness and validity of the economic and political threats to the oil-consuming nations which we currently face as a result of the concentration of proven oil reserves in a handful of countries and the ability of these few countries working together to control the price at which their oil is made available to the oil-consuming world. Given the rapid build-up in these countries' per-barrel revenues from oil from under $1 in 1971 to between $7 and $10 by the beginning of 1974 and their expectation that they will continue to rise much faster than the rate of inflation, there can be no doubt that the alternative resources will be available at costs well below the prices at which the traditional producers are prepared to market their oil. This is true in spite of the fact that the alternative oils will almost always necessarily be much more expensive to produce in a physical sense, particularly those from off-shore areas such as the North Sea, where exploration and development costs are between five and ten times greater than in traditional oil-producing areas. (Note, however, that this involves a contrast between per-barrel production costs of 10–20 U.S. cents on the one hand with $1 to $1·50, on the other, so that even the latter remains very small indeed compared with the per-barrel taxes now expected by the O.P.E.C. countries.)

Here we would hypothesize that the oligopoly will thus not be maintainable beyond the end of the present decade, because the increasingly large availability of new oil and gas resources will undermine the expected growth of the market for the oligopolists' oil and thus unstabilize the system. Western Europe's dependence on O.P.E.C. countries will start to decline by the second half of the 1970s as a result of oil and gas from the North Sea and the peak of the United States' requirement from O.P.E.C. has probably already been passed as a result, firstly, of the Arab embargo on oil to the U.S.A. in 1973–4 and, secondly, as a result of both domestic and Canadian energy supply developments. With the pressure of demand on the O.P.E.C. producers thus eliminated, and a consequential reduction in their abilities to secure revenues, the oligopolistic front will break as one or more of the producers seeks to maintain expected revenues by selling additional quantities of oil at reduced prices, so introducing a major element of instability into the controlled supply situation and leading, in the final analysis, to the re-establishment of the buyers' market in oil such as existed in the period between 1957 and 1971.

It is only in relation to this possible undermining of the oligopoly that there seems much hope for the oil-importing nations of the developing world, for which, of course, the fundamental change in the international oil system since 1970 has also eliminated their opportunity to buy cheap crude oil. Thus, from the earlier price levels of as little as $1·50 per barrel at which oil was bought by countries like Brazil and Uruguay in the 1960s, the developing nations now have to face up to the difficulties involved in importing most of their essential supplies of energy at prices which are already at least five times that level and which seem likely to rise to eight, or even ten, times the old level, as old contracts run out and the countries concerned have to bid for new supplies on the highly competitive open market.

This development very obviously spells immediate and serious dangers for the economies of such nations, with an inevitable worsening of their already generally very adverse balance-of-payments position. It is equally obvious that the international oil companies cannot, or will not, do much to help, as their search for profit maximization will not persuade them to sell oil more cheaply to a particular country just because it is poor and industrializing. Nor is there any sign as yet that the oil-producing nations are prepared to help as directly as they could by selling oil to poor countries at less than the oligopolistically determined price. Their alternative offers of loans at low rates of interest – such as that extended to African importing nations by the Arab producers – will certainly enable the importers to buy the expensive oil, but only at the cost of increasing their foreign indebtedness on a commodity which will only indirectly and after some years improve their export earning abilities.

Unfortunately most of the developing nations have chosen to adopt Western-style patterns of industrial and societal organization – with their well-known lack of attention to questions of efficiency in energy use. Road transport has been preferred over less energy-intensive rail and water transport and national transportation systems have been orientated towards road construction – even in cases where railways pre-existed. They have thus often been 'competed' out of existence. Similarly, city transport has been orientated towards motor cars and urban motorways with the private car elevated to a significant status symbol and the car-producing industry to a leading-sector role in the economy – with consequential rapidly rising petrol consumption and poorly developed mass-transit facilities. Electricity systems have also been built around large central and highly inefficient thermal power stations – so raising the demand for fuel oil – instead of being orientated towards more efficient on-site, total energy systems, making more effective use of each unit of energy input. And many developing countries' societies, with their inbuilt wide social divisions and highly skewed income distributions, have encouraged types of buildings and particular city development patterns which require high energy inputs.

With this sort of energy use in much of the Third World, there is obviously a lot that poor, oil-importing countries could do to help themselves, by paying far greater attention to the questions of energy efficiency in their economic and social systems. But such attention will, at best, only eliminate – or reduce – growth in energy demand and so leave the countries with a heavy requirement for foreign exchange to buy needed crude oil and/or oil products. And thus we come back to the significance of the low-cost loans offered to some such countries by the oil producers. This is the only immediate help likely to be forthcoming. (It can be assumed that the producers are not going to provide 'free' oil and that the developed world will remain much too busy with its own energy problems to spare even thought – let alone resources – for solving directly the energy problems of Third World countries.)

Thus, our basic hypothesis is that, in trying to help themselves, the rich energy-using countries will pursue objectives the realization of which will automatically help other parts of the oil-importing world – albeit unwittingly! Self-help amongst O.E.C.D. countries here implies the adoption of autarky as the basis of future energy policy – as, in fact, already adopted in the case of the U.S. 'Project Energy Independence 1980' – or in the ability of Western Europe to choose policies which will, as shown above, first stabilize and then reduce its requirements for imported oil. In so eliminating the hitherto expected continued growth of demand for O.P.E.C. oil, the U.S.A. and Western Europe would indeed undermine the power of the oil cartel, and ultimately achieve its disintegration, as one or more of the oil-producing nations opted out and sought to maximize sales at whatever prices it could get in a competitive marketing situation. At this stage, countries like India and Brazil, where the chances of achieving self-sufficiency in energy production remain remote, would be able to take advantage of the break in the oil system and move towards the achievement of increasing import requirements at reducing unit costs. Such a possibility does, however, imply one further line of action on the part of the rich oil-importing nations – that is, a decision to forgo their unseemly rush to secure 'guaranteed' oil imports for the long term at prices related to those of the cartel. Such action can only build unwanted stability into the present disastrous oil-price situation and eliminate the best longer-term hope for the restoration of reasonably priced energy to the world's poor, industrializing nations.

It would, however, not seem inappropriate to emphasize the need for a somewhat broader perspective. Most of the poor, industrializing nations still depend on the export of a single or a small number of primary commodities. Is it going too far to speculate that the success of the oil exporters' oligopolistic behaviour might produce a significant demonstration effect on other types of commodities from other groups of countries – say, for example, bauxite from Surinam, Jamaica and parts of west Africa; or copper from Chile, Peru and Zambia; or lead from Bolivia and Malaya; or even coffee from the handful of important producing and exporting nations. Perhaps the development we have seen in the last two to three years in the world of oil-producing nations is but a precursor to a wider and even more fundamental change in the organization of trade in the commodities which are required for development and/or for improving living standards.

In the meantime, however, we must remind ourselves that our hypothesis suggesting that the cartel of oil-producing countries can be undermined depends upon the very rapid development of alternative resources of oil and in this respect one must note an important restraint. This is the fact that most of the exploration decisions in the new areas, and the exploration and development itself, are undertaken by the very same companies which are currently responsible for oil production and developments in the traditional producing countries. They have, of course, established a relationship which is highly profitable to both parties and which will not therefore be lightly cast aside – particularly by the companies which still hold out some hope that the expropriation of their assets will come later rather than sooner. Thus, given some possibility of further mutually profitable cooperation between the parties – and with the continuing cooperation of the United States – the companies have some incentive to choose to go slower on the exploration for, and the development of, oil resources elsewhere than is required for breaking the oligopoly. Even worse, having been successful in their exploration and development efforts, they may choose simply to sit on the bulk of the new reserves in order not to upset the controlled supply situation, given that continuing to supply the consuming countries within the framework of the latter ensures higher profits for the companies than could be made out of the use of the alternative resources, the very exploitation of which could undermine the system out of which the higher profits emerge.

This possible strategy is perhaps particularly important and relevant to Western Europe at the present time. The potential danger of the less-rapid-than-possible exploitation of North Sea and other reserves requires us to take a new look at the possible alternative of the French concept of the 'special relationship', and its accompanying nationally organized refining and marketing system.

As already seen, the concept of the special relationship arose out of France's requirement for a supply of oil more secure than that which was available from the producing country/international oil company relationship. Now, at a European level, in a situation in which there are certainly oil resources locally available on a scale sufficient to meet most of Europe's total demand for oil for the remainder of this century, it seems that a more logical special relationship would be one between a European Oil and Gas Commission and those companies which have been given the rights to explore for oil in and around the continent. The special relationship would involve adequate – or more than adequate – incentives to the companies concerned to maximize their exploration, development and production efforts. In return for such guaranteed profitability, the companies would then be obliged to introduce the indigenous oil and gas into the continent's refining and marketing system in a controlled system which ensured that every possible barrel of oil and cubic metre of natural gas were used to substitute part of the flow of imported oil that would otherwise be required. This is a process which requires control over matters such as the existing right of any company to export its European produced crude oil, or products made from it; and over the schedules of the privately owned refineries to ensure that they accepted all the indigenous crude offered to them so as to utilize all the oil that can be locally produced, no matter from which company it originates, rather than giving preference to their own company's crude oil produced elsewhere in the world. Furthermore, as a background to the European system of refineries and marketing, the Oil and Gas Commission would, of course, have to ensure that indigenous oil and gas reserves and production potentials were evaluated with European, rather than individual company interests in mind, so that there is full awareness at all times of just what possibilities the indigenous resource developments are opening up for Europe's future energy economy.

In all this, the lessons of the long-lasting state-administered oil-supply system in France – as well as experience from other parts of the world where public control and/or supervision over decisions in oil resource developments and production have been important (as, for example, in the Canadian Province of Alberta) – will provide a base on which the European-wide system can be evolved as quickly as possible. Self-sufficiency in oil supply has for long been an underlying motivation for French oil policy, though the pursuit of it has been difficult given the speed with which the demand for oil has developed and the unwillingness of outside parties to contribute to its success. In the middle 1970s, at a time when Western Europe stands, in relation to its essential energy supplies, in one of the most dangerous periods which it has known, it is paradoxical that it should also be on the brink of eliminating much of its hitherto rapidly growing dependence on an insecure outside world. The luck of the occurrence of large-scale oil and gas resources on Europe's continental shelf now requires that it be used in determination and implementation of policies at a European level. These can, in part, derive from attention to long-tested attitudes and methods inherent in the French search for special relationships and a controlled system of organizing the supply, refining and marketing of the commodity. Europe's indigenous oil and gas must be utilized for Europe's benefit; in other words within the framework of an organization other than that of the traditional international oil system, in which the power lies elsewhere and the profits from which largely flow outside the continent. In the mid-1970s, this is Europe's challenge and opportunity in the world of oil power.

Day by day the oil industry continues to make news; and all too often the news items can be interpreted only in the light of the complex world oil-power structure which this book has attempted to describe and explain. Traumatic events in the oil world since the first edition was written indicate that the interrelationships of the several sets of 'actors' involved have become more, rather than less, complex. They have also produced a realignment of forces which will make the world of oil in the later 1970s and the 1980s significantly different from the one to which we have become used over the last thirty years or so. The world of oil power in 1974 is difficult to interpret in that extrapolation of previous developments is no longer valid. This last chapter of this new edition has attempted such an interpretation – and also a prognostication of where things will go. The dynamics of the international oil industry at this time are so great, however, that even the short period between writing and publication may prove the author wrong in important respects. If this has proved to be the case, then he hopes that his attempt to understand the situation will, at least, have made the reader aware of the set of fundamental issues involved in the new world of oil and so enable him to undertake for himself a re-interpretation of the position in the light of most recent events.

Suggestions for Further Reading

1. Introduction: The World's Oil Industry

An earlier book by the author, *An Economic Geography of Oil* (Bell, 1963), analyses the locational patterns of the world oil industry on a function-by-function basis. E. T. Penrose's *The Large International Firm in Developing Countries* (Allen & Unwin, 1968) in itself provides a more than adequate introduction to the economics and organization of the oil industry, but this may be supplemented by *Oil, the Facts of Life* by P. H. Frankel (Weidenfeld & Nicolson, 1962) and *The World Petroleum Market* by M. A. Adelman, published for Resources for the Future by the Johns Hopkins University Press, 1971. Two books by authors whose work as specialized journalists put them closely in touch with the working of the oil industry fill in some of the industry's political and historical backgrounds. These are *Oil Companies and Governments* (Faber & Faber, 1967) by J. E. Hartshorn, and *Oil; the Biggest Business* (Eyre & Spottiswoode, 1968) by C. Tugendhat. In contrast, H. O'Connor's *The Empire of Oil* (Monthly Review Press, 1955) and *World Crisis in Oil* (Elek Books, 1963) provide a markedly different interpretation of the history and politics of the industry. The reader seeking objectivity will want to read both points of view.

2. The U.S.A. and World Oil

M. G. de Chazeau and A. E. Kahn's *Integration and Competition in the Petroleum Industry* (Yale U.P., 1959), W. F. Lovejoy and P. T. Homan's *Economic Aspects of Oil Conservation and Regulation* (R. F. F., 1967) and E. W. Zimmerman, *Conservation in the Production of Petroleum* (Yale U.P., 1957) will give even the most avid reader enough analysis of the very closely studied U.S. oil industry. Even so, a little supplementary reading will be necessary for further background to the significance of U.S. oil import controls for the industry. Such reading was, until recently, found only in articles. Specially recommended are M. A. Adelman's 'Efficiency of Resource Use in Crude Petroleum', in *Southern Economic Journal*, XXXI, 1964; and J. E. Jensen's 'Crude Oil: Capacity, Supply Schedules and

Imports Policy' in *Land Economics*, XLIII, 1967. But now, see E. H. Shaffer, *The Oil Import Program of the United States* (Praeger, 1968), and G. D. Nash, *United States Oil Policy, 1890–1964* (U. of Pittsburg Press, 1968). For an interpretation of the more recent U.S. position, when it started to become more dependent on imports and also seriously affected by environmental considerations, see C. T. Cicchetti, *Alaskan Oil, Alternative Routes and Markets* (Johns Hopkins U.P., 1972).

3. Soviet Oil Development

A recent publication in English on the Soviet oil industry should be easily obtainable. This is R. W. Campbell's *The Economics of Soviet Oil and Gas* (Johns Hopkins U.P., 1968). U.S.S.R. and East European developments in oil and gas are covered in regular publications of the U.N. Economic Commission for Europe. See also R. E. Ebel's *The Petroleum Industry of the Soviet Union* (1961), though this book is available only from the American Petroleum Institute. It is essentially a report of the first delegation from that Institute ever to visit the Soviet Union. There is nothing substantial and objective on Soviet oil exports in general, but see J. S. Pryblya, 'Eastern Europe and Soviet Oil', in *Journal of Industrial Economics*, XIII, 1965. For a recent evaluation of the U.S.S.R.'s future potential, see *Exploitation of Siberia's Natural Resources*, the Proceedings of a NATO Round Table meeting, published in April 1974.

4. The Major Oil-Exporting Countries

In contrast there is a wealth of reading material on the oil-exporting countries – particularly the Middle East. The general oil industry texts already listed for Chapter 1 pay a great deal of attention to these countries but more specialized work includes E. Lieuwen's *Petroleum in Venezuela: A History* (U. of California Press, 1954); A. R. Martinez's *Our Gift, Our Oil* (Vienna, 1966), a Venezuelan's view of his country's oil industry; and S. H. Longrigg's *Oil in the Middle East* (O.U.P., 3rd edition 1968), a history of discovery and development by an author who was himself involved in the history as a British civil servant, military officer and oil company executive; D. Hirst's *Oil and Public Opinion in the Middle East* (Faber & Faber, 1966), which presents the development of Middle Eastern oil from a point of view which contrasts strongly with that in the previous book; C. Issawi and M. Yeganeh's *The Economics of Middle Eastern Oil* (Praeger, 1962), and G. W. Stocking: *Middle East Oil: A Study in Political and Economic Controversy*

(Allen Lane The Penguin Press, 1971) are important books on oil in this region. A. Hunter's 'The Indonesian Oil Industry', in *Australian Economic Papers*, 5, 1966; and S. R. Pearson, *Petroleum and the Nigerian Economy* (Stanford University Press, 1970), cover other producing areas.

5. Oil Policies in Western Europe

Apart from publications on oil by national governments, the European Common Market, the Council of Europe, the Organization for Economic Cooperation and Development and the U.N. Economic Commission for Europe also publish regular studies on oil in Europe. An early E.C.E. document, *The Price of Oil in Western Europe* (U.N., Geneva, 1955), was one of the most influential in affecting European policies towards the industry. Surprisingly, however, there is not yet a book which deals comprehensively with the rapid growth of the European oil industry in its economic and political environment, but W. G. Jensen, *Energy in Europe, 1945–80* (Foulis, London, 1967), goes part way towards this. A European who had a marked impact on the oil industry was Enrico Mattei, who ran E.N.I. until his death – see P. H. Frankel's *Mattei: Oil and Power Politics* (Faber & Faber, 1966). Europe's oil difficulties arising from political and military upheavals in its main supply area have been analysed by H. Lubell in *Middle East Oil Crises and Western Europe's Energy Supplies* (Johns Hopkins U.P., 1963). *The Petroleum Times* (published fortnightly in London) is particularly concerned with European oil and gas developments. For an analysis of the potential impact of indigenous oil and gas production, see P. R. Odell, 'Indigenous Oil and Gas Developments and Western Europe's Energy Policy Options', in *Energy Policy*, Vol. 1, No. 1, June 1973, pp. 47–64.

6. Japan: The World's Biggest Oil Importer

The author knows of no publications in English which are concerned specifically or mainly with oil in Japan – but the O.E.C.D. does include Japan in its area of study and its publications on oil are sometimes helpful.

7. Dependence on Oil in the Developing World

Professor Penrose's book, *The Large International Firm in Developing Countries* (see recommended reading for Chapter 1), must be the first choice for additional reading on the oil industry in the developing world. This book is also well documented with further suggestions. M. Tanzer's *The Political*

Economy of International Oil and the Underdeveloped Countries (Beacon Press, Boston, 1969) is also concerned with this subject, while P. das Gupta, *The Oil Industry in India* (Allen & Unwin, 1971), presents an important case study.

8. Oil in International Relations and World Economic Development

Most of the books recommended for Chapter 1 also provide background material to ideas introduced in this chapter. But see also G. Lenczowski's *Oil and State in the Middle East* (Cornell U.P., 1960), B. Shwadran's *The Middle East, Oil and the Great Powers* (New York, 1959), and publications of the Organization of Petroleum Exporting Countries (Vienna). S. H. Schurr and P. T. Homan, *Middle East Oil and the Western World* (American Elsevier Publishing Co., New York, 1971), is a detailed and systematic analysis of the economic implications of the dominant role of Middle East oil in the world oil economy. World Bank reports on Venezuela, Libya, Kuwait, etc., clearly demonstrate the importance of oil revenues in the economic development of major producing countries.

9. The World of Oil Power in 1974

The changes in the world oil situation described in this chapter are so recent that, as yet, there is little additional reading material of substance readily available. Some of the issues, however, have been analysed by the author in more detail elsewhere and two of these may be of interest: On the future of world energy supplies: P. R. Odell, *Energy Needs and Resources* (Macmillan Educational, London, 1974). On Europe's future energy economy: P. R. Odell, 'Indigenous Oil and Gas Developments and W. Europe's Energy Policy Options', *Energy Policy*, Vol. 1, No. 1, June 1973.

For contrasting views on the nature of the oil crisis in 1973–4 see the following articles in successive issues of the American journal, *Foreign Affairs*: M. A. Adelman, 'Is the Oil Crisis Real?' Winter, 1972–3; J. E. Akins, 'This Time the Wolf Really Is at the Door', Spring, 1973; J. Amuzegar, 'The Oil Story; Facts, Fiction and Fair Play', Summer, 1973.

The oil industry is very dynamic and some readers will want to keep up to date with events and developments. Indispensable from this point of view is the monthly publication *Petroleum Economics* (available on subscription only from 24 Ludgate Hill, London EC4). With the background knowledge and understanding of the industry acquired through reading this book, *Petroleum Economics* will make sense. One word of warning, however; the opinions it expresses very closely parallel those of the major international oil companies. It cannot, therefore, be described as reasonably objective on many important issues, particularly those on the relationships of this group of companies with governments and inter-governmental organizations.

Index

Index

Index

Index

Index

More about Penguins
and Pelicans

Penguinews, which appears every month, contains details of all the new books issued by Penguins as they are published. From time to time it is supplemented by *Penguins in Print*, which is a complete list of all titles available. (There are some five thousand of these.)

A specimen copy of *Penguinews* will be sent to you free on request. For a year's issues (including the complete lists) please send 50p if you live in the British Isles, or 75p if you live elsewhere. Just write to Dept EP, Penguin Books Ltd, Harmondsworth, Middlesex, enclosing a cheque or postal order, and your name will be added to the mailing list.

In the U.S.A.: For a complete list of books available from Penguin in the United States write to Dept CS, Penguin Books Inc., 7110 Ambassador Road, Baltimore, Maryland 21207.

In Canada: For a complete list of books available from Penguin in Canada write to Penguin Books Canada Ltd, 41 Steelcase Road West, Markham, Ontario.

Geography of World Affairs

J. P. Cole

Fourth Edition

In this latest edition the author has almost entirely
rewritten *Geography of World Affairs* and has both expanded
and reorganized its contents. The book now falls loosely
into three parts. In the first J. P. Cole sets the scene for
world affairs with facts, figures and discussion about
population, countries, European influence, politics, farming,
industry, transport, raw materials and many other factors.
In the second section he describes the countries
geographically in twelve regional groups, each in
considerable detail according to the latest and best
information available. Finally, viewing the world as a single
pitch, he comments on the interplay between nations in the
grandiose game of international relations. Seeing that the
term geography is almost indefinable, J. P. Cole's study
branches frequently into history, politics, and economics,
among other subjects.

In short, it would be difficult to name a better guide to
have lying beside the newspaper on the television set.